Praise for *The Science of Influence*, Second Edition

"As a sports and performance psychologist who promotes the positive use of persuasion and influence to turn people into extraordinary performers, I always urge clients to read Kevin Hogan's material. His new book, *The Science of Influence*, will now be at the top of the required reading list for all my sales training and coaching clients. Hogan has outdone himself this time. This is a must-read for everyone who wants to be more successful."

—Richard F. Gerson, Ph.D., CPC, CPT, CMC
Author of 19 books, including
HEADcoaching: Mental Training for Peak
Performance **and** *Winning the Inner Game*
of Selling

"Whether it is in the boardroom, on the golf course, or across the dinner table, we all struggle to unlearn bad habits, put to rest unfounded fears, and effect positive change. Kevin Hogan offers us a simple but powerful way to shape behaviors, responses, and performance—both our own and those of others."

—Linda Parker
Educator and author of *The FabJob*
Guide to Become a Professional Golfer

"A cornucopia of research-proven tips, techniques, and resources to help you unlock the key to your prospect's mind and elicit a positive response. Easier, faster, and more effective for those in business than an advanced degree in psychology!"

—Roger C. Parker
Author, coach, consultant

THE
SCIENCE
OF INFLUENCE

How to Get Anyone to Say Yes in 8 Minutes or Less!

Second Edition

Kevin Hogan

WILEY

John Wiley & Sons, Inc.

Published by John Wiley & Sons, Inc., Hoboken, New Jersey.
Published simultaneously in Canada.

For general information on our other products and services or for technical support, please contact our Customer Care Department within the United States at (800) 762-2974, outside the United States at (317) 572-3993 or fax (317) 572-4002.

Wiley also publishes its books in a variety of electronic formats. Some content that appears in print may not be available in electronic books. For more information about Wiley products, visit our web site at www.wiley.com.

Library of Congress Cataloging-in-Publication Data:

ISBN 978-0-470-63418-9 (paper)
ISBN 978-0-470-88069-2 (ebk)
ISBN 978-0-470-88070-8 (ebk)
ISBN 978-0-470-88071-5 (ebk)

Printed in the United States of America

10 9 8 7 6 5 4 3 2

For Jessica and Mark Hogan
The kids every parent asked for

Contents

About the Author

Kevin Hogan is the author of 19 books, including the international best sellers *The Psychology of Persuasion: How to Persuade Others to Your Way of Thinking, Covert Persuasion,* and *Irresistible Attraction: Secrets of Personal Magnetism.*

He has acted as a body-language expert to *Cosmopolitan, Selling Power, Woman's World, First for Women, In Touch, Star, Mademoiselle, Playboy, Success!,* the *New York Post,* the *Los Angeles Times,* and many other publications.

Truly dynamic and informative speakers are rare. Kevin has more energy than the bunny with the drum. He leaves audiences all around the globe with skills and information they never thought they would have. *Motivational* and *inspirational* only begin to describe Kevin in person. When companies need a deal closed, Kevin is often the person they call in to make the deal happen today. He has integrity, honesty, heart, and one of the most influential minds on the planet for you and your company.

Kevin holds a doctorate in psychology. His undergraduate degree was in speech communications.

Living in poverty much of his childhood, Kevin learned to sell to earn money early in life. He worked hard to take care of his family of four brothers and sisters with his Mom, after Dad left.

Today Kevin is single and the truly proud father of two amazing children, one a teenager . . . and you wonder why he stays on top of the latest in influence and persuasion?

Preface

I'll never forget the excitement of finishing *The Psychology of Persuasion: How to Persuade Others to Your Way of Thinking*. The very first review copy we sent out was to Robert Cialdini, the guru of academic influence and the author of *Influence: Science and Practice*—the work I had studied in college.

Ten years later John Wiley & Sons, Inc., asked me to pen a book sharing what was new and exciting in the field of influence and persuasion. According to the June 5, 2010 issue of *The Independent* in the UK, *The Science of Influence, First Edition* went on to be the 8th most downloaded book in the world for 2009.

Then I considered the research that has transpired in the past decade in this field. There has been research about some of the most incredible facets of influence and persuasion that I only dreamed of 20 years ago. We know so much now that we didn't know in 1990 or 1995—it is truly awesome.

The *Science of Influence* is truly a new text for influence in the 2010s. I've collected the most profound elements of influence and assembled them into one easy-to-understand, very readable book. And that's important. Scientific research can be exciting to a scientist but a sleeping pill to the nonspecialist. My work was to take all the research, test it in the real world, and describe it so that anyone can understand it—and then utilize it. My goal is for you to read this book and eventually become comfortable enough with me to have a conversation instead of engage in a science lesson. It's just you and me.

If I were a quantum physicist, I would probably write *Quantum Physics for Kids*. Making difficult things easy to understand is one thing I bring to the table that most authors don't in this very complex field of human behavior. Fortunately I don't understand quantum physics.

Some of the information in this book is information I had discovered purely by accident (the exciting work in body language and proxemics, for example). There is other information I uncovered in research papers, detailing unique and exciting studies by professors from around the world that no one has ever heard of. I real-world tested their stuff. (Ever hear of Kahneman and Tversky? Gilovich? Dillard? O'Keefe? Gass? That's what I thought—and they are the biggest names in the field!) The researchers' results that worked are in here. The stuff that didn't . . . well, I'm not going to tell them!

"Is there anything really new out there, Kevin?" People ask me this all the time. You know what? There is so much that is new and immediately useful in selling, marketing, presentation skills, even therapists, that I had to pare nearly 1,000 pages of work down to 200!

I was ecstatic to discover a new Law of Persuasion in 2001 and then another in 2009, and that information is here. These findings open new routes to positive responses that we've never used before. There is fascinating, new information about presentation order (what do you talk about when, and why). We now know answers to questions that we guesstimated before 2000. There are findings about how to deal with more than one product or option on a product or service. You will be surprised at what you learn. You're going to change the way you communicate with your friends and family as well.

I'm going to show you the ins and outs of permanent change in other people's behavior, why it's difficult—and how you can go about making it happen. You want the customer for life? It's here, for real, for the first time. No kidding.

You can count on what you read in this book. Take it to the bank. If you use this book in selling, management, therapy, or whatever, you know it is rock solid.

Finally, I want to talk about giving credit. Who discovered what? Who came up with what? I do my best to note the researchers, salespeople, and the academics. I like to be credited when I come up with a brainstorm turned tool and I want to give the same back. If you see a mistake or notice anything that needs to be changed for the next edition, let me know right away. Credit needs to be given, and I do my best to do just that. The bibliography at the back of the book will keep you busy for a few years.

This book is going to change the way you think, and that means it is going to change your life. Be prepared. Be excited.

And remember, let's have a conversation. No technical stuff. Just sit back, relax, and have fun with *The Science of Influence*.

—KEVIN HOGAN
Minneapolis, Minnesota

Acknowledgments

No book is written without influence and support.

I want to gratefully acknowledge those in my inner circle for their untiring support: Rob Northrup, Steve Chambers, April Braswell, Sonya Lenzo, Sabrina Peterson, Andrew Records, Christian Haller, Larry Hines, Michael Walker, Alam Ghafoor, David Mills, Robert Kaufer, John Bedosky, Gary Moon, Wendy Schauer, Timothy Van Milligan, Shane Kester, Scott Bell, Dale Bell, Jose Escalante, Mike Morgan, Eliot Hoppe, and our senior member Bryan Lenihan.

I'd like to thank those who have diligently helped at Influence Boot Camp: Ken Owens, Cherie Miranda, Jennifer Battaglino, Rebecca Joy, and Joshua Gretz.

I also want to thank those who have made Influence Boot Camp a great experience for the last seven years: Dave Lakhani, Gary May, Eric Knowles, Tonya Reiman, Wendi Friesen, Mark Joyner, Mark Victor Hansen, Deb Micek, Al Duncan, as well as my fantastic autumn event masters—Bill Harris (Centerpointe), Stewart Emery, Larina Kase, JP Micek, Michelle Matteson, and Kate McKeon.

I want to make a special mention of appreciation for Rich Schefrin, Brian Johnson, Jeffrey Gitomer, and Richard Brodie.

Special thanks to the staff at John Wiley & Sons, Inc.: Matt Holt, Dan Ambrosio, Ashley Allison, and Susan Moran.

Here: Mark Hogan, Jessica Hogan, and Katie Hogan.

Finally, it is required that I mention a few close to my heart that I don't see often enough . . . Mark and Kathy Ryan, Devin and Rachel

Hastings, Ron and Jeannie Stubbs, Meredith Kaplan, and Scott and Carmen Schluter.

One thing I know for certain: I've once again in my haste, missed someone so dear that when you remind me I will be calling the publisher in the morning.

1 | Influencing Others to Change

This book is about getting people to change ... something—a behavior, an attitude, a product, a service, their relationship to or with you. You want someone to do something different from what they were doing a few minutes ago. You want someone to say yes to you, now. In order for that to consistently happen it would probably be a good idea to know what it is that makes people tick. I want you to know precisely what it is that gets people to not only say yes but, if necessary, say yes all the time!

My life has been about helping people change and teaching others to change people. It's exciting, it's fun, and I've been fortunate enough to discover many keys that other promoters of influence have neglected to look for. I've also been fortunate enough to have access to a world of research from both the academic and real (i.e., private sector) worlds. The process of causing change, getting people to question the status quo, and actually implementing the change in another person's brain is an exciting process.

Short-term decisions of yes or no are much easier than achieving long-term change. Permanent change is difficult. Period. You go to the same grocery store every week. You go to the same gas stations, attend the same church, take the same route for your daily walk or jog, work out at the same gym . . . well, you get the idea. You do the same things every day, and there is nothing wrong with that. In fact, the stability of these behaviors can be very positive indeed! In this book you will learn how to get people to say "yes" to you now . . . and help them change over the long term!

Unfortunately, some of the things that people do are in direct opposition with what we *want* them to do. That's where influence and persuasion come in handy. Some people smoke cigarettes, do drugs, drink too much, beat their kids, rape, steal, eat too much, hang out with the wrong people in the wrong element, take part in self-destructive behaviors, and fail to act on living what they dream their lives should be about. People universally agree that these are things that need to change in themselves and in others. Agreement and action, of course, are often not related to each other in reality.

Even when people want change it turns out to be something that people desperately fail at. You'd think that if they *want* to change it would be easy, right? Of course it isn't that way at all. Why?

The first reason is remarkably simple. Your brain has lots and lots of highways that connect lots and lots of cells. These highways light up with activity every day when you participate in various activities. You think "walk," and you go for the same walk you always do. When you think "drink," you will go drink the same liquids you always do. Your brain is literally wired through all of your previous behavior to do exactly what it has in the past. That wiring rarely changes, except by lack of use of the highway system. However, new wiring (new highways) can come about through repetition of new behaviors and through repetition of thoughts, though with murkier results than actual behaviors such as intentionally taking a walk on a different path every day for a few weeks, intentionally eating a new food every day for a few weeks, intentionally taking part in any new behavior every day for a few weeks.

It used to be said that a new habit takes 21 days to form. It now appears that it takes five days to form a new habit that is repeated daily (i.e., to create new neural pathways in the brain). Unfortunately, creating a new habit rarely if ever erases an old habit. That means choice continues to be involved in everyday decisions and change, even though there is a new highway. Getting someone to not eat junk food today is fairly easy; getting the person to do it for a lifetime is another thing altogether. Getting the dream date isn't as hard as you might think. But getting the person to say yes to a longer-term commitment is another thing altogether.

With this in mind it can be understood that there is no reason to assume that people will be motivated, after today, to perform a newly desired behavior, regardless of what it is. The easy shift back to the strong, well-traveled neural pathways in the brain (which essentially project themselves into your external world) is not only possible, it is likely. Therefore, the person who wants to quit smoking, start eating better, or change any behavior probably won't, regardless of the motivational device, unless it is consciously and intentionally repeated time after time and day after day for months, at which point it can compete as the more likely to be followed pathway.

The status quo is the status quo for just this reason. That which is familiar is the path of least resistance. This is also why the brain reacts so strongly with a negative response to all but the most familiar requests or behaviors. It takes enormous initial effort to change because one literally must forge new highways in the brain. Once formed, the highways must be strengthened through regular usage and maintained by even further usage.

Do They Even Know What They Want?

Sit down for this one (the second reason change isn't easy): People don't know what they want, don't know how they will feel when they get it, and don't really know themselves. What does this mean for change?

We each have a conscious mind and a nonconscious mind. Even with hypnosis, you can't really have two-way communication with the nonconscious mind in any effective and reliable fashion, but you *can* communicate with the conscious mind. Even more interesting is that the conscious and nonconscious minds appear to have significantly different personality characteristics, attitudes, and motivations.

The nonconscious mind is not a six-year-old child, as has so often been speculated. In fact, sometimes the nonconscious mind is far more useful than its conscious counterpart—but not always.

The conscious mind is able to compute, calculate, compare, contrast, and perform all kinds of impressive cognitive functions. The nonconscious mind makes rapid-fire choices (though rarely decides between two options) under stress, which are more often right than wrong when there is significant experience in a situation (fighting fires, surgery, combat, etc.). The nonconscious also tends to stereotype and categorize people right down to whether someone you meet is like someone you knew in the past and if so assigning them the same traits as the person you once knew. *The nonconscious mind doesn't think per se; it simply does.* It experiences a situation and produces some behavior. Objections in sales situations almost always come from this part of the brain.

To override this behavior would take conscious effort on your client's behalf. That usually doesn't happen. More typically the conscious mind will create a reason for performing some behavior, when it really has no clue why the body is eating, going to bed, getting in the car, or taking an exit.

The nonconscious mind simply directs the body to act. Its force is usually strong and difficult to change in the short term. Because, as a rule, the nonconscious mind is rooted in deep and old brain function, it doesn't vocalize its opinions in a rational way. It simply reacts. Generally the nonconscious mind acts in a way that would be consistent with past behaviors in similar situations, meaning that it could save your life or it could overlook important new information and accidentally drive you to your demise. It is a holdover from our evolutionary history. It (the nonconscious) appears to drive almost all animal behavior, with conscious mind functions being limited to a few different kinds of animals.

> *The nonconscious mind makes rapid-fire choices. It also tends to stereotype and categorize people right down to whether someone you meet is like a person you once knew.*

The nonconscious mind deals with now. The conscious mind deals with the future. The nonconscious mind is *rigid*. The conscious mind is *flexible*. The nonconscious mind is sensitive to negative information. The conscious mind is sensitive to positive information. The nonconscious is a pattern detector. The conscious is an after-the-fact checker. The nonconscious mind is multisystemic. The conscious mind is a single system.

Conscious Mind	*Nonconscious Mind*
Future.	Now.
Flexible.	Rigid.
Sensitive to positive information.	Sensitive to negative information.
After-the-fact checker.	Pattern detector.
Single system.	Multisystemic.

Because the brain develops these two substantially distinct minds, it's important to realize that both minds have typical behaviors, and those behaviors are often at odds with each other. The conscious mind may want to be accurate whereas the nonconscious mind wants to feel good.

Internal conflict in most people is very real and very normal. Typically we consciously have an objective or goal (lose weight, get a different job, start your own business, begin a true personal-development phase in your life). However, the nonconscious mind learned early on to fear the unknown. It's a simple survival mechanism. To walk where we have walked before is generally safe. To stretch our boundaries is often something that seems risky to the nonconscious self, and, therefore, the very idea of these changes can literally feel bad. That gut instinct is probably wrong but that is what the survival mechanism in the brain sends to the body: fear, anxiety, maybe even panic.

The conscious, rational self, which hates the present job, the weak state of personal development, or the fat body, knows that change should take place, but to actually commit to a plan to overcome the status quo where the fear is present is daunting and seemingly counterintuitive.

> **Complete strangers are almost as good at predicting our behavior as we are ourselves.**

Therefore, it is critical to *evaluate the emotions of the moment* or the day and discover if there is a *legitimate, rational signal* that your brain is relaying to you. Or is the brain simply telling you it is afraid, and the fear is false evidence appearing real (fear)? If you decide (consciously) that the mind and body are feeling afraid without good cause for the situation at hand, realize that it will take some significant amount of time to overcome the fear of the situation. It certainly won't go away in a minute, an hour, or a day. Typically it is necessary to wire in a completely new set of responses to the current situation and fight through fear and negative emotions every day until new levels of comfort can be achieved.

One of the great problems of trying to know yourself is that you really can't completely know yourself. Study after study shows that complete strangers are almost as good at predicting our behavior as we are ourselves. We think we know ourselves, but we really don't know ourselves as well as we would like to. Because of the way the brain works, though, if we don't like what we see ourselves doing and thinking, we can change. It is a slow process and often difficult, but once change becomes the status quo, it becomes rigid. So select well.

Two Personalities?

Are we really two personalities woven into one person?

I confess, it's a funny thing: The personality of the nonconscious mind correlates to a person's behavior and the person's conscious mind correlates to a person's behavior—but the conscious mind and nonconscious mind of that person don't correlate to each other! Gulp. That's why people say things like, "I don't know," "I have to think about it," "I'm not sure what I want to do."

People typically look to make sense of themselves and the world around them. Because we all do and say things that truly surprise us, we must construct (fabricate) a narrative (story) that makes sense of those behaviors that conflict with our intentions. The rationales and explanations help us put the incongruency behind us and move on to other things.

What makes understanding ourselves and others even more difficult is the painfully distorted memories we all carry in the three-pound universe. The brain simply isn't a video recorder that records events. The brain is a vast array of storehouses and interpreting functions that constantly store, re-store, interpret, and reinterpret our memories and beliefs. False memories are so common that almost every conversation of any length includes reference to at least one memory that never happened.

Recognizing these two defective elements of the human experience (our suspect memory and the dual nature of our personality(ies)), one can understand the arguments, the fights, and the butting of heads that take place in relationships and communication in general between people who have lived through the same events and remembered and interpreted them so differently.

Recent research does show that there is some predictability in how we will respond to other people. For example, a person who is fond of her sister will tend to be fond of people who exhibit behaviors similar to those of the sister.

How do you actually come to know yourself? Pay attention to your behavior in any given situation and you learn who you are. However, even that is suspect because we don't see ourselves as clearly as we see others. As mentioned, current research reveals that we are better judges of others' future behavior than we are of our own. We tend to see ourselves in a much better light than we see others, and that light creates a halo effect around what most of us believe about ourselves. We tend to see others more accurately.

The brain is a vast array of storehouses and interpreting functions.

Real estate agents observe the lack of self-knowledge in others every day. They listen while their clients describe the exact house they want. The agents then show them several houses that their clients love and one that they eventually buy that has little in common with what the individuals detailed just hours or days before! Real estate agents figured it out a long time ago: Buyers have no clue what they really want.

And when we do see ourselves behave in some fashion, we often have no idea why we did what we did. A research project had women approach men on a somewhat dangerous footbridge and start a conversation. The same women later approached men seated on a bench away from the footbridge. The results were that 65 percent of the men who were approached on the footbridge asked for a date, while only 30 percent of those on the bench asked for a date. Arousal was attributed incorrectly to the woman on the bridge instead of the actual anxiety-provoking feelings that the man felt on the bridge.

Unfortunately, we don't have the ability to access the reasons we do these kinds of things, and observation helps only to some degree. Our need to find a reason for behavior, any reason, helps us make sense of our world and make us happy, even if it isn't accurate.

And what about those faced with difficult decisions in life? Beginning or ending a relationship? Buying a business or not? Buying your product or service!?

The research is compelling. After initially analyzing the problem once, the individual stands a far better chance of making a good determination than another individual who ponders for days, weeks, or months. This is true even when people write out their reasons for their decisions on paper or on a computer. In comparitive studies, individuals seem to make better decisions when gathering enough information, thinking about it, and then deciding versus writing all the reasons for and against an idea. (Ben Franklin is rolling over in his grave . . . and I'm sure I will, too!)

So, with this rather bleak picture of how poorly we make decisions and how poorly we know each other, what is the answer? How can you get people to say yes to you now and in the future?

It appears that going out into the future and speculating on what events and experiences might take place is the best option for creating the changes necessary when conflicted. To be sure, we can't accurately predict how we will feel in the future. This has been shown in volumes of studies. However, we can gain foresight by specifically seeing ourselves in future situations and determining what course(s) of action will ensure the success.

For years it was thought that journaling was a grand way to determine insight and learn about ourselves. And this is true as long as we do not journal after particularly negative or traumatic experiences that will later taint the story of our lives into being something it was/is not. Instead, it's best to journal on a consistent basis and describe events and experiences with the realization that negative emotions happen daily in everyone and that in itself is not necessarily a bad thing as long as action is taken on those states to improve the quality of life each and every day. Numerous studies have shown that people who think about the negative emotions that have been recorded actually end up far worse off than they would have had they not reviewed the emotions of the past. Such is the nature of writing history and then rewriting it without the benefit of all the other experiences that happened that day/week/month/year. Result: These people tend to predict a more negative future for themselves than those who do not ruminate. I bring up this crucial point because a lot of us sell products or services that can develop a track record. A car can appear to be reliable or unreliable, but if you just had a minor breakdown today, you will certainly be seeing the car as much less reliable than you had seen it previously.

> *After initially analyzing the problem once, the individual stands a far better chance of making a good determination than the other individual who ponders for days, weeks, or months.*

In the final analysis, the road to changing the self (yours or someone else's) is about creating behavioral change first, which will almost always lead to attitudinal change. In plain English, that means you have to get people to *do* something if you want them to say yes.

Three Ways to Change

I want to share with you three ways to change that no one wants you to know about.

What do some major corporations, all military leaders, and many major religions know that most other people don't?

The military leadership of every world government discovered this first factor ages ago. Every successful religious and spiritual organization found out how to utilize this factor in past millennia. In recent history, beyond the military and spiritual organizations, some major corporations have discovered how to thoroughly and completely change people, modify behavior, and alter attitudes. What's the first secret? Imagine: boot camp.

You arrive. They cut your hair (if you have any), issue clothing conforming to a specific standard, the same cut and color as everyone else's. You have a new place to eat and you are told specific times to wake up, eat, and sleep. Your activities are dictated from the beginning of the day to the end of the day. You are looking at dozens of other faces that you have never seen before. *Your environment has changed.*

There will be phone calls home once each week and you will not be using a telephone or the Internet for the balance of the days. There is very little contact with the outside world.

All of this is necessary to rapidly change your loyalties, behavior, and attitudes so that if you are forced into high-stress situations, like battle, your behavior will be predictable and manageable ... and you will stay alive. You will be taught to watch out for everyone else in the group, and they will be there to support you. An interdependent relationship is being created. There are no independent relationships and there are no independent thinkers allowed.

All of the needs of the military require rapid change, rapid behavior modification, and a rapid restructuring of beliefs. The same changes are facilitated in some large corporations, the large church, some schools, and a few other groups throughout society. The model is powerful and is effective with all but the most stubbornly nonconformist individuals.

The three overlooked principles to change yourself and others begin with changing a person's environment. Humans, like animals, interact with and respond to their environment far more than we are aware of at the conscious level.

- We act very differently in church than we do ...
- ... at the office, and we act differently at the office than we do ...
- ... at the football game, and we act differently at the football game than we do ...
- ... at the dinner table in our homes each night and than we do ...
- ... in our hotel rooms.

Why? Cultural rules dictate our behavior at church and in the office. Groupthink or social influence comes into play at the football game as well as the church and office. Personal relationship dynamics enter into the mix at the dinner table, joining the other environments. Finally, the hotel room is most interesting because you are a stranger in an environment without a leader or group to conform to, and often you are by yourself. Thus you are able to discover more about the true nature of who you are because you are most definitely curious about your environment and not quite certain what to do with that environment. This leaves behavior largely unpredictable for you—but very predictable for the hotel chain.

Cultural rules dictate our behavior in public.

You don't know how you will behave, but the hotel does. The hotel knows what you will do (and charges you handsomely for it). The manager knows you will do at least two of three things in your room that will generate a profit on most stays:

1. You will use the telephone (that's why local phone calls are $1.50).
2. You will eat a snack (the minibar prices for food and drink about eight times retail prices).
3. You will watch a movie (priced at three times the price of a video).

You may not know that you are going to do these things. In fact, you may bring your own cell phone, your own snacks, and your own DVD player or your computer, and you still utilize the hotel's services, and they know you will. *They know you better than you do, because the environment stimulates behavior.*

Key: If you want to change your own or someone else's behavior, *the first thing you can often do is change the environment.* If you can control the environment, you can typically predict or create a specific behavior.

It is known how people will behave in church, at the dinner table, at the office, and in the hotel. Deviations can occur, but behavior is remarkably predictable.

People learn how to behave in all of these environments and then they do behave that way. An extroverted individual will be remarkably compliant in the quiet atmosphere of the library. The introverted person will sing out in church and stand up and cheer at the football game. The behaviors are learned and reinforced. People do what they are told, and when they don't we medicate them so they will comply!

Changing the environment is uniquely powerful in changing behavior. There is no greater single influence. Not genetics, not peer pressure. Not parenting. *The environment stimulates behavior*, and changing behavior is most easily accomplished in a different environment.

And there is more. *The environment can be changed to develop different behaviors.* The positions of chairs, furniture, and decor can be altered, thus changing how much people like each other. These alterations also change how (and how much) people interact, which will directly impact whether people will like each other, be more (or less) anxious, and be more (or less) comfortable.

The colors of carpeting, furniture, and walls all change the perceptions of people in the environment and literally change their behavior.

An interesting element in changing the environment is that it tends to change behavior first, rather than the attitude of the individual. This fact is most profoundly noted in many religious institutions, the military of every government, large corporations, and some schools.

When a person is moved from one environment to another, especially when one is unfamiliar with the new environment, the brain has to change; it enters into a state of flux and typically *becomes more suggestible.*

From the standpoint of your "Self," this factor can help you determine whether you should remain in the same environment you are in or intentionally change it. From the standpoint of changing the behavior of others, this information helps you know whether you should take a person out to lunch, to dinner, or on a trip—or meet them at an international destination. The further removed from their norm, the more likely it is to gain compliance in most people.

The environment has a dramatic impact on whether someone else will say yes or no to you. It's the very first indicator that a yes or no is coming. The next indicator is equally controllable: your appearance.

2 | The First Four Seconds

SNEAK PREVIEW!

Your body language and your physical appearance will jump-start your instant likability, your persuasiveness, and most importantly how you are perceived by every person who meets you. You have less than 10 seconds and realistically closer to four seconds to make a good first impression on those with whom you come into contact. A world of research clearly indicates that you will be judged professionally and personally in the first few seconds of your meeting someone for the first time. In fact, your first impression is recorded and is used as a yardstick for all future communication by those you meet. Whatever that first impression is going to be on your part, you want it to be intentional and on purpose.

The First Impression

The second that one person sees another, a lot happens in the nonconscious mind. The conscious results are often seemingly instantaneous. Do any of these thoughts sound familiar to you?

"It's a gut instinct. I don't like her. I can't put my finger on it."

"There's just something about him that bugs me. I don't know what it is, but I can always tell."

"My intuition tells me that he's just not right."

People think and feel these thoughts when they observe mixed signals from people they meet. There is an internal conflict between the nonverbal (we'll call it body language from here on in) and the verbal signals a person receives. The sad part is that people really believe they have good instincts and that they should trust their intuition. Why sad? Because when there are mixed messages in communication, the person tends to say no because something doesn't feel right.

You see someone new: In the first four seconds of that encounter (or observation!) an incredible amount of processing happens in your brain at the nonconscious level. You'll never know what went on.

Would you like to have a clue about what is going on in the three-pound machine behind your eyes?

When you first meet someone, millions of neurons in the brain are activated. Your brain immediately wakes up. The brain instantly tries to categorize the person into a certain type. Who is she like? Is that good? Is she attractive? What's unique about her? What is familiar about her? All of this is done without thought and awareness. It's the way the brain works. If you had to consciously analyze everything about everyone you meet, you would be so busy at the conscious level that you'd have absolutely no time to think about anything but how they look. Instead, the nonconscious mind immediately goes to work, makes all kinds of judgments and evaluations, and essentially pegs the person as a winner or loser in approximately four seconds.

Sometimes all of this happens in less than four seconds and sometimes it takes a little more time, but in those first moments after one person meets another there is an intensely powerful yes-or-no response. This response is about the person. It has nothing to do with their religion, their political party, or their product or service. It's just yes or no.

When you first see someone, you instantly categorize and/or filter the person you are observing into one of many different categories. One way the brain categorizes is to make a judgment about whether the person is of high status or low status within the group. That's important because humans (and animals in general) are wired to be attracted to the more powerful and higher-status individuals in any given group. Another instant filter is whether your brain finds the person attractive, unattractive, or somewhere in between.

The brain also notes whether the individual being observed pays attention to their physical appearance.

The brain does a great deal more than just a little processing in those first few seconds. It also notes the person's intentionally chosen emblems and adornments (broaches, pins, necklace, rings, other jewelry, makeup, style of glasses, tattoos, and body markings/piercings). All of this is observed, filtered, and categorized almost instantly by the various parts of the brain. Ultimately what happens is that you get a response or reaction inside that indicates to you whether you accept and maybe like all that you see or (more likely) that you are disinterested or do not like what you see.

There is nothing fair, politically correct, or reasonable about this process. It is an instant evaluation that is almost always permanent and rarely given a conscious—or second—thought. The exception occurs when someone you see is on the edge. There are some people you see to whom your initial response to is yes. Yes, you like them; yes, they are attractive; yes, they have taste; and yes, they appear to be healthy and so on. Most people you see are processed, literally, as no. The answer to a question they might ask you is a polite but certain no. The amount of respect you would have for them is negative. They simply are no. But there is a small group of people to whom you say maybe, regardless of whether a question has been asked. This group of people includes people who are on the edge. This group is the only one that doesn't get a nonconscious yes or no. They get a "hmmmmm...." Like the yes people, they get your attention but you wonder about them. Something doesn't seem right about them. What is it?

> **When you first see someone, you instantly categorize and/or filter the person you are observing.**

It's the fact that, unlike the majority of people whom you instantly filter into yes and no piles, certain people are surrounded with ambiguity as far as the brain's processing of them is concerned. Perhaps they are not attractive, but they have taste and style, and you approve of other filters as well. Or perhaps they are attractive but they have numerous body markings and piercings that give you pause to wonder about them. These people fall into a maybe-yes category.

By the way, no question has been asked yet. No one has said hello. They may not even have looked at you, but you have already said yes, no, or maybe and you haven't a clue about who they are or whether you will meet them.

You simply walked past each other in the terminal at the airport or in the hall at the office. You don't know this person. They might have an appointment with you or you may never say hello to them in your life. But you do say yes or no long before you say hello, and that is why they must do everything they can to get you to say yes, even when they don't know you are there. *You must do the same if you are to hear yes once you communicate with someone.*

Most men don't see a woman's body type first; they see her face. Most women don't see a man's face first; they see his body type. (Throughout this book you will discover that men and women think very differently and communicate very differently. Understanding what is important to the majority of men and women will help you hear yes far more often than you will hear no.)

The instant you first see someone, and long before you even are aware that that someone is going to say hello to you, you have already said yes or no to them and they have already said yes or no to you.

> *To overcome these initial and instant impressions takes an enormous amount of conscious effort.*

To overcome these initial and instant impressions takes an enormous amount of conscious effort. The instant impression is still somewhat permeable and could be overruled; it doesn't happen often, but it does happen. It's much easier to radiate a powerful and positive impression at all times so you never have to determine whether you are exhibiting a positive impression!

In the next three seconds—long before people say hello—most decisions are becoming less permeable. Time is short for you to get from maybe/no to maybe/yes.

It makes no difference whether you are selling cars, showing real estate, going into a conference with the sixth-grade teacher, searching for a mate, or watching the church soloist. The maybe/approve, maybe/disapprove reaction is instantaneous. It's nonconscious. You aren't even aware you made the judgment except in those few cases when someone is on the edge. You simply made the decision—except you didn't. Your nonconscious mind made the decision and you had nothing to do with it!

It seems absolutely absurd to think that someone will instantly evaluate you for a job, a relationship, a business deal, or anything, for that matter, based on an instant impression! But remember, every human being alive makes these nonconscious evaluations.

The First Appearance in Action

In 2002, I asked the owner of an adult learning facility to let me host a speed-dating night. I just wanted to learn whether people could really make a no,-I-don't-want-to-ever-date-this-person or yes,-I'd-like-to-go-on-another-date-with-this-person decision in six minutes.

The promotion went in the catalog as an evening where you could have 10 dates or more with 10 different people in two hours. Total price? $49. As I expected, the turnout was impressive.

Each date lasted six minutes. Exactly six minutes. At the end of each six minutes the individuals would write Y or N on a three-by-five-inch note card with their name/number and their date's name/number. If the two people both wrote Y, the cards were put into their envelope and given to them at the end of the evening.

I observed all 18 pairs of people through each of their dates and took notes about what was happening in their particular date. I then predicted whether the pair would match or not. (As expected, the vast majority of course did not match.) Some of what I learned is detailed later in the book. Most interestingly, when I privately interviewed individuals at the end of the evening, almost everyone said they had no need for the full six minutes of date time. They knew in the first few seconds whether they would be interested in dating the person again. There were two people who said they would have liked more time than six minutes to decide with at least one other person. Other than that, everyone knew almost immediately, just as predicted.

Your perceived level of attractiveness by other people will be a significant benefit or detriment in your career, in your relationships, and throughout all aspects of your life. It isn't fair, but it is true. People who are not especially attractive learn how to deal with less than perfect physical features and work with what they have. Before we consider just how to increase your face value, let's look at the results of some fascinating studies about physical appearance.

> *Your perceived level of attractiveness by other people will be a significant benefit or detriment in your career, in your relationships, and throughout all aspects of your life.*

The Power of Physical Appearance

Did you know that, in university settings, professors who are considered physically attractive by students are considered to be better teachers on the whole than unattractive professors? Attractive professors are also more likely to be asked for help on problems. These same attractive professors also tend to receive positive recommendations from other students to take their classes and also are less likely to receive the blame when a student receives a failing grade! (Romano and Bordieri 1989)

A wide variety of research indicates that men's marriage and dating decisions are often made with great weight placed on physical attractiveness. They will often reject women who are lacking (in their opinion) in positive physical features. Women, on the other hand, place less significance on a man's physical attractiveness in considering him for a date or marriage, according to studies by R. E. Baber. Recent research in 2009 contradicts this earlier finding, so perhaps women are evolving whereas men have stopped. . . .

In studies by J. E. Singer done on college campuses, it has been proven that attractive females (attraction as perceived by the professors) receive significantly higher grades than male students or relatively unattractive females.

There is more evidence that shows you must make the most of what you have physically. Among strangers, studies by D. Byrne, O. London, and K. Reeves show that individuals perceived as unattractive in physical appearance are generally undesirable for any interpersonal relationship.

In one significant study of 58 unacquainted men and women in a social setting, Brislin and Lewis found that, that after a first date, 89 percent of the people who sought a second date decided to do so because of attractiveness of the partner.

In the persuasion process, Mills and Aronson found that attractive females are far more convincing than females perceived as unattractive.

The Two Big Questions

(1) Where does all this come from? (2) Can I be persuasive if I'm not what most people think is physically attractive? The answer to the second question is yes!

The answer to the first question is a bit of a story. It all started when you were a baby. The baby is born and in less than three days the baby will imitate simple behaviors like smiling, frowning, and sticking her tongue out. Within a few more days the baby gains a clear vision of her environment and she now is able to focus on people, easily distinguishing Mom from other people. When Mom leaves the room and the baby is shown picture after picture of stranger after stranger, the baby looks at those photographs of people who are physically attractive for a much longer time than those people in the photographs who aren't physically attractive. The desire to look at beautiful people (and symmetrical objects, by the way) is prewired into the little baby's brain.

There are more distinctions in the infant's observational patterns. The infant prefers looking at faces that are smiling to those with a scowl or frown. This response is also prewired into the infant.

Even more startling, though, is the behavior of the mother with the baby. Mothers of babies who are perceived as attractive are more likely to gaze at their babies and allow no distractions from the world around them.

Babies who are perceived (independently) as unattractive are more likely to be cared for in the sense of having their diapers changed, being burped, and being fed, with secondary attention paid to the babies' faces.

The mother, of course, is unaware of her behavior contrasted with other mothers. Her behavior to gaze at beauty was prewired in her at birth as well. The experience of the enjoyment of beauty begins in the gene and is further shaped in infancy.

It appears one reason that most children are perceived as beautiful by their parents is that the perception acts as a survival mechanism for the baby. What else would stop us from acting out when the little one is prone to endlessly whine? (There is more stopping us than the irresistibility of the infant, but it is a very good thing the baby is irresistible!)

Throughout nature the beautiful and colorful animals of a species fare better in mating, survival, and acquisition of resources. This includes humans. One recent study revealed that most of the wealth acquired by women in the world today is acquired by the most attractive women. Some of this wealth is acquired through inheritance, some through marriage, and some through the women's work.

The survival instinct is strong in women, and the genes that shape a woman's beauty and her response to beauty encourage her to optimize her appearance. This has been true for millions of years. Today, Madison Avenue exploits this survival instinct, and women drive the cosmetics and "look-good" industry to being one of the most important industries in the world. The cosmetics industry employs more people than most industries in the world. In Brazil, there are more Avon representatives than military personnel. The business of looking good continues into the twenty-first century some two million years after it began . . . and it's still going strong.

Madison Avenue didn't create beauty, though, nor does Madison Avenue set the standard of beauty. Far from it. There are more than two dozen countries in the world that place a higher value on physical attractiveness than do Americans. Typically these cultures do so because attractiveness is often a clue about the healthiness of a spouse. Countries that are disease-ridden, especially parasitic disease, are homes to individuals aspiring to mate with physically attractive people.

Volumes of research reveal that girls and women who are perceived as attractive get better grades on tests, earn more money on the job, and marry husbands with more resources (money and education, generally) than other women. Something seems politically incorrect about all of this, but the facts speak loudly. The physical attractiveness factor is important in relationships, culture, and the survival of the species—of all species.

Among men in military academies, those who are physically attractive tend to go on to better careers than those who are average or perceived as unattractive. There is also a preference for attractive men by women upon initial contact, but this preference isn't as great as other traits considered desirable by women.

It is interesting to note that attractive people tend to be more at ease and confident in social settings than others are. This is probably because of all the positive traits nonconsciously ascribed to these individuals by everyone else in the environment. If people constantly approach someone with the same positive, smiling outlook toward that person (the physically attractive individual), the person is likely to develop the typical verbal and nonverbal responses to that behavior. This means that an almost self-fulfilling prophecy happens in attractive people . . . and they don't even know it.

Standardized tests show that attractive girls and women score no better or worse than unattractive ones. Only when grading is subjective does attractiveness play a role.

A problem ultimately arises in this world that is run by personal appearance. Attractive women often find themselves strongly disliking and avoiding the company of other attractive women. It appears that this is a survival instinct. No one wants to lose access to his or her resources. Staying away from other attractive women means there is less competition when being observed by a potential mate. We all try to control our environment that we live and work in. The means and objectives are often very different between men and women.

Attractiveness is important to men and women in social settings, but it is definitely more important to men in almost all countries of the world except Sweden and Poland, where physical attractiveness requirements are similar between men and women. With these two countries being the exceptions, men place a higher value on attractiveness than women do, and this fact directly changes both nonverbal and spoken communication encounters.

Once you understand the gravity of your appearance and that it changes the minds, desires, and thoughts of everyone you interact with, you discover you have an opportunity to improve all future relationships and communication opportunities.

It's very important to look as good as you can. This might mean using makeup or not, but it probably more often means keeping your weight down. A small waist has shown to be a big factor in how people evaluate other people. Obesity is a leading cause of diabetes and other illnesses including cancer. We've all been wired to have a compulsion to invest our lives with healthy people, especially those we are going to mate with.

> *It's very important to look as good as you can.*

Now, how do we apply all of this startling information to the compliance-gaining situation?

Have you ever heard of love at first sight? Two sales were made before two people ever spoke. Both people decided that they wanted what they saw, heard, smelled, and felt inside. Sales are made and broken every day in the same manner. In this module you will learn how to help your client fall in love with you *and* your products and services, before you even say a word.

Nonverbal communication is almost always nonconscious communication. Most people have no idea what is going on at the sublanguage level of communication. This book will help you master this most critical process of persuasion.

Many self-proclaimed experts of influence and body language have misquoted a brilliant study by Albert Mehrabian. The wannabe experts state that 93 percent of all communication is nonverbal. That wasn't what Mehrabian concluded at all. However, most of the finest researchers do agree that nonverbal communication and physical appearance make up between 50 and 80 percent of the impact of a communication. The same is true for the persuasion climate.

What you wear, your makeup, your jewelry, your watch, your socks, your shoes, your coat, your glasses, and everything else about how you look can make or break a sale or a relationship, before you ever open your mouth.

The Science of Sexual Influence

Understnding sexual influence is central to understanding The Science of Influence.

The reason is simple.

What you look like matters more than you ever could have dreamed. What you look like changes how people respond and react to you in that first moment. That first moment shapes the dynamic of the entire relationship.

This didn't develop by accident. Nature has had its role and here is how it most typically plays out.

Some people are almost invisible to other people. You look out into the room and it's mostly just a bunch of faces, but a few people stand out.

When women survey the room, they aren't looking for anything. What they see, though, are the few men in the room who clearly have status in the group. Maybe it's the star player, the CEO, the manager. It could be the top Harley rider or winner of the race. Most women see status and dominance.

But women aren't blind to physical appearance. A man's physical appearance is evolutionarily just as predictive of reproductive success as a man's status or dominance in a group. The square jaw, the symmetrical facial features, each side a mirror of the other.

However, she didn't see the face first. On the contrary, unlike men, women look at a man's body and his height, and then his face, last.

Research shows that taller men make more money than their shorter counterparts and men are getting taller with each generation. Fifty years ago, a 5'8" man was average. Today, that man is close to being filtered out of consciousness by alpha females—those women who can have the pick of the litter. (*alpha females* here refers to women in the top quintile of desirability by men. Beta females are the balance of those in the top 50 percent.)

In 2010, the 5'10" man is the norm. And he needs every inch of that. For better or worse, depending on how you look at it, the taller men earn significantly more money than the shorter men. Better looking men earn a little more than their shorter counterparts.

So, if alpha women can't find status and dominance, or if status and dominance have been taken by someone else in the group, their nonconscious brains move them in the direction of the most attractive of those who remain—with a caveat: The alpha woman has her choice. The other 80 percent have the choice of what remains.

The 80 percent won't connect with the high status or highly dominant males. They won't link up with the best-looking men in the group.

But all is not lost. The beta women, the balance of those in the top 50 percent of physical appearance, will, almost to a woman, connect with those alpha and beta males of the group.

Science reveals that, as humans, we are rather shallow. Certainly women tell you they prefer a nice guy, who will care about them, someone who will respect them. And that is true on a conscious level. But conscious minds rarely make decisions in attraction.

That, however, is not what women's nonconscious minds are seeking. That nonconscious mind is fickle. It wants a man who will be successful from the standpoint of reproduction. Healthy, good looking, a man with resources, the top of the group. All these criteria are unconscious filters.

Ask women how they ended up with the last man they ended a relationship with and you'll find he was the most persistent of the men she had recent contact with. The research shows that in general, both women and men have seen plenty by the time they have dated seven members of the opposite sex.

Specifically, that means that the last seven were representative of the litter. Throw out the star and the loser and what remains is what remains. The woman, the man, has seen and dated what is in their league.

If women are shallow, men are ankle deep.

Men have filtering systems just like women, except there aren't as many filters. Men don't have a conscious or nonconscious filter for resources like knowledge, job, educational status/history, or frankly, anything. At the nonconscious level, men filter women by physical appearance.

There is, however, a different system of calculation for men than there is for women. Once men have experienced their seven relationships, whether one night or over the span of a decade in duration, they know their value on the market.

The man entering the room with a random group of women will, indeed, instantly find the most attractive of the women. Almost all heterosexual men will.

That said, the beta male will not approach the alpha female. There is a warning system for men that rejection is coming and it has a similar effect as a police car's siren or the Emergency Broadcast system. All but the alpha males will avoid the alpha females.

And how does one become an Alpha Female? Her job? Her popularity with other women? Her intelligence? Her educational background? Her propensity to smile? The warmth you feel when sitting in front of the fireplace? All meaningless.

The alpha female knows she is alpha because of the seven dates. She knows she is alpha because everywhere she goes, she experiences the same behaviors from males. Men tell her. She knows they are right. She is beautiful. And that is all that matters to the nonconscious mind of a man.

Beta females recognize they are in the top half of desirables and they know precisely what that means. They will almost always get second best, but they do fine.

As men age, their value decreases. But the dramatic declines in the alpha woman as she ages seem like a perfect example of unfairness and inequality between men and women.

And it is. Evolution is not equitable. It is not subject to law or legislation. It simply shows the same results over and over.

Attractive women enjoy a net worth that is 11 times greater than the net worth of average women. Attractive women are far more likely to get a job, get promoted, and earn more money—working for men?

No. The current research is clear. Men in the office treat the attractive woman far more equally than the other women in the office treat the same attractive woman. Women recognize alpha females and they, too, know they are in the top 20 percent of desirability. Women in positions to hire and promote consciously and nonconsciously show strong preference to attractive women.

What's more phenomenal is that mothers of children are far less likely to abuse their attractive babies than their unattractive babies. Literally, from day one, attractive children are treated very differently than unattractive children.

There is no other nonconscious filter for men. From culture to culture, there are variations on just which women are the most attractive, but if you watch international beauty pageants it takes very little scientific analysis to know that these alpha females fit the perceptual nonconscious filters of almost all heterosexual men.

And what of the beta females? What of those who miss the alpha cut? They can do quite well. They will rarely land the highest status or dominance of the alpha males. However, because there are more ways for a woman to keep a man on the nonconscious possibility list, she will actually sample from a different plate than men do.

The alpha female may sample the high status male at church. She may sample the wealthy doctor. She may sample the winner of the city's Handyman of the Year award, if that's a field she finds important.

She will certainly sample the life of the party. She will easily intuit the obviously in-charge alpha seated in the corner, holding court. Unlike the alpha male who will filter in only the top 20 percent, the alpha female will filter in a group that could consist of as many as 40 percent.

And this is why that beautiful woman can end up with that greasy looking guy—who happens to be lead singer in a band or the winner of the Handyman Award—but it rarely works the other way around.

The alpha male will rarely enter into a relationship with anyone other than an alpha female. It's not his fault. It's his nonconscious brain, just as it is for the woman.

Are there other factors involved? Yes, of course.

Beauty is one of those things that stirs emotions about as deep as anything. People want, and in fact, on some levels, people NEED to be as beautiful as they possibly can be.

Need beauty?

Yes. People need beauty.

Studies have shown that infants and children who are seen as unattractive are beaten and abused by their mothers far more often than their attractive counterparts.

We could stop there, but even if the average or below average in appearance survive childhood, their chances, particularly women's chances of ending up with a financially successful and attractive mate by midlife are greatly reduced. And what about after the mate dies?

The less attractive women end up with very little money in inheritance and accumulate almost no net worth whether from their own careers or from what they received from their hubbies in their wills.

And what if the woman decides to go into the concrete jungle? Attractiveness is crucial to their salary and advancement.

Evil men? The stereotype is not what is borne out in the science. Instead it's a different story.

Unattractive women are advanced less often and with less salary increases than their attractive counterparts to a much greater degree by their women superiors than their male superiors.

In other words, women are hiring, advancing, and paying more to attractive women than to unattractive women in a way that supersedes what men have done with women in the past.

Attraction and Net Worth

How much better do attractive women do than unattractive women in net worth? Last time I looked it was staggering. Depending on which study you look at, it's about 100 times more money accumulated in the family, usually most by the husband, but not always.

It's definitely not a pretty picture for those who aren't pretty.

And there is more.

Even Computers Know Beauty

Recently a mathematician came out with a program so that a computer can calculate whether a woman is beautiful or not. And it does so with surprising accuracy. The reason it works so well is because there are specific aspects and attributes that are visible to a machine that are quickly measurable.

To this author, it is a little unsettling that a photograph of a woman can help you predict her likelihood of success on the job, her financial accumulation, and whether she was beaten by her female parent or not.

Beauty Beyond Cultural Norms

Now there is new research that has just been released from the University of Texas, Austin that shows that things go far beyond male dominance or cultural norms.

The advantage of beauty appears to be big in one of the most important ways.

The release reporting the new study reveals that, although many researchers have believed women choose partners based on the kind of relationship they are seeking, in fact, women's preferences can be influenced by their own attractiveness.

David Buss, psychology researcher at the university, has published the findings in "Attractive Women Want It All: Good Genes, Economic Investment, Parenting Proclivities, and Emotional Commitment" in *Evolutionary Psychology*.

We used to think that what women *really* value depended on the type of relationship they were looking for. We believed that women looking for long-term partners wanted someone who would be a good provider for them and their children, but women seeking short-term flings care more about masculinity and physical attractiveness, features that may be passed down to children.

Buss and Todd Shackelford, psychology professor at Florida Atlantic University, have found women ideally want partners who have all the characteristics they desire, but they will calibrate their standards based on their own desirability.

Buss reported that women who are considered physically attractive maintain high standards for prospective partners across a variety of characteristics. The researchers identified five categories of characteristics women seek in a partner:

Good genes, reflected in desirable physical traits.
Resources (money/education).
The desire to have children.
Good parenting skills.
Loyalty and devotion.

Most women attempt to capture the best combination of the qualities they desire from the same man, but the researchers said a small portion of women who do not find a partner with all the qualities may trade some characteristics for others.

And for men? The researchers found the characteristics men desired in a partner did not vary based on their own physical attractiveness.

Does attractiveness matter for men? In fact, we know from previous research that a man's attractiveness does matter in all aspects of life.

Just recently it was found that almost all Fortune 500 CEOs are *not* bald whereas about 35 percent of men in the general population are indeed bald. We also know factually that those same Fortune 500 CEOs are likely to be significantly taller than their counterparts in the real world.

Facial attractiveness in men doesn't pay off for them as it does women, however. Attractive men don't earn significantly more than unattractive men. Attractive men don't accumulate significantly more wealth than the unattractive.

What about Romance?

In romantic attraction, however, things are different. In short, the data suggest that whether you're a man or a woman, being attractive is just as good for your romantic prospects and, to a lesser extent, so is income.

Surprisingly, other researchers who have also used speed dating have found that in addition to attractiveness, earning potential is a factor in evaluating possible mates for both men and women.

Like Attracts Like?

Physical attractiveness is important in choosing whom to date. Good looking people are not only popular targets for romantic pursuits, they themselves also tend to flock together with more attractive others.

All of this causes one question to come to mind. Do more attractive versus less attractive people filter differently when evaluating others' attractiveness?

Columbia University marketing professor, Leonard Lee, and colleagues, George Loewenstein (Carnegie Mellon University), Dan Ariely (MIT), and James Hong and Jim Young (HOTorNOT.com), decided to test this theory in the realm of an online dating site. The site HOTorNOT.com allows members to rate others on their level of physical attractiveness.

Lee and colleagues analyzed two data sets from HOTorNOT.com —one containing members' dating requests, and the other containing the attractiveness ratings of other members. Both data sets also included ratings of members' own attractiveness as rated by other members.

Consistent with previous research, people with similar levels of physical attractiveness indeed tend to date each other, with more attractive people being more particular about the physical attractiveness of their potential dates. And, people prefer to date others who are moderately more attractive than them.

Compared to females, males are more influenced by how physically attractive their potential dates are, but men are less affected by how attractive they themselves are, when deciding whom to date.

KEYPOINT: People of different physical attractiveness levels might instead vary the importance they place on different desirable qualities in their dates.

KEYPOINT: Lee and colleagues conducted a follow-up speed-dating study in which more attractive people placed more weight on physical attractiveness in selecting their dates, while less attractive people placed more weight on other qualities (e.g., a sense of humor).

Although changing facial characteristics is a tough thing to do, there are other factors in overall attractiveness (weight for example) that are controllable.

And how those factors add up can make a big difference over the course of a short life (in the case of children) or a long life (once adulthood is reached) all the way to what is left behind for the family.

Remember: Only the most attractive individual is a 10.

Almost everyone can dress like a 10, walk like a 10, and elect to look as good as they can for every dinner, meeting, and get-together. Physical features and how you utilize those physical features matter. You can't change what your face looks like, but you can change your frown into a smile and increase your face value. Your waistline is under your control and it matters. Your hair (if you have hair!) is under your control, and hair is very important in whether people filter you in or out. The first few seconds make all the difference in the world! They matter so much that you can't afford to ever neglect them again. Remember people will judge you in the first four seconds. The rest of this book will show you what to do next, whether people initially think yes or no.

Thirteen Secrets of Making a Magnetic First Impression That Will Last a Lifetime

Whether it is your first meeting with a person or a current meeting with someone you already are familiar with, the first few minutes are more than critical to the outcome; they essentially *are* the outcome. Harvard tells us that the first 30 seconds of a meeting are critical. I agree, with the added note that the first 4 seconds of any influential encounter are the most important.

With this in mind you can make some significant preparatory efforts so your message is received with the greatest likelihood to draw a positive response.

1. Dress about 10 percent better than you expect your client/customer to be dressed. Do not overdress or underdress. Both of these choices are considered disrespectful by clients.
2. People feel most comfortable when others seem to be like them in appearance, beliefs, or values. Predict the values and beliefs of your clients and customers and emulate or at least be aware of these factors so that you are prepared to make your best first impression.
3. You should be immaculate when you meet your client/customer. This means you should smell clean (not heavily cologned, as many men and women use far too much of the smelly stuff), have your hair trimmed and neat, and physically appear as good as you possibly can.
4. Find out what values are most important to a person in doing business with you and determine those values that are relevant to your product/service. "What is most important to you in possibly doing business with me?"
5. Ask your client how he knows that he has his values met. If he tells you fast service is his highest value, ask him, "How do you determine what fast service is?"
6. Ask your client: If you give him his highest value (fast service in this instance), will he work with you? If not, then what really is his highest value? (He's holding back and you have not yet developed a trusting rapport.)
7. Be certain that you know what your client *needs* your product/service to do. Needs and values are often different from each other, and we aren't interested in what your service *could* do for your customer but what it *must* do for your customer to be loyal to you. "If you had to pick one thing that our service/product must do for you, what would it be?"

8. Be certain to note the client's speaking and listening pace (they are generally identical) and match them as closely as possible. Do not speak so fast that your client fails to process what you are saying (if your client speaks slowly), and do not speak slowly if your client processes rapidly (clue: your client speaks rapidly) because you will bore him.

9. If you are nervous about your meeting for whatever reason, then your client probably is as well. Take advantage of the brain's organization and keep your client to your right if possible when shaking hands, sitting, and communicating. This accesses more of the left brain for both you and your client and allows you both to relax and perform more analytically.

10. When meeting with women (regardless of whether you are male or female) you should try to keep your eye level below that of your counterpart. Research reveals that almost all women are more comfortable and less intimidated when their eye level is higher than those around them.

11. When clients are particularly emotional, do not exceed their level of emotion as you model their behavior. Do allow yourself to be somewhat upset/concerned by the cause of their anger. "The city is making you pay an extra $20,000 for your license this year? What is *that* about?!"

12. Be familiar with the terminology of the business/profession of your clients. Research reveals that using the exact same buzzwords and corporate lingo your customer does identifies you as an insider and makes your client more likely to say yes to you.

13. Show sincere interest and fascination with your client/customer, their interests, pursuits, and business. Nothing is as important in building rapport as an honest and caring interest in the person you are trying to influence.

3 | The Delta Model of Influence

The first four seconds have come and gone. What do you do next?

Every book I've ever read about persuasion, influence, and selling neglected to put strategies and techniques into a usable sequence that would be effective for at least some presentations.

It makes no difference whether you are presenting to a group at the office, to the county commission, to the girl across from you, or making a sale to the CEO. The process is the same. Obviously minor changes will be made in each context. For example, it seems unlikely that the girl will sign and give you a deposit on your first date.

There are hundreds of ways to present information to clients, customers, prospects, and buyers. The Delta Model of Influence is one of my favorite models of selling. I call it the Delta Model because *delta* means "small" or "incremental." (Read that as *subtle*.) Remember, when you are making your presentations and proposals to others, you should note that there are seven key elements that always occur, whether it is a one-on-one lunch date or a speech before a group of 1,000. This model is effective and I recommend you utilize it often in your business. This chapter outlines the model for you so you have an idea of how to present whatever it is you want to communicate. It all begins with rapport.

The Seven Keys to Rapport

Before I delve into the subject of rapport with you, I want you to see the seven keys to establishing and maintaining rapport. Everything else you read in this chapter will then be filtered through these seven points.

1. A person of influence must synchronize with the customer using modeling, mirroring, pacing, and matching.
2. A person of influence shows true, genuine, and sincere interest in clients and customers.
3. As a person of influence, confirm you are in rapport with your client or customer.
4. Find out what is most important to your client/customer (identify *values*).
5. Ask questions to discover the rules that define your customer's values.
6. Ask questions to identify *needs*.
7. Ask questions to discover the rules that define the customer's needs.

The Bridge to a Client's Heart: Rapport

People want to be comfortable. Most people live in personal or corporate environments that either are not conducive to loving communication or, worse, are often hostile and unkind. When people are in our presence we want them to feel at ease. This sometimes means we have to do those things we know will make people feel comfortable, with that as our sole intention. Building rapport often entails doing and saying things that seem awkward but are perceived by others as loving and sensitive.

> **People want to be comfortable.**

Rapport is the perceived affinity between two or more people.

Most people enjoy talking about themselves and probably don't get to do this as often as they would like. This is one reason the Values Determination Model is so effective. When you ask people about their values, you are asking them about their most deeply held feelings and thoughts. This is an important element in understanding people and can greatly assist in developing rapport.

Your ability to build and maintain rapport in communication is one of the key skills of being a caring communicator. An excellent example of rapport building in literature (and one of my all-time favorite stories) is found in the New Testament. You may remember the story of the Apostle Paul traveling to Greece. Athens at that time had a mostly pagan culture. The city was filled with idols and temples to mythological gods. As a Jew, this was repugnant to Paul. Some of the local philosophers challenged Paul to a debate and brought him to the infamous Mars Hill. It is here that we pick up Paul's ability to create rapport and touch people.

Men of Athens, I perceive that in all things you are very religious.

This immediately breaks their skeptical pattern of thinking and creates an instant bridge for Paul to metaphorically walk on.

... for as I was passing through and considering the objects of your worship, I even found an altar with the inscription: To the Unknown God. Therefore, the One whom you worship without knowing, Him I proclaim to you.

Paul uses his rapport-building skills masterfully. The altar is one of the Greeks' objects of worship. The God Paul wants to discuss is one of the Greeks' gods. He is not going to talk about some new god!

God, who made the world and everything in it, since He is Lord of heaven and earth, does not dwell in temples made with hands.

God made the world, Paul tells the Greeks. He is obviously much too big to live in a man-made temple.

Paul continues his discourse, explaining that God gives us life, our breath, and a place to live. He explains that God needs nothing from us.

... for Him we live and move and have our being, as also some of your own poets have said, "For we are also his offspring."

Therefore, since we are the offspring of God, we ought not to think that the Divine Nature is like gold or silver or stone, something shaped by art and man's devising.

Paul once again maintains rapport by returning to and citing the Greeks' authorities. Building rapport is one step. Maintaining rapport and bridging into the message you wish to tell is another.

Truly, these times of ignorance God overlooked, but now commands all men everywhere to repent, because He has appointed a day on which he will judge the world in righteousness by the man he has ordained. He has given assurance of this to all by raising him from the dead.

Paul has reached the crux of his message and has held the attention of his audience. The rapport that Paul built with the antagonistic philosophers is the key to his successful communication here.

Rapport is much more than verbal compliments and praise, of course. Nonverbal behavior is involved as well.

Nonverbal Rapport–Building Skills

- *Physical appearance.* An individual's dress and grooming can help make someone feel comfortable or out of place. How we dress in large part determines how much people will trust and like us. Each situation has a proper manner of dress affiliated with it. To dress in a certain manner to set people at ease may seem an inauthentic way of communicating, but indeed it is very authentic. You are dressing a certain way to help the people you communicate with feel comfortable. You have gone beyond your needs and desires regarding dress to those of others.

How we dress in large part determines how much people will trust and like us.

- *Vocal cues.* It is best to gain rapport by matching the same rate and tone of voice that your fellow communicator is using. It is not necessary to mimic the other person; simply alter your speech patterns in the direction of the other person.
- *Posture and physiology.* One of the most effective methods to gain rapport is to match the posture and physiology of your partner. Sitting or standing in a similar fashion is called, pacing. You can check later in your communication to see if you are actually in rapport by leading. *Leading* means, for example, that if you are both sitting with uncrossed legs, you cross your legs. The other person will follow suit shortly, assuming you are in rapport. Once you have effectively led the other person, you can share your ideas and thoughts more constructively.
- *Breathing.* Watch how and from where the other person is breathing. You can pace the person's breathing pattern as a powerful mode to build rapport. People who breathe at the same rate are usually in sync with each other. When you make love with someone your breathing normally is matched breath for breath.

All these rapport builders lead us to an important key involving authentic communication: *You must often be more like others than yourself if your goal is to engage people in deep and intimate relationships.*

Remember a time when you were in complete rapport with someone. This is a time that you both were almost thinking the same thing. Were you sitting near each other? Was your physiology similar? Think of another time and answer the same questions. Then consider these:

During these moments of rapport did you feel that you were on a roll or experiencing enthusiasm or other intense emotion?

On a piece of paper or in a personal journal record your memories of a time when you felt very self-conscious about your body.

Write about a time when you felt very uncomfortable with another person or a group.

Using some of the information you have learned in this chapter, how might you have been more comfortable in these situations? Record your thoughts.

The 21-Point Delta Model

Having thoroughly tickled your conscious and unconscious mind, it's time to look at the Delta Model of Influence. Each point is numbered so you will be able to identify your strengths and weaknesses in this area as you progress.

1. Establishing and Maintaining Rapport

Rapport can be defined as being in sync with another person. Generally people are more likely to be in rapport with someone else if they like that person. How do you know if you are in rapport? Answer this question: Are they responding to you in a positive manner? If so, you are in rapport.

I remember what Zig Ziglar said at a seminar, "They don't care how much you know until they know how much you care." Therefore, you will want to begin to develop a sense of empathy and sincere curiosity about others. Rapport occurs on different levels of communication. You can be technically skilled at acting and appear to be in rapport, but if you don't sincerely care about your customer and the people you are working with, what is the point? There are several methods of developing rapport.

2. Using Content to Build Rapport

Discover what people's interests are, and if you are not already in tune with a customer's interest, learn about it. People like to talk about what they love and what they know about! When I teach Mind Access seminars, one of my favorite stories about building rapport is the learning-about-fishing story. Living in Minnesota, I have many clients who are avid fishermen. How would I connect with my clients if I know absolutely nothing about fishing? I grew up a Chicago Cubs fan and child prodigy in mathematics and, even though I lived very close to Lake Michigan, unlike most kids I never enjoyed fishing.

People like to talk about what they love and what they know about!

In Minnesota, a big deal is made every year when it is time for the opener. To my mind, *opener* means "opening day at Wrigley Field." The only Wrigley many of my customers know about, though, is the chewing gum. It seemed I was doomed to never meeting many of my clients at more than a superficial level ... until one day I decided to learn about fishing by asking all my clients who love fishing to tell me their favorite fishing stories. I began asking questions that to them must have seemed absolutely ridiculous. Over the past few years, I have built an array of knowledge and stories about fishing. I can direct you to all of the best lakes for fishing and I can tell you what to fish for at these lakes ... and I've never been fishing in the state, not once. You can build a great deal of rapport and long-term friendships by showing and experiencing sincere interest in what is important to other people. Sharing the experiences of your client's hobbies, lifestyle, and interests is using content to build rapport.

3. Using Processes to Build Rapport

There is more to building rapport than swapping fishing stories. Becoming in sync with another person or a group can take a great deal of skill, in addition to the sincere interest that is necessary in building relationships. Many customers will not feel comfortable discussing their families, hobbies, and lifestyles with you, a perfectly nice but perfect stranger. How does the ice get broken when stories are very uncomfortable for the customer?

Many of your customers were taught as children to not talk to strangers. Many of your customers were taught to keep private matters private. How do you help these customers become comfortable with you?

4. Pacing

When in doubt, the most effective way to begin building rapport with anyone is by pacing. Pacing is essentially synonymous with matching or mirroring. In other words, be like your customer, because he likes people who are like him. There are a number of techniques that can be used to effectively pace your client, to begin building rapport.

5. Use of Your Voice

Imagine that your customer is in an upset mood. He has a sharp edge to his voice as you get to make your presentation. Many salespeople would attempt to get him out of his mood with enthusiasm or a cheery story. In fact, the converse is a good rule of thumb: When in doubt, pace your client. If your client has an edge in his voice, let your voice have an edge. If he sounds angry, let yourself be angry, but only briefly, with something that occurred today as well. This vocal pacing will help put you in sync with your client. Eventually you will lead your client out of the negative frame of mind, if you choose to. (There are many times when a negative frame of mind is necessary to making a sale.)

There is more that you can do with your voice than match the tone of your client. We all speak with a measurable average number of words per minute. Many people drawn to the sales profession speak quickly. Part of this experience is due to the nature of the business—we are obligated to be quick and to the point. Unfortunately, if your client speaks slowly and you are speaking quickly to meet a time constraint, you probably will lose the sale. People tend to speak at a rate that is consistent with the way they process their thoughts and internal representations. If people tend to think in pictures (movies), they tend to speak very quickly. People who tend to speak very slowly process information through their feelings and emotions. In between are people we call the radio announcers who speak with more rich and resonant voices and normally think in words.

People tend to speak at a rate that is consistent with how they process their thoughts and internal representations.

Your ideal is to speak in the same rate and pitch of voice as your client.

6. Why Pace Breathing?

Admittedly, one of the more difficult pacing techniques is that of pacing your customer's breathing. Breathing is one of the most unconscious of all body functions, and pacing of breathing is one of the great rhythm generators of all time. Two people in the heat of sexual passion often are breathing at the exact same pace. Two people sitting side by side in deep meditation often experience the same exhale and inhale points. In group hypnosis, hypnotherapists find that having the group breathe together actually creates a wonderful bonding rapport in the room. As you watch your client breathe, begin to breathe in when she does. When she exhales, begin to exhale at the same time. It is best to practice this pacing technique when you are not in verbal communication with people. For example, if you are waiting in line somewhere and someone is talking to someone else, begin to pace the breathing of one of them. You can practice this at home by pacing someone without the person being aware that you are doing it. Our research shows that pacing another person's breathing results in the two people regarding each other more favorably.

7. *Physiology and Posture*

Pacing someone's posture and physiology is much easier than pacing someone's breathing. If you sit erect and stiff and your client is seated in a comfortable, relaxed manner, you are not likely to develop the rapport you hope for. Pacing physiology too closely can be a mistake, though. If every move your client makes is mirrored immediately back at him, he will begin to feel uncomfortable. The most effective manner of pacing physiology is to match the posture and general body position of the other person. The next few points on leading describe how to appropriately test your pacing skills with your client and be certain you have established rapport.

8. *Leading*

Developing a sincere interest in relationships and friendships with others is the first step in the sales process. Pacing your customer is the second step. Leading comes third. A lead is successful when the person follows you. If you are sitting across from your client and you both have similar physiology and you are both enjoying each other's company, you have an opportunity to now begin leading, which is the beginning of the active processes in selling. Will the client now follow you into the sales presentation? You have been following him for minutes and minutes. You've matched his vocal pacing and his physiology. You have shared mutual interests. Now it is time to take a nonverbal break from pacing and start leading. If your client follows your lead you have successfully built rapport at the unconscious level and you can begin your sales presentation momentarily. The next two points describe key methods of determining if you are in rapport with your client.

9. Leading with the Tone, Rate, or Pitch of Your Voice

If you have been successfully matching your client, you have an opportunity to lead by altering one of your vocal qualities. You may, for example, increase your speaking rate a little bit and induce a more enthusiastic attitude in the tone of your voice to help you bridge the conversation to your product. The context of your discussion will help determine when and if this is appropriate. When you notice that the client follows your lead with a more enthusiastic voice, an increased rate of speech, a higher or lower tone of voice, you can feel assured you have successfully developed rapport.

10. Leading with Physiology, Posture, and Movement

The simplest movements that you make will often be mirrored identically by a customer in rapport with you. Imagine that you have been sitting with a hand to your chin for several minutes, as has your customer. You believe you are ready to test to be certain you are in rapport. If you are sitting at a restaurant, you can move your hand to pick up a glass of water and watch to see what your client does. If he follows you by also picking up his glass of water, or even picking up a pen or a napkin, you have successfully led your client to the next stage of the selling process.

You need to begin the rapport process again if your client does not follow your lead.

11. Inducing Reciprocity

Building rapport begins within you. The entire process of building rapport is built on the foundation of concern, caring, compassion, interest, and a desire for the well-being of your customer. Pacing and leading comprise a process that creates comfort for you and the client to know that you are moving along at a pace that is appropriate for the client. The entire process of building rapport, pacing, and leading could take as little time as one minute and as much as an hour or more. After rapport has been established you can enter into the body of your presentation. There are many ways to begin the sales presentation, but my favorite is to give my client something. At this point, I regularly give my clients a book that I wrote called *The Gift: A Discovery of Love, Happiness, and Fulfillment.*

> **The simplest movements that you make will often be mirrored identically by a customer in rapport with you.**

You may not have a book to give, so here are some ideas to consider when deciding how you will induce reciprocity. What you will give to your customer to induce reciprocity will be in part based on the average profit per sale and the significance of your gift. Gifts tend to be reciprocated with sales in direct correlation to the dollar value of the gift that is given. Specialty items like pens, date books, and calendars are perceived as advertising items and do not induce reciprocity. You must think of something appropriate that you can give to your customer that will be appreciated. Inducing reciprocity is not just a sales technique; it is a way of life. There is almost a metaphysical energy that seems to emanate from the giving of gifts. Expect nothing in return when you induce reciprocity. The simple act of giving helps you develop a caring and compassionate personality. That is what people are buying when they buy from you: *you!*

12. Sharing Part of You with Them

Show your confidence in your customers by helping them with one of their potential clients. In other words, offer to help them in any way you can. Can you make a phone call for them as a referral? Can you help them bring more business to their store by taking 50 of their business cards? What can you do to freely help them with their business that is above and beyond the scope of your sales call? *Offer to help.* I've done this for years in selling and marketing, and my kindness has been returned a thousand times over. Would you be willing to write them a testimonial on your letterhead for them to show *their* customers? That is the kind of treatment you would like from your customers, so why not offer it first?

13. The Common Enemy

Nothing binds two people, groups, or nations like a common enemy. Find your customer's enemy and align yourself with your customer's viewpoint. Do the same people try to hurt your mutual businesses? Resonate with your customers. Once someone shares with you who his enemies are, you have built a relationship for life. Does your customer hate the IRS? Taxes? Unemployment compensation insurance? Lawsuits? Government? Criminals? Drugs? Gangs? What are the common threats to business and society that you both dislike and you both know hurt your businesses? You won't find a common enemy in every sales interview, but if you are thinking of the theme, the opportunity to put both of you on the same side of the table will occur during about half your interviews. Once you have a common enemy you have a sale and a lifetime relationship.

14. A Short Story about Someone Like Them

If you can build a reservoir of stories (short stories) about people who have become your customers, you can utilize this selling tool. Tell today's customer about another customer who recently bought from you. This customer should be someone they remind you of. You can build an entrancing sales presentation around such stories, and they make great lead-ins to the core of your presentation.

> *Nothing binds two people, groups, or nations like a common enemy.*

15. *Respect*

Sincerely show respect for the person via a compliment. Always be looking for things to like about other people. A little respect goes a long way, and you cannot underestimate the value of a sincere compliment of respect in the selling environment.

16. *Knocking Their Socks Off*

The shortest amount of time we spend with any client is normally that of the actual sales presentation. When you begin the process, the very first thing you do is this: Blow them away with an astonishing claim, an amazing fact, something that few would know. Show them something astounding that no one else has shown them. Make the biggest claim that you can substantiate. The client will always remember and consider this introduction. Start strong, finish strong. Your claim for your product or your service should be colossal and it must be true. Knock their socks off.

17. *Always Giving More Than You Promised*

Napoleon Hill always made sure his audiences knew the principle of going the extra mile. Follow the examples of those who sell who become millionaires. If you promise something, make sure that your customer gets exactly what you promise and then some. Remember that phrase: . . . *and then some!*

18. *The Power of Understatement*

After making your claim, you can quickly work your way into your sales presentation. This is the time to make sure you don't overinflate your product or service. You made your claim; now support it with the power of understatement. In other words, if your mutual fund portfolio has a track record of 12 percent return per year over the past 10 years, then understate that by saying, "Now, if you average 10 percent per year. . . ." For 10 years you have earned a 12 percent return, but you are being conservative for your client and he knows it and appreciates it.

19. Be Precise: Then Beat Your Precision

If you know that this automobile is going to get your customer 19 miles per gallon, tell him that. Then tell him a secret. "But if you use Mobil One oil you can literally add an extra three miles per gallon of gas, and that translates to an extra $100 of gasoline savings per year." Be precise; then be better than precise.

20. Get It Done Faster, Easier, Better

You live in an age when your customer wants everything to be better, cheaper, faster, quicker, smarter, easier, more luxurious. So promise what you can, and then deliver ... *and then some*. If they tell you that your competitor will get them X, then if you can really do it, you tell your customer that you are going to get them X + 2. Never be beaten because of the lack of going the extra mile. What can you do for your customer that no other agent will do for them? What can you do for your customer that no one else in the business does? Answer these questions, then do it.

21. Be on the Edge of Your Seat

Pay attention with bated breath to every word your customer has to say. It should be clear that what your customer has to say is the most important thing in either of your worlds at that moment ... and it is. If these were the last words you would hear while you were alive you would want to know what your customer has to say. Live your sales presentation as if the significance of each word will change your very life. Relationships are cemented when you do this. With the attitude of respect, going the extra mile, and showing intense excitement about your customer and his life, you won't need to use a multiplicity of closing tactics on your customer. He will demand that you sell him your product—now!

> *Pay attention with bated breath to every word your customer has to say.*

Fifteen Never-Before-Revealed Secrets to Optimize Your Persuasive Messages

Revelation is exciting! Over the next few pages you will discover some of the most powerful secrets of influence.

Primacy and Listing Order

Knowing what *order* to present information in makes all the difference in the world, literally.

I think most people would agree that, in elections, when the voter is not familiar with the names on the ballot, it is simplest to choose the *first option*. What's interesting is that research clearly shows that order makes a difference even in large-scale elections with recognizable names of candidates!

As reported by Jon Krosnick, in the 2000 presidential race, George W. Bush received *9 percent more* votes among Californians in districts where he was listed first on the ballot than where he was listed later. Even in high-profile elections, such as the presidential race, name order in balloting *does* make a big difference.

In general, we know there is a huge advantage to being listed first. In multiple-choice questions, people often choose "A" simply because it is listed first. But knowing that the world can change due to list order is amazing! In all three states where name order was studied (California, North Dakota, and Ohio), Bush got more votes when listed first on the ballot. Other candidates studied also received more votes when listed first. Name recognition and other factors may make a difference, but the impact of name order is clear.

Peripheral Cues and Central Cues

Being listed first on the ballot is what's called a *peripheral cue*. A peripheral cue is a factor that is not relevant to the main factor. It is a factor not central to the decision in question. *Central cues* are the main factors involved in making a decision.

Do not underestimate the value of the information in this piece of research. Bush received *9 percent more* votes when he was listed first. That is upward of 100,000 votes or more! You will need to utilize this information when you are positioning yourself in your sales and speaking and persuading career.

In a three-choice list, you should be first or last. In a list of more choices, most people won't get to the end of the list. When presenting information to others, you want people to select your choice. That means describing and detailing it first (or last).

Today we take the process of persuasion and help you tailor your message with some pretty shocking tactics. A tactic differs from a strategy in that a strategy is more of a plan. A tactic is one element, a smaller piece of the strategy.

I confess that there is some knowledge in the arena of influence that even I simply don't like to part with. The value is so great that it's worth keeping quiet about it. Yet, when I started the Science of Influence series of CDs (the foundation for this book), I was compelled to put (almost) everything on the table for the program. This is one of the dozen or so in a collection of secrets that I didn't plan on bringing out because the material is so profound that it will soon be replicated by others and will bring the cumulative value of the information down in five years. Nevertheless, I want you to have it. This collection of secrets is about optimizing your persuasive message.

> ### *In a three-choice list, you should be first or last.*

After producing the first 72 CDs in the Science of Influence series, one thing is now clear to me. A plethora of variables, useful tactics, powerful strategies, and precision models in the process of gaining compliance exist and now can easily be made operational. There are also numerous models of persuasion and influence that can help you gain compliance rapidly.

Did you know that for a significant number of sales calls, persuasive presentations, and proposals you should *not* mention the benefits of you, your product, service, or idea? Heresy, you say? Heretical, yes; and absolutely proven factual.

Did you know that different people need different amounts of information, and if you guess wrong about how much and what you say, you lose the client, the sale, the date, and the deal? True.

And that's just the beginning.

Knowing When Enough Is Enough: Before You Begin

"Too much information!" You hear that sometimes when you tell someone something that they really didn't need to know. Maybe it was about an operation or some bad food or changing the baby's diaper. Just about anything about these subjects will draw the response "too much information!" from some people.

What about in selling? In the process of persuasion? How about asking for the date? Closing the deal?

Is it possible to give too much information and lose the sale? Yes, it happens all the time.

Is it possible to not give enough information and screw up the sale? Yes, it happens all the time.

Can you predict *when* to give *what* amount of information? Yes!! In fact, this one factor is so important that if you guess wrong you will definitely lose the sale. Period.

How much information to give someone is just one crucial piece of information you must know to optimize every persuasive presentation. How you determine this is based on whether the person you are communicating with is likely to mentally process your information *peripherally* or *centrally*. (Now, don't freak out!)

That means, are they actually considering, pondering, analyzing, and thinking about your message? Or are they relying on other cues like positive images or positive values for the answer? (Your appearance, your expertise, your status, your company reputation, and so on are all examples of *peripheral cues* that have nothing to do with your actual message: your presentation.)

The more information your clients consider and the more they evaluate, the more information you need to give them. The less information they want, the more likely they will say no if you go into great detail.

There are other things that are crucial to success as well. *Message repetition*, *prior knowledge*, *self-referencing*, and other factors will determine whether you will be successful in persuading someone to your way of thinking.

How much information to give someone is just one crucial piece of information you must know to optimize every persuasive presentation.

Repetition

Remember the old Budweiser commercial where there were three frogs sitting on their logs and they repeated the words, "Bud," "Weis," "Er,"over and over and over until it was ingrained in your mind. So, the next time you were presented with a choice to order a beer, what did you say? "Bud-Weis-Er." *Repetition* (a peripheral cue) makes a difference in decision making.

When making a presentation, the simple repetition of key thoughts, ideas, and concepts can pay off big time. In a presentation about how to give a speech, this is what Speakers Bureau owner Dottie Walters said: "Tell them what you're going to tell them, tell them, and tell them what you told them." That was it. There is a lot to be said for the ancient tactic of repetition.

Dramatic Difference

What is memorable about you and your product? What is the *dramatic difference* between you and your competition? If your customers don't remember what it is, they will say no. Stress the dramatic difference between you and the person next to you. Show the quality difference, and repeat it over and over. They may not hire you today, but in the future they may. When they think of you, they will think of the dramatic difference, and it will make a difference in the outcome of their decision.

> *"Tell them what you're going to tell them, tell them, and tell them what you told them."*
>
> —*Dottie Walters' Repeatable Message*

I can't stress enough the importance of a *repeatable message*. Find a way to put your message in a form that is easily repeatable. When I have made mistakes in the past in influence, it has been when I failed to create a meme, or a message that can be easily replicated. Memes are ideas that pass from person to person to person. These are the ideas that spread like wildfire—and result in lots of sales!

Remember the beer commercial that showed the Bud Bowl? As the Super Bowl progressed, the beer bottles played football just like the real players in the game. Budweiser is expert at using peripheral cues to sell its beer. Bud Bowl/Super Bowl. Who always wins? Bud. Bud. Bud.

Miller Lite also used the concept in its "Tastes Great/Less Filling" campaign. Remember this? An interesting sidebar on this campaign is that after the Miller Lite commercials, the concept of light beer hit big, and every brand came out with a light beer. Light beer became so generic that Miller had to let go of the concept.

Prior Knowledge

How much do your clients know about your product beforehand? When they already know about your product, you should not share the benefits with them. When they already are experts and have that knowledge, you must speak to that *prior knowledge* in great detail. When your customer is not an expert, in contrast, you must share the benefits with them.

Physical Attractiveness

Surprising research reveals that your *physical attractiveness* makes a difference when communicating with an expert. When you're talking about the numbers, statistics, and details, physical appearance does not seem to matter. But when you are simply verbally communicating with an expert, you should always look your best.

How Much Is Too Much?

Here is a good rule of thumb about *how much information* to give someone: The more expert a person is in a given area, the more features (not benefits) that person needs information about to make a decision. Knowledgeable people are going to match your message to what they already have stored in their memory and mind. If you come across as not knowing the actual working details of whatever your idea or proposal is, you lose. If you have quality information, you engage the client and optimize your chances of making the sale.

When a person is not an expert in a certain area, less information is generally more likely to be processed more quickly and favorably. In this case, because less is better, you want that message to be very different. You want to share benefits and not features with this client. When the client is not an expert, peripheral cues become crucial.

Self-Referencing

When you are communicating with your clients/customers, be absolutely certain to paint them in the picture of your presentation. Research clearly shows that your clients will give far more consideration to your proposal and will remember it in greater detail if your presentation encourages them to see themselves using your product or service. Remember that *self-referencing* is a peripheral cue. If *you* are the expert or your sources are and the client has marginal knowledge, then self-referencing is a powerful peripheral cue to use. However, if your clients have tons of product/service/idea knowledge and you spend time on getting them in the picture, you are wasting your time and blowing the presentation!

> *The more expert a person is in a given area, the more features (not benefits) that person needs information about to make a decision.*

The more people self-reference the more likely they are to buy, and the more likely they are to remember you and your services.

This is true for almost all advertising when the customer/client has some motivation to use your services. (If the client has no motivation to make use of you, all the self-referencing in the world won't make the sale!)

Remember the controversial commercial that lasted for perhaps three months in 2003? Two beautiful and scantily clad girls were wrestling in the mud. It drew everyone's attention. It aired a lot in those few months but then was pulled. Why? Because of the controversy? Not at all. No one could remember what they were selling. If you guessed beer, you got that right. But what brand? Right—most other people don't know, either. It was Miller, but you get the point. Viewers may have a great feeling toward mud in the future but they are unlikely to find a particular brand of beer interesting because of the advertisement.

Why? There was no viewer involvement with the product. Had the catfight girls sipped on the beer during their bout or had they used the beer cans as defensive weapons, then the viewer could have referenced the product. But there was no linkage between the commercial and use of the product, and, therefore, the commercial ultimately failed.

So what did the Miller folks do when they finally figured this out? They pulled the plug on the catfight girls and added Pamela Anderson in lingerie in a bedroom scene. Certainly that is enough to get anyone's attention, and hold it, but, does she hold a Miller Lite? Does she drink any Miller Lite? Does she have a tattoo of a Miller Lite? Does she in any way talk with you the viewer about buying her a Miller Lite (self-referencing!) No. She holds a pillow and throws it at another beautiful woman, making for an enjoyable 30 seconds, a controversial TV spot, and of course ultimately another 1 to 2 percent market share lost. No self-referencing—no money made!

> **Remember that self-referencing is a peripheral cue.**

Perhaps you recall the controversial and sexy Calvin Klein commercial where the models all appeared to be under 18? The press went nuts. Eventually Calvin Klein got what they wanted. They had 18-year-olds posing as 14-year-olds in hot jeans that teens could identify with (self-referencing) *and* they had all the free advertising from the controversy. The commercials became news and thus were running for free (genius)! However, the key difference was the self-referencing for the target audience. The teens could see themselves wearing the jeans and ultimately did indeed buy them, making for a brilliant campaign.

This tactic has been used by Calvin Klein several times and each time it works brilliantly. Not only does it draw attention, it draws anger from religious parent groups, which, to teenagers, are outgroups.

Because, by nature, we do the opposite of what an outgroup does, their anger, ire, rage, and press accomplished what Calvin Klein knew it would: millions of dollars of free press and sales that skyrocketed. Watch for the next time Calvin Klein is at the center of controversy. Now you'll know why they do it, and, more importantly, how.

Authority

In a presentation, a person who is considered a credible source, an *authority*, is more likely to make the sale. In the next chapter, I share with you this research on credibility.

When talking with your clients, you must make it known that you are the source, the expert. (But you should also be aware that source credibility does not convince those who also are experts.) The fact that you are an expert can tend to create competition in the mind of your buyer. Short-term, anyone can be an expert. Long-term, if you can show that you are the expert, you can make the sale.

With this group of people, it is not the message that matters, it is the fact that you are the source, the expert. With non-experts, you focus on the message.

Arousal

Arousal decreases central processing in the brain and increases peripheral processing. If you want your clients to be persuaded by central cues, you will need to keep arousal to a minimum. If you want them to be persuaded by peripheral cues, you should utilize covert tactics to increase arousal and make them open to the peripheral cues you are optimizing. Keep in mind that arousal can be excitation, happiness, and/or enthusiasm.

Directed Thinking

You want to be able to *direct your client's thinking* in the persuasive process. You would like to be able to get across the idea of finding the difference between you and the norm of the category. Once you have them thinking about that, you've locked in a piece of the sales puzzle.

For example, what is the difference between Kevin Hogan and other speakers? I do not have a prepared presentation. Mine is a stream-of-consciousness presentation, and one speech is never the same as another. Other presenters try to make you believe their speeches are not prepared, and they may get lost in their presentations. How is my speech a little different from theirs? I don't want to be totally different from the rest. Show that you have made alterations, improvements, and adjustments from others. Now we return to the concept of the dramatic difference. This is a great place to share what that is with your client.

Unusual Claims

When trying to hook the client, you can use the tactic of *unusual claims*. Examples would be:

"I'll show you seven things no one has ever shown you before." "Here are three new ways to clean your shower without putting on gloves." "Pay your bills without ever writing another check."

Checklisting

If you look at a successful hotel ad or credit card brochure, you will see a list of benefits you will get with the product advertised. Then next to that list will be the competitor and *its* list of benefits—which always comes up short.

The competition has fewer items checked off. The comparison is presented clearly. We have more benefits! *Checklisting* is one of the most powerful tactics you can use in your advertising and promotion.

4 | Credibility

The Pivot Point of Persuasion

Perception of Credibility: Do You Have It?
It Means Everything

Barack Obama, His Holiness the Dalai Lama, John F. Kennedy, Ronald Reagan, Bill Clinton, Oprah Winfrey, Adolf Hitler, Osama bin Laden, Benjamin Franklin . . . all masters of persuasion. They differ(ed) very much in their goals, objectives, and vision but they are/were all successful at influencing the masses. Why? Credibility. Among those they wanted to influence, they are/were believable. They knew their business. They knew their outcomes. They were incredibly competent.

Credibility is one of the common denominators of success at influencing others. Credibility . . . is the "perceiver concerning the believability judgments made by a communicator" (O'Keefe 1990, 181).

Credibility Is the Pivot Point

Credibility matters. Credibility is the pivot point in influence. Unfortunately, it doesn't initially matter whether you *have* credibility (or are credible); it matters whether *you are perceived that way*.

The perception of your credibility is critical to your being recognized as a person of influence. Credibility is an emergence of six component factors of which the first is most crucial to success in persuasion.

What factors make up credibility?

1. Competence.
2. Trustworthiness.
3. Expertise.
4. Likability.
5. Composure.
6. Sociability.

Competence is the first major component in the credibility puzzle. Go back to the list of the names at the beginning of this chapter. They are/were all very competent people. Competence is a cornerstone of credibility. (Notice that competence isn't correlated with having good values, morals, or the best interests of others.) You can fake competence for a while, but eventually competence is tested and it makes or breaks you. Competence is expertise. It is your qualification(s).

Golden Key: Building your true competence level and building the perception of your competence are two separate projects: You must be the expert, and you must be perceived as the expert.

What specifically do you want to work on? (McCroskey and Young 1981) You want to work on the Seven Scales (continuums) of Competence (being experienced, informed, trained, qualified, skilled, intelligent, and an expert) with those two goals in mind.

Key Point: You want to be competent, and you want to be perceived as competent. It does you no good at all to be competent and be perceived otherwise.

Do an important exercise. Answer these 14 questions. Take your time and assess yourself with great objectivity. If you do this and don't fly past these questions to the next set of techniques, you will make great strides in determining your real and perceived credibility.

1. Are you experienced or inexperienced?
2. Are you perceived as being experienced or inexperienced?
3. Are you informed or uninformed?
4. Are you perceived as being informed or uninformed?
5. Are you trained or untrained?
6. Are you perceived as being trained or untrained?
7. Are you qualified or unqualified?
8. Are you perceived as being qualified or unqualified?
9. Are you skilled or unskilled?
10. Are you perceived as being skilled or unskilled?
11. Are you intelligent or unintelligent?
12. Are you perceived as being intelligent or unintelligent?
13. Are you an expert or not?
14. Are you perceived as being an expert or not?

After answering all these questions, you must construct a competence-building and perception-of-competence building system. If you aren't experienced, you need to become experienced. If you aren't perceived as experienced you must make clear verbally, in writing, via testimonial or in some covert fashion, that you are experienced.

If you look in the yellow pages you may come across words and phrases that attempt to establish credibility, because this is such a big piece of the influence puzzle.

Licensed.
Certified.
MD.
PhD.
Has 27 years of experience.
Harvard educated.
Black belt.
Award-winning.
Internationally known.

On television you see Michael Jordan lend his credibility and competence as the world's greatest athlete to everything from hamburgers to batteries to underwear. This is roughly what a testimonial on the back of a book does for the author. It is called the halo effect. You are borrowing someone else's credibility to build your own. It's smart to do and something you should pursue as well.

Competence is the cornerstone. *Covertly make your client base aware of your competence.* (Have awards on the wall of your office. Have testimonials in your portfolio.) Then, make it certain that, in all of your interactions with your clients, every single one of them knows that your knowledge runs deep and wide. You are the obvious expert in your field.

There are four pieces of the persuasive setting. The first three all demand the dimension of credibility for success.

1. The environmental context.
2. The persuader.
3. The message.
4. The audience/recipient.

Of course, having credibility and presenting a credible image to your customer are very different things. Here is a list of a number of characteristics of credibility building. These words identify areas of credibility that you must have to be a person of influence.

Trustworthiness.
Character.
Safety.
Goodwill.
Personal integrity.
Expertise.
Competence.
Qualification.

Here are a few words you can utilize when you communicate your message of credibility to the public:

Experienced.
Informed.
Trained.
Qualified.

Skilled.

Intelligent.

Expert.

". . . as seen on TV" (hard to believe but true).

Has 25 years' experience.

Credentials

In any given situation you have four ways to show your credibility. Within each of these factors are some polarities that form a continuum of your behavior. Where would you be seen by most people in each of these areas?

1. Extroversion:
   Bold/timid.
   Verbal/quiet.
   Aggressive/meek.

In any given situation you have four ways to show your credibility.

---

2. Composure:
   Poised/nervous.
   Relaxed/tense.
   Calm/anxious.
3. Sociability (likability):
   Good-natured/irritable.
   Cheerful/gloomy.
   Friendly/unfriendly.
4. Being inspiring to others.

Once again, don't fly past these characteristics. Go back and look at the characteristics again. Where do you find yourself among them?

Seven Ways to Increase Your Credibility: The Nucleus of Influence

---

Current scientific research reveals that credibility is one of the golden keys to getting anyone to say yes to you. Very few people have credibility in their profession because they don't understand what it is and why they need it, and they certainly have no idea about how to acquire it.

Write down the following formula and keep it nearby at all times. Whether you are a therapist, a small business owner, or a sales manager at a major corporation, this is the formula that will determine whether anyone will ever listen to you:

$$\text{Expertise} + \text{Trustworthiness} = \text{Credibility}$$

Imagine these two lists of topics about which a company might want to hire Kevin Hogan for training, consulting, or a keynote speech:

Group A: Sales, Influence, Marketing, Body Language, Unconscious Communication, Persuasion, Motivation, Goal Achievement, Personal Authenticity, Communication Skills.

Group B: How to Be Politically Correct, Union Power, How to Change the Oil in Your Car, Government Support for the Arts.

You get the idea. You can see Kevin Hogan making major progress in the company about Group A topics because of massive credibility in those areas.

$$\text{Credibility} = \text{Expertise} + \text{Trustworthiness}$$

I have no expertise in Group B topics and certainly would have no trustworthiness if I claimed to support those issues (although oil changes are very important, and I love the arts—just not the government support of them). It would be inauthentic to promote myself as a sensitivity trainer or someone who wants people to communicate anything but the gentle truth to their company.

Nothing persuades like credibility in people's decision-making processes. You need it, I need it, and indeed everyone needs credibility or we will all ultimately fail at whatever we do. Consider the following example.

Martha Stewart

That name not long ago was perceived as having massive credibility. Not long ago Martha Stewart had a TV show, a profitable publicly held business, and her own magazine: massive credibility. But then one day it all slipped away. *Poof.* In a matter of days Martha Stewart had zero credibility. It's hard to trust the Martha Stewart name today, and when there is no trust there is no credibility.

Nothing persuades like credibility in people's decision-making processes.

Your Mom?

Remember when she said, "Get with a big company that gives you lots of benefits and retirement"? Then millions lost their retirement pensions, their jobs, and many their self-respect because of the corruption of a few in their companies and a bad economy. Lesson: Don't trust everything to anyone. How many people look back at the lousy advice someone they loved gave them only to have been hung out to dry—innocent and well intended as the advice giver was? Mom. A great Mom, lousy business adviser.

So what are the seven research-proven ways to build your credibility?

Daniel O' Keefe discussed these seven in his book, *Persuasion*. My take is a bit different from his, but you get the idea!

1. ***Stress your education, position, and experience.*** The evidence is overwhelming. People respect someone who has a higher position (MD vs. orderly), more extensive education (PhD vs. high school), and more experience (20 years of X vs. just out of school). You cannot immediately change your education but you can reframe your position and frame your experience so that it accents you in the best possible light. You should never lie or exaggerate, but definitely put yourself on stage at the better angle.
2. ***Be a fluid communicator.*** Again, the evidence is overwhelming: Communicate your message without the use of "uh" or slips of the tongue.

Don't mispronounce words. Each flaw counts against the communicator. It is so important that the lesson is clear. A fluid communicator will not read a script or use notes to any significant degree. You need to know everything about your topic, product, or service. You need to be able to influentially communicate that information, and don't even try until you are ready.

3. ***Pick up your speaking pace.*** The research is mixed here, but usually a slightly faster than normal pace is superior to other options. The reason is simple. You can't communicate quickly if you don't know the answer/information.

4. ***Cite evidence.*** I always tell people to never buy a book without a bibliography unless they enjoy fiction. No sources means no credibility. It's better to say, "Daniel O'Keefe says," than to say, "research shows." One shows you are well read, while the other shows you read *The National Enquirer*.

5. ***Argue against your point of view.*** Every great speaker knows that when you bring up the point of view that disagrees with your own you are more likely to win the audience over. Why? That is what they are thinking, and you defuse or inoculate your audience to the opposite point of view. The more you say that surprises your audience/client in this respect, the more likely you are to gain critical persuasion points.

6. ***Be likable.*** This quality won't affect your listener's perception of your expertise, but it will affect their perception of your trustworthiness, and that is the second key aspect of credibility. Being likable doesn't happen overnight. Read a book like my *Irresistible Attraction* or *Talk Your Way to the Top* to enhance your charismatic influence on others.

7. ***Use humor . . . carefully.*** Humor can increase the trustworthiness of a communicator *if* the humor is appropriate to the context and it is not excessive. A little humor can really help your persuasiveness—a little, not a lot!

5 | The New Principles of Influence

Over the years there has been a lot of animosity between academics and street-smart businesspeople. Academics don't go out and actually do the work; they study and research things. Street-smart businesspeople (including salespeople) don't actually know specifically what they are doing that is working. When you take the two worlds and bring them together, you get ... this book. For 20 years I've been interested only in what works. You have the same interest or you wouldn't have picked up this book.

Before we move on to the universal principles of influence in business and relationships, I want you to take a little self-test with me. Throughout the book you will get an opportunity to participate in lots of self-tests. In each of the tests, the questions have been used in numerous studies before. The answers you give will help you understand how you think, and as you go through the book you will literally come to understand how people in general think and decide. Ultimately you will learn how you can utilize all this new learning to be far more influential.

Framing a Question

For your first dip in the pool of new knowledge, I want you to participate in a decision-making game that comes from Kahneman and Tversky (1984). Simply read this scenario and write down the answers before going through the evaluation.

Imagine that we are preparing for the outbreak of a dangerous disease that is expected to kill 600 people. Two alternative programs to combat the disease have been proposed. Assume the following scientific estimates of the consequences of the programs:

- If program A is adopted, 200 people will be saved.
- If program B is adopted, there is a one-third probability that all 600 people will be saved and a two-thirds probability that no people will be saved.

What do you advise—program A or program B? Once you record your answer, read on.

There are two other options now:

- If program C is adopted, 400 people will die.
- If program D is adopted, there is a one-third probability that nobody will die and a two-thirds probability that all 600 people will die.

Write down your choice of program C or D; then read on.

Kahneman and Tversky found that 72 percent of their subjects (medical doctors in this case) chose the "sure thing" (program A) over the "risky gamble" (Program B). However, the researchers obtained almost the opposite results when the alternative options were offered (C, D).

Then 78 percent of the same people (doctors) chose option D, which is identical to option B (C is identical to A).

In other words, someone who chooses A logically must also choose C. Someone who chooses B logically must also choose D because they are the same exact results. However, the different framing or perspective that is given shifts people's thinking in a dramatic fashion.

Fear of Loss versus Possibility of Gain

Key to Influence: The majority of people will do far more to avoid losing something they already have than they will to get something they don't have.

Key to Influence: Fear of loss is a much greater motivator to most than the possibility of gain.

Need more evidence? (Say "yes," as that is the logical response!) The same Princeton University researchers who did the framing research project looked at another situation. They told one group of students to imagine they have arrived at the theater only to discover they have lost their tickets. Would you pay another $10 to buy another ticket? A second group was asked to imagine they are going to the theater but they haven't bought a ticket yet. When they arrive at the theater, they realize they have lost a $10 bill. Would they still buy a ticket?

In this study, 88 percent of those who lost the $10 in cash said they would buy the ticket, but only 46 percent of those who lost the ticket (for which they paid $10) would buy another ticket!

There is nothing logical or rational about the way people buy or make their decisions to buy from you.

Logic would tell you that people want the best product.

They don't.

> *There is nothing logical or rational about the way people buy or make their decisions to buy from you.*

Logic would tell you that people want the most choices possible and that they make decisions logically.

Nothing could be further from the truth.

I have a confession to make. I'm not completely logical, either. I haven't worn a seat belt (except in Seattle, Warsaw, and Boston) for 20 years. My stepdad was nearly killed in a car accident. In 1979 he was struck by a farm vehicle and didn't have his seat belt on. Had he been wearing it, he would have been crushed to death in the car. Because he didn't have it on, he was thrown through the window—140 feet—and barely lived . . . but lived. That emotional imprint has kept the seat belt off me for years; and yet my kids wear a seat belt or we don't put the car in drive. How's that for crummy logic?

Now let's talk about how all this should change the way you sell, buy, and influence others to your way of thinking.

Freedom of Choice . . . or Barrier to Selling?

Even more interesting is research that was just released from a joint study between Stanford and Columbia Universities (*see* Iyengar 2000). Researchers went to a grocery store and set up tasting booths there. On one table they had 24 jams that the people could taste. On another there were six different kinds of jams. As you would expect, 60 percent of all people who stopped at the table with 24 jams tasted a jam. Only 40 percent of those stopping at the table with six jams tasted there.

What's shocking? Underline the following two sentences; then highlight them in yellow:

Thirty percent of all people who stopped at the table with six jams purchased one of the jams.

Only 3 percent of people who stopped at the table with 24 jams purchased any of them!

The ramifications are enormous. The larger number of options (in jam, religion, spousal choices, jobs) creates what we call *cognitive dissonance*. Cognitive dissonance is what happens when you hold two or more beliefs or ideas and don't know which to choose. It makes you feel overwhelmed. People like to have choices; it gives them freedom. But if you give people too many choices they will simply freeze and do nothing.

This is clear in a casino (where I have been known to spend a few hours). Bettors will drive themselves crazy trying to figure out which team, horse, or color to bet on. When they place their money, they become certain they are on the correct side. Later, when their team loses, they can say, "I knew it was going to go that way. I should have listened to myself."

Similarly, people do this when they buy clothing. They see blue; they see black. They stand there helpless. Finally they buy the black and then they feel better inside . . . in fact relieved!

When faced with too many choices, most people can become paralyzed and do nothing at all. People who feel overwhelmed simply drop everything. They do nothing and give birth to procrastination.

If you tell someone, "You can have any of these 100 choices of paint," there is a good chance the person will typically suffer information overload and may very well walk away. People are *not* used to deciding among so many options. They won't be able to decide what to do. If you say, "I can give you one of these four options," then the person finds it much easier to choose.

The truly devastating impact of the internal desire to be directed instead of being given a few options happens in brainwashing and sudden conversion experiences. Here, there is only one correct way or ideology and all others are wrong. This solves the problem of cognitive dissonance and creates what Eric Hoffer called *True Believer.*

Key Question for You: How will you utilize your newfound knowledge about cognitive dissonance in the selling and persuasion process?

> *When faced with too many choices, most people can become paralyzed and do nothing at all.*

Quick Summary

1. People crave direction. Give them direction that wires into their non-conscious drives.
2. People want to believe they are in control, and feel better when they perceive they are.
3. Help people resolve their cognitive dissonance by narrowing options and alternatives quickly and decisively.
4. Realize that your profits will increase with fewer choices for your clients and customers. There are not 64 color choices for the new Lexus or Honda. There are seven choices.
5. Too many choices means that people will freeze and not know what to do. Always be prepared to direct people to the best choice for them.

Your First $10,000 Key: (A $10,000 Key is different from a Key to Influence because the ultimate value of these special keys is found in their ease of application in all walks of life, sales situations, and communication.) *People want what other people already have.*

Your Second $10,000 Key: People overestimate the value of what they already possess.

Every four-year old child will tell you that the most important toy in a room full of toys is the one that the other child is playing with!

Always think long term. Your clients look to you for guidance and will remember the results.

Mine Is Best

In the first part of this chapter, we discussed how the vast majority of people do not normally make buying decisions (or any decisions, for that matter) in a logical or rational fashion. In fact, you found just the opposite.

1. You found that people make decisions based on how a proposition is framed (positive versus negative, for example).
2. You also found out that people who have purchased a ticket to the theater and lose it are not likely to replace it, but someone who loses money (the cost of the ticket) will still buy a ticket. Owning money and owning a future event are different things.
3. You discovered that people typically are more likely to purchase something when there are fewer options to choose from instead of having many options.

None of these things should matter when it comes to buying or not buying, but they do. Just applying these three simple facts should be enough to help you increase your sales by 15 to 25 percent if you apply them to your product, your mode of receiving payment, and your specific situation. Now, how can we top paradigm-shaking facts like these?

Glad you asked!

You've probably thought that, as a therapist or a salesperson (the two largest demographics of my readers around the world), if you could just get people to change their attitudes, you could get them to change their behaviors (in fact, you could say that persuasion is about influencing attitude, and compliance is about changing behavior).

But perhaps you haven't thought of the opposite: *Change the behavior first and you can change the attitude forever.* Here are some examples of successful behavioral changes to influence long-term attitude change. Once people own their actions or once people own something, their behavior and attitudes both begin to change. In fact, once people own something or possess something, they believe that what they own is worth more than it really is, whether it is an idea or something tangible.

Once people own their actions or once people own something, their behavior and attitudes both begin to change.

Ziv Carmon, a French marketing professor, and MIT's Dan Ariely divided a group of nearly 100 Duke University students into two groups. One group was asked to state the highest price they would pay for a ticket to the National Collegiate Athletic Association (NCAA) Final Four basketball tournament. The other group was told to imagine they had such a ticket and were asked for the lowest price at which they would be willing to sell it. The median selling price was $1,500. The median buying price was $150! The sellers perceived their ticket to be worth 10 times what the buyers thought it to be worth!

(Could it be that what a person will lose once they no longer have their product/idea is a cause of the inflated price? Keep reading and you will see that you are right! Fear of loss plays a big role in decision making . . . a much larger role than it should!)

Endowment Effect

This effect has been exploited for generations. In the profession of selling, everyone knows the puppy-dog close—the technique of getting your product into your customer's office or home for a short period of time. Why? Because, like taking a cute puppy dog home, once we possess something, we value it more highly than we did when it was in the store. Once we do that, the price of the goods goes up in the human mind. That price is more than its price tag at the store, and the individual then buys it. What marketing strategies currently utilize this psychological quirk in human nature as an influential strategy to make sales?

- Book–of–the–Month Club.
- Columbia House CD Club.
- Magazine subscriptions.
- Office supply sales (especially photocopier machines).
- Art galleries.

So many different companies utilize the endowment effect in selling, it's a wonder that everyone doesn't. Key learning strategy for today: How can you use the endowment effect without actually having your product/idea in the customer's possession?

From Your Life

Have you ever had people from a church or group invite you to their meeting or service? That didn't change your attitude (or, say, your religion). You simply went as a favor. But then, after some period of time, you decided that you liked this church or group and decided to join. Later, as time went on, you decided that your newfound group was indeed the right group to belong to.

Many groups do not ask you to change what you believe; they simply ask you to take part in their service/group/organization and test-drive it to see how you feel, for example, and see if it works for you.

The brain is a funny thing. Once you start to perform a set of actions, you become accustomed to the actions, and you would feel a void if those actions were no longer there. Therefore, your attitudes begin to change.

Now, none of this is good or bad; it's simply an example of how you can utilize actions that you own to change attitudes. In fact, there is little that is more effective in changing attitudes than regularly performing a set of actions or rituals. Rituals are remarkably important in attitude change.

Key Question for You: How can you get people to take an action instead of persuading them to change an attitude or belief?

There are a few multibillion-dollar corporations that know how to reach the inborn genetic programming within each of us so we will be inclined to purchase their products. You are going to now learn a few of the secrets of these multibillion-dollar international successes. The world's best advertising is not geared at just our behavior but at something that is next to impossible to change: our DNA. We aren't going to take you through a scientific explanation of how each of these mind access points works. That would take a set of encyclopedias. What you are going to learn is how to apply the research that we have done in the sales situation so that it is easy for you to utilize.

> *The world's best advertising is not geared at just our behavior but at something that is next to impossible to change: our DNA.*

All people need food, clothing, and shelter in our society. Those are inborn requirements to survive. You must have some kind of shelter for inborn needs of security and territorial ownership. Beyond this, there are very few inborn needs, but there are many inborn tendencies that drive human behavior as your customer grows and becomes an adult.

Your Appeal Should Be to the Many or Greater Cause, Not Just Your Client

Our genes do not simply generate the tendency for us to survive and care for the self; they virtually command and carry out a powerful compulsion to care for the larger groups that we are part of. In fact, almost all of our genetic makeup is so designed that we will help the larger groups we are part of survive before we will save ourselves.

Have you ever seen a news story where a man raced into a burning building to save a young child? Not only is that an altruistic act, it is part of most people's genetic programming. The compulsion to care for others in our group is very powerful.

Almost all people are preprogrammed to act in the best interests of:

- Themselves.
- The family.
- The group.
- Society.
- God.

The big mistake that salespeople make is that they appeal only to the customer's best interest when they should be appealing to the customer's interest in how your product will help his family, his employees, his civic groups and church organization, society as a whole, and even God. It was only in 1998 that there was discovered a portion of the brain that is activated when communicating with the divine.

There is an old McDonald's commercial that ran for a decade or more, and it illustrates how to appeal to the greater genetic needs. The theme song, "You deserve a break today, so get up and get away, to McDonald's ..." plays in the background. The image is that of a man who has had a long day at work. The genetic motivator, however, is not self-satisfaction. The motivator is when you see Dad and Mom and the kids all driving off to McDonald's together.

Exercise: In order to motivate a person you often must widen the context for the emotional reasoning to engage. Describe how you can do this for your product(s) and/or services.

Competition Is a Driving Genetic Force of Survival

The field of evolutionary psychology has taught us that competition between individuals and groups is what naturally selects winners and losers in society. When you are appealing to your customer to purchase your products and services, appeal subtly to the fact that owning your products or services will give him an advantage in society, within the group, or against his competitors. The makeup of the individual is to survive competitively. The world's greatest competitors are those who become the wealthiest individuals. Bill Gates, Ted Turner, Warren Buffett—all of these men are very good people, yet brilliant competitors. Bill Gates doesn't seek to own a share of the market with Microsoft—he seeks to dominate the market with Microsoft and does so by providing outstanding products at reasonable prices. Microsoft seeks to dominate with great products and services. You can do the same by appealing to the competitive nature in your customers. Do so quietly and with careful subtlety. *It is a genetic fact that those who opt out of competition reduce their level of prestige on the societal ladder.*

The world's greatest competitors are those who become the wealthiest individuals.

Exercise: Realizing that competition is one genetic component of what creates success and failure in society, take your time and carefully answer the following three questions.

1. How can competing to dominate your market with great service and great products help you and your family ascend the ladder of success?
2. How can you sell more of your products and services by appealing to the need in our customers to be at or near the top of the success ladder?
3. How does being competitive enhance the quality of your life?

The Principle of Larger Numbers

It is a known fact that madness is the exception in individuals and far more common in groups. Most normal humans would never throw ice balls at unprotected innocent people walking down the street. Watching a football game in season would never convince you of this truth as referees are constantly on the lookout for spectators who they know can generate great harm. Soccer fans have been seen on numerous occasions to literally kill people at soccer games because of the intensity generated during the competitiveness of the game.

Every public speaker knows that persuading most of the people in a large group is far easier than persuading one individual in a one-on-one setting. There is an almost evident IQ deficiency in groups. Groupthink takes over and people will follow the vocal proponents of a proposition. Most people in a group are like sheep waiting to be herded.

Scientific research clearly shows that the more people there are in a group the more likely that the vast majority of the group will comply with whatever the leader is proposing. The fascinating caveat is that there is a very common fear of speaking and presenting before groups.

People act like animals in groups and are easily herded. However, you cannot expect or even consider having 100 percent assenting opinions in group settings. In all groups there are individuals who rise above groupthink. When facing their objections, always honor and respect their viewpoints and continue on with your presentation. The vast majority will always rule and you will nearly always succeed in group selling situations if you follow all the key elements presented here.

Remember the truism from the nineteenth century: The larger the lynch mob the more brutal the lynching. Those in an emotional frenzy lose all sense of ethics. Think of experiences that you have had that make this fact clear to you.

Those in group settings tend to be led by the nonconscious minds of the rest of the group. The average intelligence of a group is very low. People in groups either don't think well or they succumb to groupthink quite easily. At this point, the conscious minds of people tend to wind down. The nonconscious starts to drive the human brain in groups, and that nonconscious mind is far more reactive and emotional than the analytical individual conscious mind. The conscious mind rests in group settings, making an easy target for the ethical salesperson or the unethical swindler.

Principle of We All Need Someone to Love

All humans need to feel wanted. Science and medical research clearly reveals that feeling unwanted stunts all forms of human growth and development. Physical, psychological, and emotional growth all are influenced by a person's perception of feeling wanted. In fact, people who say they don't need to feel wanted are literally lying or psychotic. The need is preprogrammed.

All humans need to feel wanted.

You need to make it clear to your customers that you are interested in them as more than customers. People can literally sense genuine interest, and when they do they are likely to develop the long-term relationships with you that will create win–win selling situations.

One medical study (Ryan and Lynch 1989) concluded that "a lack of warmth and meaningful relationships" is a significant cause of heart attacks in many people. What does this tell us about needs preprogrammed into our behavior? We are physically influenced by love, compassion, and relationships.

Dr. Dean Ornish published a wealth of material about the fact that closeness can literally heal people and separation from loved ones can kill. Understanding this biological fact can help us influence others in a powerful way.

Aside from the lack of closeness with others, why is it that people are impotent when it comes to influence?

Why do most people fail at selling (and hate to sell)? People go to motivational seminars. They come back. They go to work Monday. . . They still sell only 10 percent of the time. Why?

They are smiling and motivated. Because far more in the realm of selling and persuading others is about nonverbal behavior and context than anything anyone will verbalize.

Actually, *motivation* in the sense that most people think about it, has very little to do with influencing or selling or much of anything.

However, there are factors that do matter in whether someone will sell a whole bunch more stuff, a little stuff, or no stuff at all.

Positive attitude might sound trendy, but it doesn't rank in the top 10 factors that affect selling. For several years we've known, for example, that, on average, when a product is shown first or last in a presentation or grouping of many products or people, it is more likely to be selected or bought.

This is true whether the context is someone hiring a new employee after many interviews with others, or selling. It's true across contexts. We know that those products/items/people shown **last** are significantly more likely to be selected than any other choice.

For example, on American Idol, the contestants who perform last are far more likely to advance to the next show and, in fact, to win the overall competition.

What we didn't know until very recently was what happens when you show products/items to buyers who are *happy*. All of a sudden things get **really** interesting.

Influence and Mood

Participants were first asked to write about either a happy or a sad event in their lives, to help establish their mood.

They were then presented with several mango-flavored desserts, and 69 percent of happy participants chose the first option they saw, compared to only 38.5 percent of unhappy participants.

The researchers also found that when happy consumers were asked to withhold judgment until all options were presented, they tended to prefer the last option they saw.

In another study, three dessert options—blueberry, almond, and plum pie—were presented sequentially, and consumers were explicitly asked to withhold judgment until all options had been presented.

Happy consumers chose the last item 48 percent of the time, compared to just 26 percent of unhappy participants. Researchers offer the following explanation:

If consumers are exposed to multiple options that differ only in global aesthetic aspects, they tend to evaluate each option spontaneously at the time they first encounter it.

On the other hand, if consumers are exposed to multiple options that differ in important descriptive features, they may withhold their evaluation until they have seen all the options available and evaluate the last presented (most recent) option first.

They conclude:

Altogether, these findings suggest that the influence of mood on comparison depends on which alternative in a choice set is the one being evaluated first. (Cheng and Yeung 2008)

Influence and Product Placement

A can of Coke next to the word *awesome*; a can of Pepsi next to a picture of a happy couple. Seem too basic to be effective advertising?

Prior research has shown that reported attitudes toward brands are not affected by such simple juxtapositions. However, a new paper in the *Journal of Consumer Research* examines our implicit opinions—and finds that we may actually be more susceptible than we think (*see* Gibson 2008).

Bryan Gibson (Central Michigan University) showed undergraduate psychology students pairings of well-known cola brands with words and images. Some had positive associations: a field of flowers, the word *awesome,* or a mother holding a child. Others had negative associations: people at a gravesite, the word *terrifying*, or a person in a contamination suit.

Participants were then distracted by an unrelated thinking task—memorizing an eight-digit number—and offered a can of Coke or Pepsi to take home with them.

When distracted, those who were initially neutral toward both brands strongly tended to choose the brand that had been paired with positive images or words in the earlier task.

Interestingly, this happened even when the participant couldn't remember which brand had been paired with positive information.

Those who had an established preference for one brand before the experiment, as established by a pretest, were not affected by the inclusion of a distracting task while making their choices.

In an April 21, 2008 press release, Gibson said:

These results have implications regarding how consumer attitudes are formed, and how they are then applied in brand choice situations.

This suggests that implicit product attitudes may play a greater role in product choice when the consumer is distracted or making an impulse purchase (*see* Gibson 2008).

Influence and Community

I've made a great deal of fuss about persuading not just the individual about his or her self/best interest, but in the interest of the group, the community, or for God.

People act in their own best interests, according to traditional views of how and why we make the decisions that we do. However, psychologists at the Universities of Leicester and Exeter have recently found evidence that this assumption is not necessarily true. In fact the research, funded by the Economic and Social Research Council, shows that **most of us will act in the best interest of our team—often at our own expense.**

Psychologists carried out tests of team reasoning theories by measuring two well known views of how people behave.

Orthodox or classical game predicts that people will act for selfish reasons.

Team reasoning theory suggests individual self-interest is not always what happens in the way people act because they will act in the best interest of their team.

In an April 28, 2008 press release, lead researcher Professor Andrew Colman, of the University of Leicester School of Psychology, said:

> We have shown that, in some circumstances, decision makers cooperate in their collective interests rather than following the purely selfish predictions of orthodox game theory.
>
> We carried out two experiments designed to test classical game theory against theories of team reasoning developed in the 1990s by British game theorists.
>
> Theories of team reasoning were developed to explain why, in some circumstances, people seem to act not in their individual self-interest but in the interest of their families, companies, departments, or the religious, ethnic, or national groups with which they identify themselves.[1]

On a larger level, people don't always just think of themselves. Perhaps we aren't as selfish as we once believed.

---

[1] For published results, please refer to: Colman, A. M., B. D. Pulford, and J. Rose. "Collective rationality in interactive decisions: Evidence for team reasoning." *Acta Psychologica 128*(2) (2008): 387–397.

Next, let's look at a very microlevel of influence princples. Here are a handful of tactics that will accelerate the process of persuasion.

Loss-of-Ownership Tactic

Humans are "possession creatures." Research is clear that simply by holding an object we value it more in financial terms. Bidding on an item on eBay increases the perceived value of an item. Once we own an item or even a person, in our minds or in reality, we place a much higher value on it than we do if someone else owns/holds it. Therefore using the loss of ownership tactic can be powerful in gaining compliance (technical term for gaining agreement or a specified behavior).

Here's an example of this tactic:

"Dr. Johnson, I understand you earn X dollars per year."

Now, which approach is going to work better in causing compliance?

- "I would like to show you how to make 25 percent more next year."
- "I'm worried about your income dropping 25 percent. . . ."

If you said the second choice, you were right. We are much more afraid of losing what we already possess than getting anything of similar value. People will do a great deal to protect an intiial loss from happening.

Disconfirmation-Doesn't-Cut-It Tactic

- Once people have a belief, they filter out *all* other information.
- They do *not* look for information to disconfirm their beliefs.

No matter how wrong someone is about something, no matter how obviously they are shown to be incorrect, they will continue to look for information to support their original belief. Therefore, don't try and point out what won't fit through someone's mental filtering system.

Instead, cause them experience alternatives so they can disconfirm their own beliefs.

If someone thinks that one brand of gasoline causes better gas mileage, simply do a test to show that gasoline is gasoline. But don't tell someone that. When people have beliefs that are erroneous, the best way to eradicate them is through their own personal experience.

The Mistake of Asking the Wrong Question

People don't know why they say yes or why they buy something, so don't ask.

> "We decided to buy that house because it was close to a good school . . . ."
> "We decided to buy that car because it gets good gas mileage."

These kinds of statements are the results of someone asking a question that has no real answer. By asking these kinds of questions you put yourself at risk of causing the person to say no to you.

Instead, ask questions that cause someone to reflect on actual behaviors and have them describe actions or behaviors to you. Unless you have a well-planned strategy, don't ask why they said yes to him and no to you. They simply don't know.

Note-Taking Tactic

It's hard to overstate the value and effectiveness of this tactic.

When people are in a decision-making process, do anything and everything you can to have them take notes. Encourage them to write facts, figures, and ideas onto a piece of paper. (Using a computer doesn't have quite the effectiveness, but it is better than doing nothing at all.)

- To get people to stick to their decisions, get them to write them down.
- This works far better than asking for people's decisions and having them stick with them.

Getting people to write anything down creates involvement. If they were even to write down the possibility of doing business with you rather than not, they *still* have written down the possibility of doing business with you! *That* increases compliance.

People Can't See the Future, So Get Them to Commit to It, Not Pay for It

Temporal reasoning—that is, thinking about time—is something people aren't very good at. People tend to overestimate the amount of time and money they will have this time next year or in five years or even at retirement.

Two things are certain.

1. People want to buy your X today. They want to go have fun today.
2. People would prefer not paying for your X or having fun today.

People want gratification and their addiction fixes right now in this moment. Having people pay for that gratification is another thing altogether. When putting the payment off into the future, the individual is much more likely to comply with a request right now.

- They can see the car.
- They can see food.
- They can see today.
- Therefore, you must often move the painful end of a commitment into the future to hear yes today.

The future is impossible to imagine for most people. Therefore, get them to set the payment date a great distance into the future. Then, all you need for commitment is a yes or a signature today. Study after study shows that people are comfortable agreeing. They are uncomfortable with money.

The Inconsistency Tactic

- After making perceived progress in some way toward a goal, a person becomes more likely to do contrary behaviors.

The person who just lost 10 pounds is quite likely to celebrate with a pizza (or something similar). The person who makes a donation is likely to splurge on themselves. The person opening a retirement account is more likely to buy a new car.

Watch for opportunities. When someone does something foolish, have them then agree to do something in their best interest. Timing can sometimes be everything in persuasion.

The Single Differentiation Tactic!

People can typically repeat one message about another person or product.

> "He's a jerk."
> "It's a piece of junk."
> "This thing is a monster."
> "It's a cash machine."

What *one* factor, element, or benefit of you, your product, or your service makes you worthy of going viral?

> Focus a great deal of attention on one benefit. (For example, increases word of mouth ... easier to spread quickly!) What makes it easy to differentiate you from the competition?

Nine Golden Keys

You learned in this chapter that:

1. People make decisions based on how a proposition is framed.
2. People do more to avoid losing than to make an equal gain.
3. Reduce choices in order to increase sales and compliance.
4. Change the behavior first and you can permanently change the attitude.
5. People overestimate the value of what they own.
6. Appealing to higher values is more important than appealing to the individual.
7. People want to be at the top of the pecking order.
8. It's much easier to influence a group than an individual.
9. People will do much to be part of a group.

6 | Introduction to Omega Strategies

Before you learn about omega strategies, I want to give you your first Influence and Persuasion Quotient (IPQ) test! (Do I have you in suspense?)

In the preceding chapter, you decided how you would react in a couple of different hypothetical scenarios. Now, I want you to discover where you are at in terms of your understanding and ability to apply some of the principles of influence. This test is one that I gave in "Coffee with Kevin Hogan" (if you don't subscribe, my goodness, go to www.kevinhogan.com right now and do so!), and the response was one of great appreciation. Even if you may have taken this test already, please do so again.

Testing Your Influence and Persuasion Quotient

Wouldn't it be great to know how to frame your products, services, and ideas—yourself—so that others simply fall over as they try to get to you? Over the next several months, I will be releasing on my web site the culmination of years of research and meta-analysis of what works and what doesn't in the fields of influence, persuasion, and compliance. All of this material is 100 percent ready for use in selling and marketing. Virtually all the information is new and has never been shared in anything that I have ever released.

To gauge your current knowledge of what works in influence, let's start with a test that you can take to see what your IPQ is. You'll need a pen and paper and about five minutes of your time. Write all your answers down. This is crucial, as you will see.

1. Imagine you are considering purchasing a CD player but you haven't decided which brand or model you want to buy. You walk past an electronics store and see a sign in the window advertising a popular Sony CD player that is on sale for $99. You know that price is well below the standard retail price.
   A. What percentage of people would buy the Sony, according to recent research?
      24 percent.
      48 percent.
      59 percent.
      66 percent.
   B. What percentage of people would wait to learn about other models, according to research?
      76 percent.
      52 percent.
      41 percent.
      34 percent.
2. Now imagine the same situation except that the store is also advertising a high-quality Aiwa CD player for $159. Like the Sony, this player is a bargain.
   A. What percentage would buy the Sony, according to researchers?
      11 percent.
      27 percent.
      39 percent.
      51 percent.
   B. What percentage would buy the Aiwa, according to research?
      11 percent.
      27 percent.
      39 percent
      51 percent.

C. What percentage would wait to learn about other models, according to research?

62 percent.

50 percent.

46 percent.

10 percent.

(If you knew the answer to just these two questions, you would have an enormous understanding of what causes people to buy now, and how people make choices. But there is more you can learn. Continue with question 3!)

3. In a research project by Kahneman and Tversky (1984), researchers offered individuals their choice between a Minolta X-370 camera priced at $169.99 and a Minolta Maxxum 3000i priced at $239.99. What percentage of people chose the Minolta X-370 at $169.99?

10 percent.

30 percent.

50 percent.

70 percent.

4. The same researchers as in question 3 also offered a different group of participants the same two cameras noted in question 3 but also offered the Minolta 7000I at $469.99.

A. What percentage of people chose the X-370?

21 percent.

31 percent.

41 percent.

51 percent.

B. What percentage of people chose the Maxxum 3000i?

47 percent.

57 percent.

67 percent.

77 percent.

C. What percentage of people chose the Minolta 7000I?

2 percent.

12 percent.

22 percent.

32 percent.

Knowing how the wild card of the third product, which is new, significantly more expensive, and probably better, changes the buying decisions of individuals is absolutely essential in understanding how to communicate with and influence people. Before we talk more about that, score your self-test right now!

Scoring

Question	Answer Points	If Correct
1A	66%	3
1B	34%	3
2A	27%	4
2B	27%	4
2C	46%	5
3	50%	4
4A	21%	4
4B	67%	4
4C	12%	4
Total		35

Your score:

30+ Superb. You have a solid understanding of the dynamics of influence. Well done! You are in the top 10 percent.

20–29 Not bad. You have some of the basic concepts of influence down and a good intuition. The Science of Influence series of CDs and home study manuals will help you enormously.

11–19 Don't worry. More than 50 percent of the marketing and salespeople we work with are in this category. You aren't alone and we aren't telling anyone! Order the first volume of the *Science of Influence* and start utilizing its cutting-edge information.

10 or fewer points. Almost 30 percent of sales and marketing people fall into this category. The Science of Influence will change your life and your income forever!

As you have learned, adding the Aiwa CD player to the decision-making process caused people to not know what to do—46 percent of the people couldn't decide, so they put off their decision! Among the half that did buy, they were evenly split between going for the bargain and opting for the better product. Unfortunately, cutting your sales this much will kill most businesses. Don't make this mistake!

The next thing we learn from our test is that, when given the two original forced choices between the two cameras, people were split between the bargain and the higher-quality option. However, adding another choice, the very expensive camera, caused a large majority of individuals to buy the *middle*-priced product.

Pay close attention: In numerous research studies in catalog promotions *the addition of an extremely expensive, high-end product causes people to buy the next highest product with a great degree of consistency.*

Reducing Resistance in Relationships, Business, and Life

I've held you in suspense long enough. What is an omega strategy?

An omega strategy is a strategy that is specifically planned to reduce resistance to your message and, as such, has nothing to do with adding value to your offer.

Here's what to do before they say, "I shouldn't have listened . . .":

Broadly speaking, there are two ways you can be more persuasive and gain compliance. You can make your offer more attractive or you can reduce the resistance that you experience with the other person. Most books in the world of selling, persuasion, and influence deal with making your offer more attractive. This article, however, is going to show you how to reduce resistance. It's something that hasn't been dealt with much in the literature, so it might take a bit to lay out this mind-blowing information from all angles.

Do you remember the last time someone said, "I think you should . . . ," or "If you do this, it will work," or "Do this," or "Do that," or "If you buy this . . . , " or "I'd do X if I were you"? And then, for some reason, you not only didn't do it, you did the opposite! This is called a polarity response, or in psychological terms, reactance. Eliminating or reducing the polarity response and reactance is what this section is all about. There's nothing easy about understanding all of this, but if you stick with me over the next few pages, you will be astounded by what you learn. That's a promise. If you don't read these pages, you will always regret that you didn't learn this information and begin applying it in your life, your relationships, and your business!

My life's work is in large part about influencing the human mind (yours, mine, our client's and customer's, and the public's—everyone's!) for health, wealth, and happiness. You and I are always fascinated by the processes that people use to decide between X and Y, realizing how the choice will, perhaps, change their life forever.

You can make your offer more attractive or you can reduce the resistance that you experience from the other person.

Before we go on with why we sometimes respond negatively without a great deal of thought and conscious cognition, I'd like to share with you a story of how one simple decision that started with a "no way" knee-jerk reactance could alter the course of a person's work and life.

It was 1998 and Archie Levine was the event planner for a small non-profit organization. He asked me to speak at its convention in Seattle. (I had been going to speak for this group the previous year but it didn't happen. I had been on the last flight of the day, and it was canceled due to mechanical difficulties. Yes, another stellar moment for the airlines.) When Archie quoted me the fee, I immediately said, "Sorry, I can't do that." To myself, I said, "No Way!" But due to other circumstances that would soon materialize, I decided to speak at this convention—not because of the convention and certainly not because of the money—but rather because when I announced I might be there, a cyber friend, Richard Brodie (inventor of Microsoft Word and author of *Virus of the Mind*), said if I came he'd introduce me to the audience. Well, I could hardly wait. I loved his book, and he said he found my book, *The Psychology of Persuasion,* fascinating. (He was obviously the genius that everyone claimed he was.)

Yes, I was going to Seattle to speak, but the fee wasn't even close to my standard fee. The nonprofit group just couldn't afford it. My incentive was that I was going to have dinner with Richard. That was really why I was going to go to Seattle. The convention—well, I'd give my 1,000 percent, but to dig into the brain of Brodie was the real enticement to me! So, I went.

Richard and I met, and we hit it off from the first. He and I would become good friends. Since we met, Richard has written testimonials for three of my books, and he wrote the Foreword to *Talk Your Way to the Top*.

Meanwhile, because I decided to go to Seattle, I also met the woman who would become the co-author of two of my books (*Irresistible Attraction* and *Through the Open Door: Secrets of Self-Hypnosis*). Mary Lee LaBay is an excellent writer and has a sharp mind. Her contributions to these books helped make them among my favorite books. She also worked with me on developing training sessions in Seattle, where she brought me several students, including Ron Stubbs, Bev Bryant, and Katherin Scott, who are now partners with me on various other projects.

Three years later, on a trip to Las Vegas with Richard, I met his good friend Jeffrey Gitomer, who is the author of *The Sales Bible*. Jeffrey is a rough-edged guy with a heart of gold. We became friends and eventually he wrote the Foreword and testimonials for my recent book, *Selling Yourself to Others*. He's one of the nation's highest-paid and finest speakers.

There is a lot more that came out of Archie Levine's phone call to me six years ago, but the point, of course, is that my decision to go was a life-altering decision in every way.

Key: My initial gut reaction to this offer was, "No way!" The money was lousy, the venue was mediocre, and I saw nothing attractive about the convention from a professional standpoint . . . until I had more information, and it took weeks to get the information I needed to make one of the best decisions of my life.

Wouldn't it make sense for you to make sure that your decisions and the decisions you influence others to make are the best ones?

Two Kinds of Resistance

Broadly speaking, there are two kinds of resistance. The first is because of reactance (a knee-jerk deflection of anything that infringes on our personal choice or freedom), and the second is because of anticipated regret of complying or failing to comply with a request.

Did you know that very few people will trade a lottery ticket they have just purchased for the original dollar they paid? Now, at best, a lottery ticket is worth 50 cents on the dollar. (This is complicated to explain, but if you bought $100,000,000 of lottery tickets you'd win about $50,000,000 for a net loss of $50,000,000—that is, 50 cents of value for every dollar spent—a terrible gamble for you and a moneymaker for everyone else involved.)

Now, why do people want to keep their lottery ticket once they possess it? Why don't they want to part with this terrible investment?

The reason is that people anticipate regret regarding of what would happen if the ticket happened to win! They'd feel terrible, and they don't want to live with that feeling. Thus they keep the ticket! The person thinks, "If I sell this ticket back for $1 and it wins, I will feel like an idiot!"

In this case, the lottery ticket is perceived as a positive, and the regret is about how the person would feel on missing out on the positive experience of winning.

The next section discusses just how to turn a no into a yes, before they say no!

Exercise: Draw these distinctions and ask these questions in your mind: *What is the difference between reactance and anticipated regret? How do these two critical concepts relate to your business or life situation?*

Overcoming Resistance with Omega Strategies

From what we already know about influence, people make knee-jerk reactions to people's requests for compliance on issues. We often say no without knowing why—it simply feels right.

From the point of view of persuasion, it's important to not allow that negative reaction to take place, and if it does to disarm it as rapidly as possible. Once people have taken a public stand on an issue, it is increasingly more difficult to get them to change their minds.

> *Once people have taken a public stand on an issue, it is increasingly more difficult to get them to change their minds.*

In the *Psychology of Persuasion* you discovered the Law of Consistency. This law states that people will behave in a way that they believe is consistent with their past statements about an issue and their past behaviors about an issue. This is backed up by numerous studies in social psychology.

Even more interesting is that research shows that if people pass up on an opportunity once, they will almost certainly pass up on that same opportunity in the future (Tykocinski and Pittman, 1998). Their behavior sets a precedent. Once someone passes up an opportunity, no matter how positive, they tend to decide that way in the future as well.

In general, people will avoid doing something that could be in their best interest simply because they have avoided doing it in the past.

Dr. Matthew Crawford of the University of Arkansas did an experiment in which a confederate was placed in the room with subject after subject. The confederate would encourage the subjects to bet on the confederate's choice of the winner of a given football game. The confederate working for Crawford would say, "You definitely have to pick team X."

Crawford soon discovered some interesting things.

Half the subjects were instructed to notice and record how much they would regret their decisions if they chose X and Y won versus if they chose Y and X won. In the end the majority of the subjects said they would feel much worse defying (choosing team Y) and losing versus complying (going with team X) and losing. The result was that 73 percent complied with the confederate and chose team X.

But when subjects were not asked to consider how they would feel about their decision (no instruction was given at all) if they chose X and Y won, or Y and X won, things were very different. Only 24 percent of this group chose team X!

Without the contemplation to consider the regrets they would have, people typically respond with a polarity response, also known as a cognitive reactance. They have a knee-jerk negative response hardwired into their brains.

Finally, in Crawford's study, all subjects were informed that their team lost. Results: Those who complied with the confederate felt much worse than those who reacted with a polarity response. (People are lousy at predicting their future feelings!)

$10,000 Key to Influence: Having the subjects focus on the regret of both complying and reacting (polarizing) helped to increase compliance and overcome resistance.

I know what you are thinking! You are wondering, "How could it be that actually putting attention on the negative ('No, I will not. I am a free person and I will do as I please!') helps subjects to be persuaded to do what they are resistant to?"

The question makes complete sense. The fact is that people would like to comply if they can see a way to do so. They simply don't want to have regrets about it, so the best thing to do is to evaluate what happens if they do *and* if they don't comply. This very exercise of looking at both sides increases the chance of compliance dramatically.

When a confederate is in the room and supposedly siding with the person/subject whom we are trying to persuade, the confederate can actually help our cause by defiantly standing up for the point of view held by the subject. The confederate literally can say, "I haven't made up my mind. It's my choice, and I'll choose what I want."

According to Crawford,

This reinstatement of personal freedom, a release from reactance, actually increases the percentage of participants who choose Alternative A, *beyond* that of a group that *never* had its personal freedom threatened. . . . Thus the arousal of reactance and the subsequent reduction of this resistance is an effective way to increase compliance. [All emphasis mine.]

The four steps:

1. The participant's/person's/subject's freedom of choice is threatened.
2. Focus is placed on the person's feelings of the threat to their freedom.
3. The threat is negated.
4. Persuasion is accomplished with future regret verbalized or focusing on the threat to personal freedom.

The key is to go quickly beyond reaction on the person's part (an *unconscious* reaction) and focus on anticipated regret (which is conscious and controllable). By doing this we dramatically increase compliance. You might feel that this is counterintuitive, but it overcomes the reaction of a knee-jerk, negative response!

This brings us to a key question that Crawford has asked and answered and to which I will add my comments.

What causes people to be this way at the unconscious level?

Crawford believes that mainstream culture values autonomy, self-determination, and independence, and that the importance of these values is reinforced at an early age.

I agree, but I would add that this reactionary behavior is genetically wired. Any animal that feels it is trapped and doesn't have freedom to escape will prepare to fight or flee. That's the negative response!

Therefore, the human animal when trapped will say no, but when asked to ponder the feelings of the future instead of the personal freedom that is threatened, the individual will focus on anticipated feelings of regret of not doing what they are being asked. Therefore, the individual is more likely to say yes and comply. The conscious mind (left brain, say) is likely to override the unconscious mind (right brain, say) and consider the options in a nonreactionary mode.

Most people aren't very good at predicting what emotions they will feel when they make a choice that doesn't work out for the best. People often believe, "I will regret this decision so much" when in fact they later do not feel that way when things turn out badly. The exception to this rule is people who are constantly planning for the future and anticipating future events. Research does indicate that these people do have a better grip on what their emotions will be in the future. However, these individuals are in the minority, so when someone tells you that they will feel a certain way, remember that the statement is a guess and not a fact.

> **Most people aren't very good at predicting what emotions they will feel when they make a choice that doesn't work out for the best.**

Mastering Omega Strategies

Time for another measure your of IPQ and a sly way to reveal more principles of influence to you!

1. In a study using students posing as beggars, would the students receive more or less when requesting a specific amount of cash?

2. Are people more or less likely to have a knee-jerk reaction of resistance when they've been taken advantage of in the past?
3. Do hotel bellmen receive larger tips for delivering better service?
4. What can waiters and waitresses do to increase their tips?
5. What are the top three reasons some waiters and waitresses receive more money in tips than others do?
6. What percentage of men believe they are above average in appearance?
7. What percentage of women believe they are above average in appearance?
8. What is the earning power of above-average-looking men and women versus average-looking and below-average-looking men and women?

Bonus Question: How would a waiter or waitress offering a piece of chocolate candy with the check affect the amount of tip received?

Here are the answers, and the research that backs them up.

1. *In a study using students posing as beggars, would the students receive more or less when requesting a specific amount of cash?*

Students posing as beggars found that they received money 44 percent of the time when they didn't ask for a specific sum. If they asked for a specific single coin, they got it 64 percent of the time. But if they asked for an arbitrary amount, such as 37 cents, they got it 75 percent of the time. What can we learn? The more precise the request, the more likely it is to be fulfilled—the more irresistible it is.

2. *Are people more or less likely to have a knee-jerk reaction of resistance when they've been taken advantage of in the past?*

Once people learn they have been fooled and taken they develop much more resistance. Detecting and avoiding cheats is one of the most powerful driving forces in human behavior. (Brad Sagarin, Northern Illinois University)

3. *Do hotel bellmen receive larger tips for delivering better service?*

Taking a few extra minutes to (1) inform guests how to operate the television and thermostat, (2) open the drapes in the room, and (3) offer to bring guests ice doubled a bellman's tips! He received an average tip of $4.77 when he did these things and an average tip of only $2.40 when he did not do them. Providing these extra services increased tips from men as well as women and from young as well as elderly guests (Lynn and Gregor 2001).

4. *What can waiters and waitresses do to increase their tips?*

Data was collected in 1991–1992 on a sample of 207 dining parties at a Mexican restaurant and on a sample of 148 dining parties at a Chinese restaurant in Houston, Texas. The servers used a coin toss to randomly determine whether they would stand or squat when first interacting with a table. They also recorded the customers' experimental condition—bill size and tip size.

A waiter at a Mexican restaurant increased his average tip by $1.22 (from 14.9 percent to 17.5 percent of the bill) by squatting down next to the table when introducing himself to his customers. A waitress at a Chinese restaurant increased her average tip by $0.72 (from 12 percent to 15 percent of the bill) by squatting down next to her tables (Lynn and Mynier 1993).

Once people learn they have been fooled and taken they develop much more resistance.

—*Brad Sagarin*

---

5. *What are the top three reasons some waiters and waitresses receive more money in tips than others do?*

Data were collected on a sample of 51 servers at a Mexican restaurant in Houston, Texas, in the early 1990s. Servers posed for photographs and completed a questionnaire that included questions about their service abilities and questions from the self-monitoring scale. Ten judges independently rated the photographs on physical attractiveness. An assistant manager at the restaurant recorded the afternoon and evening charge sales and tips of each server at the restaurant for a period of six weeks. The relationships among the variables measured in the study were analyzed using weighted multiple regression.

Servers received larger tip averages to the extent that they were physically attractive, to the extent that they rated their service abilities highly, and to the extent that they were sensitive to the situational appropriateness of their own behavior. Physical attractiveness had a stronger effect on the tips of waitresses than on the tips of waiters, whereas self-rated service ability had a stronger effect on the tips of waiters than on the tips of waitresses. However, all these effects were observed only for evening tip averages. None of these variables predicted servers' average lunch tips. In fact, even servers' average evening tips were only weakly related to their average lunch tips (Lynn and Simons 2000).

6. *What percentage of men believe they are above average in appearance?*
7. *What percentage of women believe they are above average in appearance?*

A study by Michael French, "Physical Appearance and Earnings," suggests attractive women earn more money. Hospital and school district workers provided the following self-report of women's and men's physical appearance:

	Men	Women
Above average	47	33
Average	49	61
Below average	4	6

8. *What is the earning power of above-average-looking men and women versus average and below-average-looking men and women?*

Michael French found that above-average-looking women earned 8 percent more than average women. There was no statistical difference related to physical appearance of men.

Bonus Question: How would a waiter or waitress offering a piece of chocolate candy with the check affect the amount of tip received?

In a study of tipping, a waitress working for David Strohmetz of Monmouth University at a New Jersey restaurant offered one, two, or no pieces of chocolate to 80 dining parties (293 people). No candy? The average tip was 19 percent. Two pieces, 22 percent. When she gave one piece of chocolate and then offered a second piece, her tips averaged 23 percent.

Exercise: What are three ways you can implement this information today in your business and in your relationships?

The Power of the Future . . . in the Present

Alpha strategies are those that make an offer more attractive. Omega strategies are those that reduce resistance. Resistance is a thing that can be used up and replenished like water in a tank.

In an experiment, students were divided into gullible and skeptical groups based on interview questions. Each of these was then further divided into four subgroups.

The first subgroup was shown seven video clips of unfamiliar candidates running for office and where they stood on the issues. One group was asked to pay particular attention to the first clip. The other three groups were told to pay attention to the last. Two of these last three groups were shown a travelogue of Fiji before the last video was shown. One of these two remaining groups was told to think positively about Fiji. The other remaining group was told to make a list of all things that could go wrong on a trip to the islands. Finally, all subjects had to criticize each advertisement and candidate.

Gullible subjects used up their resistance to advertising early on. They became less critical of the candidates as the experiment proceeded even though the clips were shown in different orders to different students.

Reaction to the final clip depended on the approach that had been taken on the travelogue. If the subjects criticized the Fiji trip, they were more likely to look at the final candidate positively. If they were told to look positively at the Fiji trip, they were more likely to criticize the candidate.

Skeptical subjects reacted differently. Skeptics were least critical of the first candidate and became increasingly more critical as time went on, regardless of the Fiji travelogue.

Key: It is possible to *use up* resources for resistance, thereby making people less likely to resist your message.

Exercise: How can you use up resistance early on with your clients and customers, making them more susceptible to your message?

Using Time Perspective

The Tenth Law of Persuasion, as you know from my books *Covert Hypnosis* and *Selling Yourself to Others*, says, "Changing someone's time perspective helps them to make different decisions. When people change their time perspective they change how they feel about something and the decisions they make in regard to it."

Having carefully looked at the work of Steven Sherman, Matthew Crawford, and Allen McConnell, I find their research dovetails in some very unique and special ways with the Tenth Law of Persuasion, time perspective.

I must confess that when I discovered this missing piece in the persuasion and influence models a few years ago, I truly felt I had singularly come across one of the missing links in the science of influence. However, it is more than instructive to discuss the work of these leading academic researchers because it appears that my work was concurrent with theirs. I want to offer full credit to these men for the work they have done and the information that they have brought to light.

When I was just starting my career in selling, I found that asking people to commit to buying something from me in the future was a very powerful strategy to actually having people follow through later. I also learned that having people envision being happy with their purchases in the future was an excellent way to increase my personal sales.

When I wrote scripts and trained fund-raisers for nonprofit charities, I discovered that having people envision feeling good in the future about decisions to give today literally increased donations dramatically. The only thing was that I had no hard data, just case studies and personal experience from my work as a salesman, fund-raiser, and trainer.

Today we have the real-world experience and the academic documentation to show an overwhelming amount of evidence that shifting a person's time perspective really is one of the most powerful tools of persuasion and influence imaginable.

When I sold life insurance in 1985 for Farmer's Insurance Group, I felt very comfortable asking my future clients to imagine how they would feel if they died and left their spouse with no money to pay the bills, pay off the house, to put the kids through college, and so on. I then would look at the spouse and say something like, "Doesn't it feel good to have a spouse who wants to take care of you long after he isn't here to do so?"

I meant every word of it. I had learned the value of not having a parent with life insurance very early in my life and again later in life. It can be devastating. For the tiny amount of money that life insurance costs someone (for term insurance) I was 100 percent appropriate by asking my clients to imagine the future and look at what it would be like when they were gone.

I'm not the only person to have done this as a salesperson. Many individuals have intuitively utilized the principle to aid in decision making. Many use this theme manipulatively. Many use it because they care. One fact is certain: Asking your client to see themselves in the future and imagine what it would be like is strikingly powerful in increasing compliance and gaining agreement.

> *Asking your client to see themselves in the future and imagine what it would be like is strikingly powerful in increasing compliance and gaining agreement.*

In 1996, I developed a psychotherapeutic tool to be used in hypnosis called the Time Track Therapy Intervention (see my *New Hypnotherapy Handbook*). This intervention focuses in large part about having a client go into the future and imagine in detail some of the good things their life might offer them. The handbook instructs therapists to create a positive, believable, and realistic future from which they can look back toward the present and see how they took the steps toward this new and compelling future. The results of this intervention have proved to be healing and dramatic in ways I never would have imagined. The e-mails and testimonials are abundant. However, they don't represent scientific proof that the intervention is successful. Case studies are useful, of course, but they may or may not represent the norm.

Returning to the more traditional settings of influential behavior (directed at the goal of gaining compliance) we have always wanted documentation about what specifically is effective and what is not. The need for external and reliable validation now appears to be near completion for the experience of having individuals see the future, good or bad, to gain compliance, and this is where I truly appreciate the work of Sherman, Crawford, and McConnell.

In addition to the aforementioned influence researchers, Robert Cialdini has discussed the notion that the principle of scarcity (see *The Psychology of Persuasion* or *Selling Yourself to Others* for detailed information about scarcity) is similar to the notion that people lose freedom (choices) in the future if they do not comply with a proposal today. This is in line with the anticipated regret model. Scarcity has certainly proven to be an effective principle for gaining compliance. So is the utilization of fear.

Key: Fear has proven to be effective in the vast majority of studies researching the appeal to fear when combined with highly effective persuasion messages. However, fear appeals generate a polarized response when combined with ineffectual persuasion messaging (Witte and Allen 2000).

What else helps overcome resistance and the knee-jerk negative response?

As noted earlier, literally asking the individual to consider the future is an excellent technique for gaining compliance. Instead of telling someone what to do, which typically generates the knee-jerk response, asking the person to tell you whether they would do something if someone asked them to do it is the key strategy that has been successfully studied by Sherman.

Crawford has discussed some truly remarkable research, which serves as a template for influencing using these future pacing themes. Researchers asked some individuals to give an afternoon of their time to charity. Two percent of those asked complied. Researchers also asked other individuals to tell them what would happen if someone asked them to give an afternoon to charity. Of this group, 40 percent said yes. Two weeks later this group of individuals was called again (the people who were asked to predict the future), and 38 percent said yes—they would comply in helping the charity. Numerous studies show that individuals agreeing to do something are much more likely to do so when the time actually comes when compliance is requested than simply directing individuals to comply.

Individuals also are influenced by their own beliefs and imaginings about the future. When asked to describe how team A might defeat team B, those individuals then tend to believe that team A will actually win the game. The effect is observed when other individuals are asked to imagine how team B might defeat team A.

Sherman also found that individuals who were asked to explain their hypothetical future success or failure at completing an anagram task were *all* likely to do better than control groups who were given no opportunity to explain their future success.

People who imagine a positive future appear to succeed and do better than those who do not. This indicates that stopping the knee-jerk no is very possibly the right thing to do in addition to being the most influential option.

> **People who imagine a positive future appear to succeed and do better than those who do not.**

Finally, in another study done more than 20 years ago, Gregory, Cialdini, and Carpenter found that individuals who were asked to describe how much they would enjoy owning cable TV later were found to be much more likely to actually purchase cable.

The evidence is strong. Having individuals imagine the future is a powerful tool for gaining compliance now . . . or in the future.

Exercise: What can you do to implement the concepts of bringing your clients out into the future in your business and relationships?

Mastering the Science of Influence

To know that reciprocity is effective is one thing. To know how and when to induce reciprocity is quite another. To know that asking for a favor can be a powerful technique of influence is different from knowing when to ask—and how. I want to show you how to communicate persuasively using a couple of separate techniques of influence . . . and I also want to show you what *not* to do.

"Son, if you do that you will kill yourself," said Mom—and the son went right back to doing it . . . remember?

Mom neglected a key factor of influence that almost everyone forgets:

$10,000 Key to Influence: *Give specific instructions or steps when directing or attempting to influence behavior.* Simply telling someone to stop doing something or to get a job or behave or shut up is utterly and completely destined to fail because these are not instructions.

Decades of research reveal that *specific instructions are necessary to influence and induce compliance.* What does this mean to you? It means that you need to walk people step-by-step through a process that leads them to the door you ultimately want them to open. Anything short of doing this is unlikely to succeed in the short or long term.

I want to direct your attention (did you catch that?) to another technique that can be remarkably influential or explode in your face. Fear. Fear is something we are all wired to fight or flee from. Our irrational fears are those that we attempt to conquer and overcome. No one likes to experience fear. Fear literally can motivate people in ways few other things can.

"If you have sex without a condom you could get AIDS!"

That statement could induce fear or not. It could induce a behavioral change but it probably won't. The word *AIDS* now is a bit like *accident.* The public has been inoculated to the word through overuse.

"Imagine that you keep smoking those cigarettes and what you see is your kids and your grandkids coming to look at you in your casket, crying because they can't speak with you anymore because you committed a slow suicide with tobacco. Your face is shriveled and they will never think of you in the same way."

Now, that is a scary scenario for most people with children. (You've used fear in a powerful fashion.) Let's follow it up with "And if you cut down to half a pack of cigarettes each day this month and to a cigarette each day next month and finally throw the pack away, wouldn't it be something to see you healthy and happy, having fun, playing with those grandkids?"

What happened here? We scared the hell out of our friend and then we gave a specific set of instructions to follow. That's persuasive. However, cigarette smokers may have heard it 50,000 times, in which case they are vaccinated against your proposal and they will not pay attention to your petition. Once a person has heard the same words or concepts over and over, the warnings lose their power. What to do?

And are alternative actions ethical? That's an interesting question and books have been written about such things! I don't know the answer to the question but I'm glad we brought it up. A good rule of thumb is to always act in the very best interests of everyone you communicate with.

The lesson here is simple. If you are going to use fear in a communication in order to foster change or alter behavior—or encourage someone to buy your product, idea, or service—you must also include a step-by-step set of instructions in your message in order for it to be successful.

This formula, therefore, is:

Negative Emotions + Behavioral Plan → Behavioral Change

What happens when two scary or anxiety-producing experiences compete with each other for the person's behavioral response?!

Academic researchers have been studying *anticipated regret* for the past few years, and here is a scenario that was proposed to 164 UCLA students.

You've parked your car in the lot and you are rushing to class for an important quiz you don't want to be late for. You realize on the way that you may have left your car unlocked!

A number of students were then told to imagine how they would feel if they went back to the car, found it was locked all along, and now had missed the quiz. Others were told to imagine how they would feel if they didn't go back to the car and instead took the quiz, only to discover afterward that the car had been vandalized. How would they feel then?

All students were asked whether they would go back to the car or go to take the quiz. Of those told to imagine the car vandalized, 69 percent said they would return to the car and check to see if the doors were locked. Of those who were told they would miss the quiz, 34.5 percent said they'd go back and check on the car. The control group showed 46 percent returning to check on the car.

> ***Once a person has heard the same words or concepts over and over, the warnings lose their power.***

Lesson: In general when the students experienced anticipated regret, they said they would take the action appropriate to prevent the regret from happening.

We all know that what people say they will do and what they actually do in real life are very different things. Later research has in fact validated this fact. When people experience anticipated regret, they tend to take action to prevent the regret. As people of influence, that's a mighty important thing to remember!

Exercise: Write down 10 things you can do in your business where negative things will happen to customers if they don't take advantage of your product or service. In other words, how can you take advantage of the concept of anticipated regret?

7 | Framing Principles, Persuasion Techniques, and Influential Strategies

More about Framing

No often means "no," but it doesn't have to! Allow me to keep you in suspense for just a few moments and let you indulge yourself with another game you can play and compare your results to the majority of the population:

> ***Situation A:*** In a game, you receive $1,000. In addition, you have a choice between a certain gain of $500 *or* a 50 percent chance of winning an additional $1,000 and a 50 percent chance of winning nothing. Which do you choose?
>
> ***Situation B:*** In a game you receive $2,000. In addition, you have a choice between a certain loss of $500 *or* a 50 percent risk of losing $1,000 and a 50 percent chance of losing nothing. Which do you choose?

Before you read on, please do make your choice.

These are the situations that Kahneman, Slovic, and Tversky (1982) presented to hundreds of subjects. Situations A and B are 100 percent identical, but most people choose differently in each situation because of the framing.

In both situations you are deciding whether you want $1,500 guaranteed or have a 50–50 chance of ending up with either $1,000 or $2,000.

How do most people respond?

In situation A, 84 percent of people choose the certain $1,500 (the first option). Only 16 percent gamble on the 50–50 chance of ending up with either $1,000 or $2,000.

In situation B, 31 percent of people choose the certain $1,500 (the first option). A full 69 percent are willing to gamble on the 50–50 chance of ending up with either $1,000 or $2,000.

The situations are 100 percent identical, yet the manner of framing makes all the difference in the world about how people decide.

Question: Examine the two situations carefully. What is the difference between the way each is framed, and why do you think people choose the way they do? How might you utilize your hypotheses in your own interactions?

Here are a few lessons we learn from research that examines frames and choices:

Lesson A: People do not necessarily decide what is best for them; they decide what presentation of facts is more attractive.

Lesson B: Because we all succumb to the presentation of facts (and fallacies) and not to reality itself, we all need to look at any important decisions from all points of view.

Lesson C: People will lock in a sure gain in favor of any risk in the future, but they will let their losses run. (Example: People hold a stock today at 10 that they bought at 70 because they have so much in the stock. This is one of the stupidest things people do. They should take the money and invest in the instrument that holds the highest probability of appreciation.)

Let's move this to a more real-world scenario and see how the way people think causes them to make bad decisions, and how you can influence them to do what is in their best interest once they blow it.

Scenario 1

You see a brand-new car that you have been drooling over for months. It's priced $500 below invoice and offers a $2,000 rebate! But because money has been tight, you decide against buying the car. Three months later, your financial situation has improved, and you see the same car still priced at $500 below invoice. However, the rebate program ended last month. Do you buy the car?

If you are like most people the answer is no. Why would that be? You can get a car at below invoice. (That's supposedly what the dealer pays for the car, not the retail price on the car!) The reason is that most individuals experience what is called avoidance of anticipated counterfactual regret. In simple English, that means that if we bought the car now, we would feel as if we had missed out on last month's bargain and don't want to regret it. To avoid that pain, people will continue to pass up great opportunities, even though they aren't quite as great as the one that got away.

However, if you drive past the dealership every day on your way to the office, the repeated exposure to the car is often enough to overcome the inertia of inaction and allow you to change your mind and buy the car. You're going to be seeing what you could have had every single day, and, therefore, you are experiencing regrets of another kind anyway, so you become more likely to stop back and buy the car.

Now, if you can understand this, you can influence others to your way of thinking in ways you have never dreamed of.

- You've met with a client or customer and given them a grand opportunity, which they declined. How can you stay in front of that customer over the weeks and months so they ultimately will do business with you? (Out of sight = out of mind.)
- How can you change an offer or restructure an offer so that the clients/customers feel as if they are getting the same original price on something and, therefore, they do not need to psychologically avoid buying from/saying no to you?

Scenario 2

Another example might be a TV that you know retails for more than $600. In the Sunday paper you see it on sale for $397 but it's for one day only. It's a super bargain if you ever saw one, but you decide against it for some reason. The following Sunday the set is still on sale, but this time for $497. You missed the first opportunity for some reason or other and now you have an opportunity to still get the TV at a big discount . . . and of course you don't buy it because you will feel the loss of the $100 that you would have saved had you purchased it last week!

The research of this phenomenon shows that *inaction inertia* occurs when the second action opportunity is in some sense worth substantially less than the initial opportunity, even though the current action opportunity has positive value in an absolute sense (Tykocinski and Pitman 1998).

Therefore, once a customer or potential customer/client says no to you, you must develop a strategy to overcome inaction inertia or you will lose this client forever.

How can you structure your initial offer so that it is a tremendous value while allowing the customer to feel the perception of a similar tremendous value later . . . if they say no to you now?

In the case of the TV, perhaps you might include a service contract at no cost. This costs the company next to nothing and is quoted at $80 to the customer.

In the case of the automobile, you could offer to do 18 months of free oil changes and tune-ups. Total value could be as much as $500 and the real cost is next to nothing because a tune-up might not be needed, especially in the first year and a half, and the cost of oil and a filter is negligible compared to the profits on the automobile sale.

A person of influence must preclude the no reaction in the first place. The best way to do this is by utilizing tools of anticipated regret that overcome resistance.

Publishers Clearing House has done this for years. (Many would say unethically and I might not argue about that.) Here's how it has used anticipated regret in its mailings in the past:

Suppose we told you . . . you were recently assigned the winning super prize number, but you didn't enter, so we gave the $10,000,000 to somebody else! Deciding not to enter our sweepstakes is serious business.

That's pretty powerful stuff, isn't it?

Asking a person to engage in counterfactual thinking means you are having someone consider alternate realities that could be true had someone taken another course of actions. Counterfactual thinking generally is related to regret, and Publishers Clearing House has mastered the concept of regret in marketing, as you can see!

Here is your homework assignment that will help you build your powers of influence.

1. List four specific ways that you can utilize anticipated regret with your products and services.
2. List four specific ways you can keep your product/service/ideas in front of your prospects who have temporarily said no to you.
3. Write down how you normally frame your offers and see if there are other ways that you can frame your offers to make them more appealing.

Foot in the Door: A Proven Persuasion Strategy That Leads to Yes!

(Bonus: This is a $10,000 Key that I have shared with numerous companies. It's now yours free for reading. Use it wisely.)

You can't persuade someone if you can't get in front of them to communicate your message. For hundreds and thousands of years businesses, merchants, therapists, and salespeople have used the foot in the door (FITD) technique to gain access to the person who can say yes. Does it really work as well as salespeople think?

You already know that every persuasion and influence strategy that works in selling works in therapy, works in marketing—well, you get the idea. We tend to say yes or no based on the interaction of certain measurable variables.

I favor any strategy in the field of influence that is tested and proven to be effective. I want to share two powerful techniques that increase your chances of getting the result you want: the FITD technique and the amendment technique.

FITD Technique

The FITD technique is a simple concept. The idea is to get your client/customer to say yes to a simple and small request immediately before you ask for a *big* yes.

Remember the old days when an encyclopedia salesman would come to the door offering a free three-book set of a thesaurus, dictionary, and grammar book if you simply listened to his presentation about his encyclopedias? I do. I still have the Britannica in the office. This is the perfect example of the FITD technique. You ask your client/customer to say yes to a small request so that you can have an opportunity to ask your customer to say yes to a large request.

Effective?

You can't persuade someone if you can't get in front of them to communicate your message.

More than you know!

The FITD strategies are the strategies that have sold billions of dollars of time-sharing (one of the worst investments you can make—though it can be fun!). How? Most resorts will ask you to give them 90 minutes of your time in exchange for a free television, tickets to Disney World, or a free weekend at the resort. The 90 minutes they want is a structured high-pressure presentation designed for the person who has predetermined that "There is no way that we will buy." The strategy has been effective for decades.

Pharmaceuticals are getting their foot in the door in a positively brilliant fashion now. Instead of having doctors give away free samples, many pharmaceutical companies are having the doctor give the patient a free prescription coupon redeemable at the pharmacy and all the doctor has to do is write the prescription. The pharmaceutical wins big because, not only is the prescription written, but when the prescription is used up, all that needs to be done is call the pharmacy for a refill. Absolute brilliance that didn't always work when the M.D. was giving free samples to the patient.

More recently researchers performed a meta-analysis of FITD data and it is best summed up in this one experiment. Researchers turned out participants to go door to door asking homeowners to place a large sign in their front yard. It said, Drive Carefully. It was big and ugly, according to the researchers. Seventeen percent said they would comply.

A second group of participants asked homeowners to place a 3-inch card in their home. The message was the same.

Two weeks later the participants returned with the big and ugly sign to each homeowner who agreed to put the 3-inch sign in their home.

Seventy-six percent agreed to place the big and ugly sign in their yard! All of this sounds amazing. Does the research tell us anything else?

Research shows that *using FITD can increase compliance in many situations by as much as 200 percent!* Here are a few facts that have been discovered:

1. The larger the first request that is agreed to, the more likely the person/company will say yes to the second and more important request.

$10,000 Gift for You. This was borne out with one company I consulted with that used coupons to discover which coupons would draw more people and what the retention rate of each coupon was. The discovery was that the higher the price paid on the first coupon, the larger the retention rate. The lower price/greater discount on the coupon had a much higher usage rate but a much lower retention rate. Read this 10 times and calculate the implications for your situation!

2. Do not use money to induce compliance to the first request. When this is done, the FITD does not work.

    In other words, don't offer someone money as an inducement to do business with you or to buy your product/service.
3. The receiver of the FITD must actually do something, not say they will do something, for FITD to be effective (Burger, Chartrand, and Pinkert, 1999).

Always remember: What people say and think they will do bears little relationship to their actual actions. It's not that people are ill willed or have bad intentions; people simply are lousy predictors of their future actions. In fact, simply go with this: What people say they are going to do is relatively meaningless. Observe what people have done in the past and you can predict what they will do in the future with greater accuracy than by asking what they intend to do in the future.

4. If the request has some prosocial aspects (Dillard, Hunter, and Burgoon 1984), people are sometimes significantly more likely to comply than they would in situations that are clearly for profit only.

The FITD technique is one of the most powerful persuasion techniques, and there are reams of research studies in the literature that prove this beyond a shadow of a doubt. It's time to start putting together a plan on some level about how you and your business/company can utilize the FITD technique!

Exercise: How can you apply the FITD technique to your specific persuasion scenarios?

> ***What people say and think they will do bears little relationship to their actual actions.***

Four Tested Ways to Be More Persuasive with Framing

1. Get something of yours (your product, your idea, your service) that has value into your customers' hands/minds as soon as possible! As soon as someone possesses something, they perceive it to be more valuable than they did immediately prior to owning it.

   Research by Kahneman and Tversky (1984) brings these examples to our attention:

   - Individuals who ultimately bet on team A in a football game are often ambivalent about which team to select until they actually place their bets on team A. Once they have placed their bets, they tend to dramatically favor team A and show little hesitation in sharing their certainty that team A will win.
   - Students receive mugs in a research setting and are given the opportunity to sell the mugs. Other students are given the opportunity to buy the mugs. Students will not take less than $7.12 on average for the mugs they have taken possession of. The other students will not pay more than $3.12 on average for the same mugs. Lesson: Once you own something you value it more highly than those who do not own it—even if it has been owned for only 10 minutes!

2. *Create a frame (a word picture in your customer's mind) that your product/ service/idea is something that they already possess . . . so that it becomes the* status quo *in their thinking:* For example, "Once our lawn service is yours we help you eliminate all that crabgrass that the old services you used to use never were able to control."

- Students in one class were given a decorated mug as compensation for filling out a questionnaire. In another class, students received a large bar of Swiss chocolate. When given the opportunity to trade with members of the other class, only 10 percent of students traded their item while 90 percent stayed with what they had.
- More impressive: 45 students received a gift package of a Stanford calendar and a free dinner at MacArthur Park Restaurant. In another group of 45, the students received a Stanford calendar and a certificate for an 8 × 10 professional portrait. Later that day, all the subjects were told they could trade their current package for either *two* free dinners at MacArthur Park Restaurant or a professional portrait sitting including an 8 × 10, two 5 × 7s, and a wallet photo. The results were that 81 percent of the dinner/calendar group swapped their package for the two dinners.

Lesson: People want what they have and more of it!

3. Create a word picture that creates a moderate amount of tension if the client doesn't do business with your company. In other words, what will the clients lose if they do not do business with you?
   - Research: In one experiment with gambling, individuals were given the opportunity to flip a coin and bet $10. Most were willing to gamble only with a payoff of $25 and a possible loss on the individual's part of $10! That's a 2.5:1 ratio for a 1:1 bet!
   - Research on real-life applications: Loss aversion is more pronounced for personal safety than for money. (People will do more to protect themselves than their money.) Loss aversion is more pronounced for income than leisure. (Losing a chance to travel isn't as powerful as losing income.)

Lesson: People move away from loss. Determine what people lose if they don't do business with you and artfully develop word pictures that clarify the hurt they might experience. For example, "You are seven times more likely to become disabled than die in any given year, and if you become permanently disabled, your family will lose everything because you will be unable to work and they will have the added expense of taking care of you. If you carry insurance against this enormous risk, you avoid losing everything and have the ability to maintain a high standard of living no matter what happens to you."

4. *Don't confuse opportunity costs with out-of-pocket expenses.* Your customer doesn't and is watching you to see how you promote your business. The following research was conducted in two cities by telephone sampling:

Scenario 1. A shortage has developed for a certain popular make of automobile, and customers must now wait two months for delivery. The dealer has been selling the cars at list price. Now the dealer prices the cars at $200 over list. Is this acceptable or unfair?

Acceptable 29 percent.

Unfair 71 percent.

Scenario 2: A shortage has developed for a certain popular make of automobile, and customers must now wait two months for delivery. The dealer has been selling the cars at $200 below list price. Now the dealer sells this model at list price. Is this acceptable or unfair?

Acceptable 58 percent.

Unfair 42 percent.

Scenario 3: A company is making a small profit. It is located in a city experiencing a recession with substantial unemployment but no inflation. The company decides to decrease wages and salaries this year by 7 percent. Acceptable or unfair?

Acceptable 37 percent.

Unfair 63 percent.

Scenario 4: A company is making a small profit. It is located in a city experiencing a recession with substantial unemployment and inflation of 12 percent. The company decides to increase salaries by only 5 percent this year. Acceptable or unfair?

Acceptable 78 percent.

Unfair 22 percent.

Each pair of scenarios presents two identical situations. (Scenarios 1 and 2 both involve a price rise of $200; scenarios 3 and 4 both involve wages 7 percent below the inflation rate.) However, the consumer reacts very differently to each option. Consumers do not want to perceive money coming out of their pockets. Be certain to frame every promotion in such a way that the consumer is clearly saving (and assume no mathematical ability on the part of the consumer).

Consumers do not want to perceive money coming out of their pockets.

Mastering the Science of Influence: Priming the Pump

Do these four thought exercises with friends, groups (best!), or on your own.

1. Read this scenario:

   John is intelligent, industrious, impulsive, critical, stubborn, and jealous.

   Mark is jealous, stubborn, critical, impulsive, industrious, and intelligent.

   Quickly, which person do you think you would like more, John or Mark?

   You have a lot of company if you said John. Most people do, and the reason is simple. Although the same traits were used to describe John and Mark, the principle of primacy primes the mind to filter everything else you learn about someone through the first characteristic, that of being intelligent in John's case and jealous in Mark's case As each characteristic is mentioned in order, it becomes less and less important.

2. *Guesstimate the total of each of these multiplication problems.* Show the first equation to one person and the second equation to another. Each person gets only five seconds.

$$1 \times 2 \times 3 \times 4 \times 5 \times 6 \times 7 \times 8 = ?$$

$$8 \times 7 \times 6 \times 5 \times 4 \times 3 \times 2 \times 1 = ?$$

   The average guess for the first problem is 512. For the second? 2,250. The correct answer is 40,320! Why the big difference in guessing and the huge distance in both cases from the right answer? People group the first few numbers together in each set and then guessed based on this information.

3. Group 1 (or person 1 if you are doing this with only two friends) is shown these words and asked to remember them: "adventurous," "self-assured," "independent," and "persistent."

   Group 2 is shown this set of words and asked to remember them: "careless," "conceited," "solitary," and "stubborn."

   Now, each has 15 seconds to describe and evaluate the following person: Donald is a parachutist.

   The descriptions given by the individuals or groups will be heavily slanted toward the words they had to remember. Group 1 typically finds Donald a free spirit. Group 2 typically finds Donald careless and a daredevil.

$10,000 Key to Influence: Whether you realize it or not, everything you watch, listen to, read, and think about influences the next thing you consider.

4. Say the following word five times, then continue reading:
blood.
What color does a traffic light have to be to proceed?
Did you say, "red?"
Go back and look at the question. Interesting, eh?

These four scenarios all take advantage of our brain's programming for primacy. We tend to lose the ability to consider much information after the first important piece, and, in fact, we tend to filter or disregard information that doesn't match our current information, regardless of whether the new information is valuable.

Key to Influence: There is an enormous amount of research, old and new, that confirms that what happens first in some experience, event, or situation alters our perceptions of everything that follows. There is also an equally large amount of research that shows that what happens last in some experience, event, or situation is extremely important in our perceptions and beliefs.

Are the two findings in contradiction? No. The brain tends to remember what happens first and last in sequences, events, and life in general. The balance between the two (primacy and recency) is very interesting. One experiment shows that when two speakers are giving speeches, one right after the other with no break, the first speaker tends to be received better and appreciated more. However, when speakers (say candidates for office) can choose between speaking before a group this week or next week, they should choose the later event because people (when they go to the polls, say) will forget what happened last week, and the freshness of this week's speaker and her message will ultimately be seen in a much better light. When considering going first or last, the key determining factor for positioning is the elapsed time between the events. The shorter the elapsed time, the better it is to go first. The longer the elapsed time, the better it is to go last.

Let me ask you a few questions, may I?

What was the first school you attended?
What was the second?
Who was the first person you kissed?
Who was the second?
What was the first apartment you rented?
What was the second?
What was the first car you actually owned?
What was the second?
What was your first job?
What was your second?

I think you get the idea!

So we know we have a hard time remembering things in the middle! We are good at beginnings and endings. How do we use this enlightening information?

Priming people to accept a message is all about starting out with a great impression—something big, a promise, a big smile, something that sets the stage for everything that can happen later. Remember that what happens first will be remembered and will serve as a filter for everything that comes after.

Quick! Get a pen and paper. Choose which you prefer (you're making monetary bets). Circle or write down your choice.

Alternative A: A sure gain of $240.
Alternative B: A 25 percent chance to gain $1,000, and a 75 percent chance to gain nothing.

Choose which you prefer:

Alternative C: A sure loss of $750.
Alternative D: A 75 percent chance to lose $1,000, and a 25 percent chance to lose nothing.

Kahneman and Tversky (1984) found that 84 percent of people choose alternative A over B.

First Key: When people have a sure thing in hand, they tend not to go for the potential bigger gain and lose what they have. People hate to lose what they have.

Second Key: Instead of the sure loss, people will gamble at an even greater loss for the chance to break even. (This is why casinos have big chandeliers, big-name acts, and the best hotel rooms on the planet.)

When people feel pain or have experienced loss, they will spend more to get out of the loss or come out of the pain, even if the odds are against success.

In fact, 73 percent of all people choose the AD combination even though BC is a better choice (only 3 in 100 will choose that combination) and the one that is the logical choice. And so it is with our species. We are a rationalizing people. We make emotional choices and then rationalize (make them seem logical, whether correct or incorrect).

Most people respond or react to the fear of loss and the threat of pain in a much more profound way than they do to the potential for gain.

Third Key: How a question, proposal, idea, product, or statement is framed can largely determine what the majority of people will decide and actually do.

Most people respond or react to the fear of loss and the threat of pain in a much more profound way than they do to the potential for gain. This does not mean, however, that all of your influential messages should be couched in the language of fear and threats. Far from it. In fact, in some situations fear and pain will turn someone away from your attempted persuasive communication.

Once you begin to understand when it is appropriate to use prohibitions, losses, and fear in your message and when it is appropriate to use allowances, gains, and positive messages, you will find yourself influentially succeeding in ways you didn't think were possible.

We pride ourselves on being in charge, in control, intelligent, great decision-making beings . . . until we are exposed to the truth. Sigh. . . . We often respond to others in ways that make absolutely no rational sense whatsoever. Becoming aware of most of these mechanisms of stimulus/response, environment/response, frame/response, perception/response will help you become a superb decision maker and open the door for you to become a remarkably influential person.

What about educated people? Medical doctors? How do they decide what to do, and how will they influence your decision?

A 1987 study in the *New England Journal of Medicine* involving 1,193 participants revealed this:

Which of two treatments would specialists prefer—surgery or radiation therapy for cancer? It depended on how the question was asked!

If the medical specialists were asked the question in terms of "surgery will yield a 68 percent chance of surviving after one year," then three-quarters of the time surgery was chosen. If the question was asked in the mortality (death) frame (32 percent will be dead by the end of one year), then only 58 percent of the time did the specialists choose the surgery option.

Fourth Key: The frame of a proposal can alter life-and-death decisions, even though the identical data is used to make the decisions!

Hypnotic Confusion

Milton Erickson, MD, was one of the twentieth-century's best-known hypnotherapists.

Erickson utilized the tactic of confusing his patients so they would go into a trance and be distracted from resistant thoughts they would have toward Erickson or hypnosis in general. Erickson believed that whatever suggestion followed the confusing tactic he would use would be more likely to take hold and succeed.

Some hypnotic confusion techniques have proven to be counterproductive and actually increase resistance, but simple disruptions followed by an elegantly simple reframe actually have been proven to be successful in influence. In the following examples, "control" is a presentation or communication that is "normal" (where there is no miscommunication or speaking error). A "mild disruption" is where the experimenters intentionally misspoke in a briefly confusing fashion, and a "significant disruption" is where experimenters were intentionally overly confusing.

Example 1: The Cupcake Study

People coming to the Psychology Club's bake sale table on campus used the following answers in response to the question, "How much are they?", posed by the salespeople at the table.

> Control: "These cupcakes are 50 cents; they're really delicious."
> Mild disruption: "These half cakes are 50 cents; they're really delicious."
> Severe disruption: "These *petits gateaux are 50 cents; they're really delicious.*"

What worked for making sales?

Mild disruption: 74 percent.
Severe disruption: 67 percent.
Control: 46 percent.

Does this work with anything other than students selling cupcakes?

Example 2: The Donation Study

Students asking for donations to their Richardson Center asked people to donate "some money" in the control and "money some" (just those two words in their door-to-door presentation) in the disruption condition.

A third condition was tested using "money some" and the name of the organization incorrectly stated as "Center Richardson." This was a severe disruption.

> Results:
> Disruption: 65 percent of houses donated.
> Control: 30 percent of houses donated.
> Severe disruption: 25 percent of houses donated.

Exercise: How can you use the technique of hypnotic confusion in selling your idea or product (or yourself)? List three ways.

The Amendment Technique

There are different ways we can present our price to our client. Look at the following two ways.

1. "These cupcakes are 50 cents."
2. "These cupcakes used to be a dollar, but now they're 50 cents."

What difference can that little bit of wording make? A *big* difference. The sentence you want to use, of course, is the second one. We are telling our customer that we have amended the price. The power is in its startling the client with the original price, and then revealing the new reasonable price.

How can we use this data to our advantage? You tell your customer that your bicycles were $129.95 each, but now they're $99.95! People appreciate knowing how much something did cost, and what is a reasonable amount for that product today.

Bonus: Price Points

In the United States, we think of money in terms of our standard currency. We have $1, $5, $10, $20, $50, and $100 bills. These are all what we call price points. A price point is a point at which going over that price will make our customer hesitate, or even refuse to buy.

The most common ones are $.99, $9.95, $19.95, and $99.95.

What about $20,000? A car for $19,995 is much cheaper than one for $20,195, right?

Exercise: How can you use the amendment technique in your business today? List three ways. How can you take advantage of price points in your industry?

How Most People Make Bad Decisions and How You Can Help Them Make Good Ones!

Our life experience is largely a combination of our state of mind, communication, relationships, actions, and decisions. If someone is to achieve success in some area of life, certainly making well-considered decisions is critical. Learning how you make decisions and how others make their decisions will not only allow you to become a more influential person, it will help you grow yourself—with fewer regrets and more wins!

> *People appreciate knowing how much something did cost, and what is a reasonable amount for that product today.*

Is it time for a career change?
Which job should you take?
Should you marry this one?
Should you divorce this one?
Should you buy this car?
Should you buy that home?

Before you make that big decision you may want to read this set of articles, which will shed light on not only our decision-making blind spots and errors, but also how to actually make great decisions.

Reams of research show that in general:

- People assume when they decide on something and it turns out well that they made a good decision—when it easily could have been attributed to chance (luck).
- People tend to overemphasize the importance of pain by about 2.5:1 in decision making. (People may not need to feel great but they don't want to hurt at all.)
- People rationalize their emotional decisions instead of making rational decisions.
- People make their decisions emotionally when the answer to a question or proposition isn't obvious.

- People make their decisions impulsively, then stand by their impulses as if their decisions were made rationally.
- People make their decisions based on their own experiences and not the experience of the masses.
- People make decisions based on the socioenvironmental frames they put the decisions into. (A woman going to Planned Parenthood for counseling will get different advice than the woman going to her conservative pastor.)
- People tend to make decisions on their own instead of seeking the counsel of numerous others who can give additional perspectives.
- People are unaware of the enormous power of the actual words that are used to ask the question, and how the phrasing can make an enormous difference in the actual decision that is made.
- People are unaware about how the influence of specific questions changes their minds unconsciously. ("Are you sick of driving that old junker?" versus "Are you thinking of buying a new car?")
- People tend to avoid what they perceive as risky.
- People tend to lack the skills to calculate the chances that events will or won't happen.
- People tend to decide on the sure thing even when it doesn't make real sense to do so. They will take a sure $100 instead of a 50–50 chance at $250, for example.)
- People tend to make decisions without a solid understanding of the real-life likelihood of events. (Read that as mathematics, statistics, and probability.)

Not only do most of us make lots of bad decisions, we also tend to dramatically overrate our decision-making skills! We tend to remember our good decisions and think we're actually good at decision making. But wait! It gets worse! We tend to overestimate everything about ourselves from the income we earned last year to the grades we got in elementary school. Here are just a couple of examples of how people perceive their judgment in the real world to be in contrast to how it really is.

Ninety-six percent of all men rate their physical appearance as average or better!

Ninety-four percent of all women rate their physical appearance as average or better!

What's wrong with this picture? (Obviously only 51 percent are average or better. The other 49 percent are below average.)

Ninety-one percent of all business leaders believe they are good or very good decision makers.

Eighty percent of businesses fail in the first four years.

Ninety percent of new products fail to make a profit.

What is wrong with this picture?!

Now, with these amazing facts behind us, it would seem that seeking expert advice from your broker, your agent, your attorney, your therapist, or your mom would be helpful (maybe), but don't get too excited until you look at this:

Here's an example of how we tend to overrate expert advice:

About 20 percent of all stock mutual fund managers select stocks that ultimately do better than the S&P 500 index, often called the market. In other words, only 20 percent of experts—people paid millions of dollars per year to beat the market—succeed at doing so. Think about that. Given reams of computer analysis, data, and information, a full 80 percent of the world's smartest professional investors cannot do better than the person who claims to know nothing about the market and simply invests in the 500 companies in the S&P 500!

Why are these experts so poor at deciding what stocks to buy?

- Past performance is *not* always an indicator of future results . . . but most experts still make investment decisions as though it is.
- Most experts don't consider the factors that really will influence the future.
- They believe their own publicity clips.

Almost every decision we make in business, relationships, or life is a function of probability. That means that you don't actually know the outcome of the decision in advance. When you get in your car and drive to work, you are deciding that people will drive carefully on their side of the road while you speed along at 55 mph on your side of the road with two painted yellow lines dividing you. Indeed, when you look at it this way, that is a decision that is fairly risky, but in reality the probability of disaster striking (someone running head-on into you and killing you) is very slim. In this case, our day-to-day experience and our illusion of control (we're driving so everything will be okay) confirm for us that, although we see a lot of accidents, we know that almost everyone is safe driving to and fro. So we drive.

> *Almost every decision we make in business, relationships, or life is a function of probability.*

But the same set of factors can work the opposite way in making decisions.

Millions of people buy lottery tickets every day. The lottery (like Powerball) is one of the worst bets on the planet. The odds are 55,000,000 to 1 that you will lose—and, yes, eventually someone has to win, but let's put those chances into perspective: If you have been struck by lightning 40 times or have died in 20 plane crashes, then you might just be the person to win the lottery—those are the same odds as winning the jackpot in the Powerball game! The fact is that you aren't going to win the lottery and neither am I. It is a terrible decision to buy a ticket. Just take your dollar bill or $10 bill and burn it. Feel better? Ouch!

What about the easier lotto games? What about games where you only have to match three numbers to win $500 for your measly $1 investment? From 000 to 999 there are 1,000 total numbers that can be drawn. Your odds of winning, therefore, are 1 in 1,000. That means that, on average, for every $1,000 you spend on the lotto you will get $500 returned. You should get $1,000 for a winner but the government/lottery sponsor is giving you $500. I don't know how much you earn, but a lot of people make only $500 per week and it's worth considering that the government, which regulates the lottery, is really extracting a stupid tax from those foolish enough to decide to play. Now, could you pick the winner tonight in a 1 in 1,000 event and win the $500? Sure you could. Lots of people will. But it's still a foolish decision to buy the ticket just because it *could* happen.

So how do you make a good decision?

There are lots of factors involved. Dozens actually. Let's look at one simple factor and key to making good decisions.

Key to Influence: What is the chance of something happening versus the payoff? If the payoff is worth more than the risk, then the decision is a good decision even if you are wrong. If the payoff is worth less than the risk, the decision is a bad decision, even if you are right.

Example: Several years ago, I won a nice sum of money on the Super Bowl. I use a modeling tool for predicting the outcome of football games. Some years the model does better than others. My model said that New England would beat St. Louis about one-third of the time in this specific game. The casino was offering about $450 for each $100 bet if New England did indeed win. It was very difficult to put money on New England (because they should lose two-thirds of the time in this game), but clearly, because they should win one-third of the time (assuming the model is right) and the casino was willing to pay off more than double those odds, I had no choice but to bet it all on New England. In other words, according to my model, the casino should pay off only $200 in addition to getting my $100 back, but it was offering $450! I had to make the wager. I did. They won. It was good.

Now, New England could have lost, and it still would have been a good bet because the casino was going to pay me more than twice as much on a win as they should have. It's no fun when your decision turns out wrong, but you can learn to make the best decisions possible. We'll talk much more about just that in later chapters.

> *It's no fun when your decision turns out wrong, but you can learn to make the best decisions possible.*

It's sometimes difficult to calculate the probability of life events.

"If I buy the Palm Pilot will I really use it?"
"Will I be happier if I divorce him?"
"Will I be happier if I go out with Jane instead of Betty?"
"If I quit the job will I find a better one?"
"If I take the job will I be happy there?"
"If I marry Bill/Bonnie, will he/she be a good spouse?"
"If I have children, will they be born free of major defects?"

For these questions it is more difficult to determine what the right decisions are because they include numerous variables that need to be weighed and all possible options explored before such decisions are finalized. (Once a decision is actually made, most humans are unable to change their minds because they will appear to be wrong in their own minds, to their peer group, or to society in general.)

8 | Applying the Laws of Influence

You drive down the street. You have to stop at stop signs, yield to on-coming traffic, and even keep to the speed limit (at least when you see a highway patrolman!). These are all simple laws. Laws created by society for the safety and betterment of the masses aren't necessarily perfect, nor are they absolutes. Laws of society don't always work.

However, universal laws like the law of gravity always work. If you drop 10,000 baseballs off the top of the Sears Tower in Chicago, the balls will all drop to the street below, probably doing major damage. None of the balls will rise up toward the atmosphere as you drop them off the Sears Tower.

These are universal laws that never change. If you try to break a universal law, normally you won't get a second chance to make things right! Legislated laws are different. If you follow them, you will probably live longer and pay fewer traffic tickets.

The laws of influence aren't quite like the laws of society or the laws of the universe. In fact, most people aren't even aware of the laws of influence. They simply tend to act in accordance with the laws at a completely un-conscious level. There are major prices to pay when the laws of influence are broken. The problem is that most people aren't aware of the laws in the

131

first place. If people unconsciously follow the rules, they will be happier and communicate well with others. If people don't follow the rules, they will run into lots of problems, experience broken relationships, earn less income, be more readily downsized in corporations that are cutting back, and—well, you get the idea.

There is nothing you do that is more important than communicating with others. There are very specific laws that govern not only the communication process but also the sales process. It's interesting because sometimes when you drive past the highway patrolman at 75 mph you don't get a ticket. Sometimes you fail to yield to oncoming traffic and you don't get in a car accident. Every now and then you run the stop sign and you don't hit a pedestrian. The laws exist, though, and when they are followed they tend to work in favor of law-abiding citizens. When they are broken, the chances that something will go wrong are dramatically increased. The same is true in this respect for the laws of influence.

How can there be laws of selling? How can something like sales or communication have laws? As our species has evolved for millions of years, we have discovered that we tend to need the cooperation of others to succeed. Gaining the cooperation and compliance of other people is absolutely critical to the persuasion process and the continuance of society as we know it.

In this chapter you will learn how to apply the 10 Laws of Influence. Following each of these rules is important in gaining compliance from others. In most situations on most days of your sales career, if you follow each law, you will find selling to be a fairly simple experience. What's better, if you utilize these 10 laws in all of your communication you will find that your sales career is fun, sometimes challenging, and always rewarding.

Law of Reciprocity

When someone gives you something of perceived value, you immediately respond with the desire to give something back.

It's December 24 and the mail has just arrived. You open a Christmas card from someone you had taken off your Christmas list. This is a crisis! "Honey, are there any more Christmas cards left?"

"Yeah, in the drawer."

"Thank God." You go to the drawer and sure enough there is a card there—but there are no envelopes to fit the card into! You search and search, finally deciding to use an envelope that isn't quite large enough . . . but you have to use something!

You sign the card, and yes, you personalize it! (You write something special just for the sender.) You stuff the card into the envelope that is still too small. You slide a picture of the family in, and you even find a leftover newsletter that tells everyone what your family has been up to all year.

"I'll be back in a while, I have to go to the post office and mail this card."

Why do you have to go to the post office?

You have to go because the letter must be mailed with a postmark before Christmas! December 24 will show that you cared. December 26 will show that these people were an afterthought in your mind, not worthy of sending a card to before Christmas. You race off to the post office—and you have just discovered the power of reciprocity.

You were taught to share your toys and your snacks and your space and your time with all those around you. You were scolded when you were selfish and you were rewarded with kind smiles and pats on the head when you shared. The Law of Reciprocity was installed at a very early age.

The world's greatest people and marketing mavens give something to their clients—and I don't mean a business card.

- Have you ever received a bar of soap in the mail?
- Have you ever received a box of cereal in the mail?
- Have you ever received return-address labels from a charity in the mail?
- Have you ever received a handful of greeting cards from a charity in the mail?
- Have you ever received a sample-size shampoo bottle in the mail?

These are all examples of what we call inducing reciprocity. The practice is very simple, yet absolutely brilliant. If your product is top quality and it is something that everyone can use, send everyone a small sample of it, and they will be more likely to buy it the next time they go to the store for two reasons.

First, they will recognize it as something they have used. The brain picks up on what is familiar. (Have you ever noticed how many cars there are like yours on the road? What happened to all the rest?!)

Second, reciprocity has been induced when someone gives you something and you give them something back. Reciprocity has also been induced when someone gives you something and you *feel compelled* to give something back. Kellogg's was nice enough to send us their free box of cereal, and because it tasted good we should at least buy their cereal this one time. We return the favor.

Reciprocity, based on scientific research, appears to be the single most powerful law of selling persuasion there is, but is there a problem?

- If you sell life insurance, you can't give away $10,000 of free coverage.
- If you sell real estate, you can't give away bathrooms.
- If you sell speaking services, you can't give away free speeches.
- If you are a stockbroker, you can't give away 100 shares of Microsoft.

What do you do if you don't have sample-size products or services? How do you take advantage of this powerful law of share and share alike?

> Give away something of perceived value to someone, and others will feel compelled to do likewise.

You do not have to give away free samples to utilize reciprocity. You must only give away something that has perceived value. My favorite method of inducing reciprocity is taking someone to lunch or sharing a valuable tip related to building that person's business or income in some way. (I like these approaches because they are measurable and the person knows that you really helped them when they follow through on your suggestion.) Taking someone to lunch is usually an inexpensive way to induce reciprocity, and you have the added benefit of meeting one of your client's 16 basic desires (the desire to eat). Sharing helpful secrets that are truly specialized knowledge is also an elegant way to induce reciprocity. One simple idea can often help someone earn hundreds or thousands of dollars per year more in income.

Here are a few creative ideas for people to use as inexpensive giveaway items.

Life Insurance and Financial Products

Give away a free report that lists all the top-performing investments for the past three years (even if it contains information that is positive about your competitors!). Give away a handy chart that people can place on the refrigerator that shows the 10 questions to ask telemarketers to determine the legitimacy of investment opportunities and requests for charitable donations.

Real Estate

Estimate the amount of the loan the client will take out and run several amortization tables showing how small extra payments each month will cut years off the life of the loan, save the client tens of thousands of dollars, and create long-term financial freedom. If the client is already putting every penny toward the 30-year mortgage, give away a handy booklet that shows how to do simple maintenance on the house, how to find good service people to work on the home in the future, and how to keep the home in top-dollar condition should they decide to sell.

Automobile

If you sell a great car, give away a recent *Consumer Reports* article comparing your car with others in its class. If you sell a car that is a good car but not listed as one of the best, give away a list of the top 10 strategies to keep the car running cheaply and its resale value high.

The message to you is that everyone can give something away for free with nothing expected in return. It is a scientific fact that reciprocity is effective. The key is that what you give away must have perceived value on the part of the client. Traditional promotional items like personalized pens and date books may be useful or they may not be. You can test them to see if they assist in making sales. It doesn't matter what your giveaway actually costs you. What matters is the value the client places on the item, report, or product.

Exercise: How can you utilize the Law of Reciprocity when selling your products or services? Be very specific.

Law of Time

Changing someone's time perspective helps them to make different decisions. When people change their time perspective, they change how they feel about something and the decisions they make in regard to it.

Time is the subtle equalizer in life. No matter how rich or poor you are, time is the one commodity that is the same for everyone. Everyone has this moment of experience only. What happens in this moment is normally not a matter of conscious choice or thought.

Quite often when you walk into a client's office or you contact them in some other way they will immediately equate you, at the unconscious level, with all of the other people they have ever met. In all probability they have more negative experiences than positive experiences with people.

Two things need to happen. You must distinguish yourself from all the other people they've known, and you need to move their time filter from the past to the present or future. People have emotional responses that are attached to various stimuli. You are a stimulus. You trigger positive or negative experiences in all of your clients' minds regardless of whether each client knows it. What's more interesting is that this response isn't necessarily linked to *you!* Most people see you as a salesperson and they have a negative emotional response to all salespeople. Therefore, in most cases, you are a bad salesperson when you walk in the door. You haven't opened your mouth or asked any questions, and you are already a bad salesperson. Ready for more?

When you walk out the door, your client is going to think differently of you, but by the next time you talk with your client, his brain will be back in bad-salesperson mode for two reasons. First, he will confront many other idiots posing as salespeople between now and then. Second, his past emotional memories are not going to be wiped away by a fun one-hour meeting with you!

Therefore, you must become an expert at altering time. You must become a master of moving people through time so that they are not affected by their past programming and emotions. You must be able to get them to look at your product and service from a completely different perspective! And you can.

Time plays a big role in people's decision-making processes. There are three fundamental ways that people experience time: past, present, and future.

Past: Some people live in the past or use the past as their guidepost for all decisions they will make in the present and future. These people are often cynical and depressed. They also make fewer bad decisions than other people. Their guard is up and they will make fewer errors because of this. They will also miss out on opportunities because of their past experiences. You will need to remember this!

- "I was ripped off once before doing this."
- "I ate at a place like this once and it was terrible."
- "I got conned the last time I bought a car."
- "I never get a good deal."
- "The stock market always goes down when I invest."

These are all common experiences for people who process all information through filters of the past.

Present: Some people live in the present moment. These people tend to have much less stress and to give little thought to the past or future. They tend to be lousy planners and to seek instant gratification. Usually their credit cards are maxed out because they have sacrificed a future they cannot see for the pleasure of the moment. They think like this:

- "I know it's right when I feel it."
- "I do what feels good."
- "I just wanted to have fun."
- "It looks like fun so I'm going to do it."
- "I never thought I'd get pregnant."
- "Who'd have thought I'd lose all that money?"

Future: Some people filter most of their thoughts in terms of the future. They tend to live in the future, delay instant gratification, and have determined that the past, for better or worse, isn't that relevant for them. People who live in the future are constantly planning, organizing, preparing, and sacrificing. They sacrifice the moment for a brighter tomorrow. They think like this:

- "I could buy a car now but that money is better off invested."
- "I'll wait for retirement."
- "I could buy that now but I'd like to watch that money build up over time."
- "I better not do that because I might get pregnant."

Once you know how people generally filter their information, you can have them look at different events in the past, present, or future, *or* you can change the perspective from which they are looking.

You can change someone's time perspective with some linguistic maneuvers that rival the martial arts.

To get your clients out of the mistakes of the past, get them to see things from a future perspective.

Client: "Look what happened to the market this past year. It went to hell. Dropped by 50 percent. Why would I want to invest in your mutual funds?"

Salesperson: "You might not want to. But the next time the market doubles or triples wouldn't you want just a little piece of that for your future?"

Client: "My experience is that I listen to a salesperson and I get ripped off."

Salesperson: "When you go out 10 years into the future and look back, what do you do right to correct that?"

Client: "Last three times I bought a big yellow pages ad I lost my butt."

Salesperson: "I understand. If we can create an ad that will pull in the future will you be up for that?"

Client: "I tried hypnosis before and it doesn't work."

Salesperson: "So you had someone who didn't know what they were doing. If you were to work with someone who was adept at his art and knew how to help you, would you be willing to do that?"

Law of Contrast   139

Exercise: How can you utilize the Law of Time when selling your products or services? Be specific.

Law of Contrast

When two things, people, or places that are relatively different from each other are placed near to each other in time, space, or thought, we see them as more different, and it is easier to distinguish which one we want more.

There is a wonderful piece of television history from the archives of the *Tonight Show with Johnny Carson.* Carson hosted the *Tonight Show* for almost 30 years. One night, Johnny had the number-one Girl Scout cookie salesperson in the country on. He asked her the secret of her success. She said, "I just went to everyone's house and said, 'Can I have a $30,000 donation for the Girl Scouts?' When they said 'No,' I said, 'Would you at least buy a box of Girl Scout cookies?'" The audience couldn't stop laughing and neither could Johnny. The little girl had mastered the contrast principle, at age eight.

Have you ever walked through a grocery store and watched people take two competing products and put one of them in each hand, then look at them side by side, literally weighing which one they should buy? The principle that guides people in this product choice is called the Law of Contrast.

Psychological studies have shown that people can use the Law of Contrast in a very specific and predesigned fashion. If you can show your expensive product or service first and then show what you would like to sell (what you think creates the best win–win with your client) second, the client is very likely to purchase the second item.

When you were a child, you would go into a store with one of your parents and as your parent shopped, so did you. You may have picked up two or three items to propose to your mother for possible purchase. Time after time, your parent programmed into you either one of two themes:

1. They're too expensive—you can't have either of them.
2. You can have the little (cheapest) one.

You soon learned that the best method of selling your parent was to note how little the item cost. "It's only a dollar," your voice would resonate in a pleading fashion. With the proper eye contact and pitiful face the strategy regularly worked.

The Law of Contrast doesn't say that you will always sell the less expensive of two products. It does say that if you put two products or services close together in space, in time, or in a person's mind, the person will begin to clearly see the differences, and their programming will help them choose which to buy instead of whether to buy. Price was the most common programming installed into most of us as children, but there definitely were many parents who programmed the theme "it's junk—don't buy garbage" into their children. These adult clients now buy higher-quality items when possible. The Law of Contrast acts within each of us to help us choose which of a number of items to buy.

> Show your client the product you believe is the best option and/or least expensive last. The client is compelled to own something and normally will take the least expensive item if it is shown last.

Real Estate

First, show your clients a home that they do not like first; then show them a home that meets all of their buying criteria. People tend to buy what they are shown or experience second.

Financial Products

Tell your clients you have two products to show them. The best financial fit for your clients to own is a diversified portfolio of mutual funds. You first show them an expensive annuity product and then follow that with a brief explanation of another option, that of owning mutual funds that require a smaller investment and offer easier access should they need their money. The better product and lower price both come second in this case, creating a compelling unconscious urge to invest in the mutual funds.

Clothing

Once the client has agreed to buy the suit or dress, now present a tie, a scarf, a new pair of shoes, or a nice necklace as an absolute must. If the client has purchased a $400 suit, isn't a $37 tie a necessary purchase?

Electronics

Your customers have said yes to the computer; now you can show them the extended service plan, a piece of useful or fun software, or an extra battery for emergencies. These $100 items contrast nicely to the $2,000 they just spent on the computer and almost seem irrelevant.

First, let your clients buy one of several necessary items; then let them buy the add-ons or accessories. In contrast to the large main investment the accessories seem small and a good value.

A useful rule to remember in any sales situation is that, when someone mentions that your product or service is too expensive or costs too much, you respond with a gentle, "Compared to what?" "Compared to what?" is a question that puts your client's thoughts into perspective and allows them to rethink their apparent negative response. If your client was heading toward a negative response, "Compared to what?" may often bring them back to the positive response.

Exercise: How can you utilize the Law of Contrast when selling your products or services? Be specific.

Law of Friends

When someone asks you to do something and you perceive that the person has your best interests in mind, and/or you would like him/her to have your best interests in mind, you are strongly motivated to fulfill the request.

How many times have you experienced someone knocking on your front door asking you to donate money for some cause? Compare the number of times you donated to the cause when you knew the person who asked you to donate in contrast to how often you donated when you didn't know the person who asked you to donate.

If you are like most people, you have donated more often when your neighbor has come to the door asking you to donate. You felt empathy for the person you know who is possibly being put upon by this charitable request. The people who solicited from you less regularly received fewer donations because they didn't have that same empathy or trust. We tend to say yes when we know someone or perceive that they are our friends.

In a similar context, most people would never go to a meeting for multilevel marketing if a friend or acquaintance didn't ask them to look at this business opportunity. The greatest strategy a multilevel marketing corporation can utilize is the friends-and-family strategy, using these people as the first contacts in the multilevel marketer's early days in his new business. These friends and family are the most likely to say yes to actually going to a meeting.

As people develop relationships with their clients they become friends. Friendships grow and become special, and future sales are all but assured with the ongoing relationship.

An extremely powerful persuasion tool that few salespeople ever use is that of pointing out the negative aspects of their products and services. One of the most effective ways to influence people is to argue against your own point of view or argue against your own self-interest so that it appears that you are being unbiased in your proposals.

One group of researchers had a heroin addict tell people that there should be stricter courts and more severe sentences. The researchers found the heroin addict to be more credible than others presenting similar points of view. This was one of the few instances when people believed someone who was not perceived as physically attractive. When the message conflicts with the expectations of your buyer you'll be perceived as more serious. This is a powerful point, and when you utilize it with careful skill you will regularly bring out any minor negative aspects of your products and services.

> Help people see you as their friend and someone who cares about them, and you will dramatically increase the probability of their compliance.

Be eager to point out any negative aspects of your proposal. This accomplishes two important things. First, it makes you appear far more trustworthy, and second, it allows your clients to be set at ease as you are doing their job of finding the drawbacks of the proposal.

Financial Products

Tell your client a story of how you recently helped your family members with their finances in the same manner that you are going to help your client. When they understand that they are going to be treated exactly like family, they perceive you also have *their* best interests in mind.

Real Estate

Share with your client why you would *not* buy a specific house. If it is clear that your client is *not* interested in the house, and you don't like it, either, explain why this house is not something you would recommend your friends buy and then explain why in detail. This strengthens your bond with your clients.

Exercise: How can you utilize the Law of Friends when selling your products or services? Be specific.

Law of Expectancy

When someone you respect and/or believe in expects you to perform a task or produce a certain result, you will tend to fulfill this person's expectation, whether positive or negative.

There is a famous study from the 1970s by psychologist Dr. R. Rosenthal that reveals that the expectation of one person can radically alter, both positively and negatively, the actual results of how people will perform. Students were divided into what teachers were told were bright and dull groups of students. The students were told nothing. The group that was made up of supposed high-IQ students performed at an average of an "A" level in their schoolwork after eight months. The group that was made up of supposed low-IQ students performed at an average of a "D" level after eight months. In reality, there was no difference in the IQs of the students. They were randomly divided into the groups, and the only variable in the study, which was immediately discontinued, was the expectation of the teachers involved.

In psychology, the placebo effect is a well-documented and scientifically measurable response on the part of the body to be healthier (or in the case of a nocebo, to be sicker) based on expectancy, suggestion, and belief. In the Korean War, there were thousands of casualties and not enough morphine to relieve the pain of the suffering soldiers. Medics and doctors were forced to give sugar pills and to suggest to the soldiers that they would shortly be out of pain. Approximately 25 percent of all soldiers taking the placebo had their severe pain relieved.

This same level of expectancy is necessary as a belief in yourself about your abilities to be successful and also about your influential ability with your clients to win them to your products and services.

Exercise: How can you utilize the Law of Expectancy when selling your products or services?

The behaviors you expect of yourself and others are more likely to be manifested in reality. If you believe that your clients will most certainly buy from you, they probably will.

Law of Consistency

When an individual announces in writing (or verbally to a lesser degree) that he is taking a position on any issue or point of view, he will strongly tend to defend that belief, regardless of its accuracy, even in the face of overwhelming evidence to the contrary.

- There is much research about consistency that you might initially think isn't about consistency. I want to bring this to your attention now so that you understand consistency as you never have before. I want to show you a very important factor of how the mind operates and how you can construct influential messages with ease! Consider this from Plous (1993) and the joint study between Stanford and Columbia Universities cited earlier:
  - In a nationwide opinion poll, 70 percent of Americans once gave an opinion about a legislative act that didn't exist. Some felt the states should take care of the responsibility; some felt the federal government should.
  - When asked their opinion on how easy getting a divorce should be in the United States, more than 40 percent more Americans chose the last option of three, regardless of which option was offered last.
- Sales of jams in a store increased 10 times when people could stop by and sample up to six jams versus those days the store offered 20 samples.
- College students reported cheating to be wrong when given the opportunity to fill out anonymous forms. Even those students reporting strong attitudes against cheating on exams immediately cheated on their exams when given the opportunity.
- When pollsters asked people what was the most important issue facing the nation, people respond with hundreds of different answers that were completely different and in greatly differing percentages than when pollsters ask people to choose from a list of options the one they considered to be the most important issue facing the nation.
- When people are asked about such hot topics as nuclear weapons, they respond with opposite opinions, depending on how the question is phrased.

From these and dozens of other valid and reliable studies you can conclude six crucial points:

1. People's opinions, thoughts, and desires are often molded by the questions they are asked.
2. People's thoughts, opinions, and desires are often created in the moment and have little or no relationship with what they will actually do or what they will believe later.
3. Many people have beliefs about things that are not real, based on fictitious questions (like acts of Congress) and not knowledge.

4. Most people are fairly automatic in their behavior. They see a commercial and because they believe what they see without critical thought, they decide what drink to drink, what restaurant to eat at, which tax preparer to use, all based on suggestion.

5. Once most people choose something, write something down, or say something, regardless of whether it makes any sense, whether it is in their best interest or not, they tend to stick with that decision, regardless of how that decision was made.

6. People don't like cognitive dissonance. Most can't hold two opposing thoughts in their minds, so they simply pick the thought/decision/belief they currently hold and eliminate the rest without further consideration.

All of this is part and parcel of the Law of Consistency.

Your clients' past decisions and public proclamations dramatically influence their beliefs and attitudes. Once people have publicly said, "I'll never X," they normally never do. Many people make public statements that they have not thought out, and those public statements often turn into beliefs and permanent attitudes. The reason is simple. We are taught that our word is our bond. When we say something, you can count on us.

Did you know that 70 percent of all people are the same religion they were raised in as children? This is the Law of Consistency in real-life action! People respect consistency and predictability.

A recent research study had subjects make decisions among various choices.

Group A was asked to remember their decision.

Group B was asked to write their decisions on a magic slate and then pull the sheet up, erasing their decisions.

Group C was asked to write down their decisions on paper with ink and hand them in to the researchers.

Which group stuck with their decisions? Right. Group C stuck with their decisions more than three-quarters of the time.

Group B kept their decisions half the time, and Group A tended to change their minds. The lesson is to get your client to write things down as he participates in the sales process. He could write down anything from goals for the coming year to what he would really like in a car, a house, a stock portfolio, or a vacation time-share package. The key is to get a pen in the client's hand and have him write!

Never ask a question that will pin the client down to a permanent no response.

Exercise: How can you utilize the Law of Consistency in selling your products or services?

Law of Association

We tend to like products, services, and ideas that are endorsed by other people we like and respect.

Tell me, what is it that Michael Jordan knows about underwear that I don't? Didn't Michael sign a $40,000,000 deal with Calvin Klein to do a few commercials about underwear? Now, it's my opinion that I know as much about underwear as Michael Jordan and I would have shot those commercials for half what he got! But Kevin Hogan is a name known in the field of selling. Michael Jordan is a name known throughout the world. Michael Jordan was paid two cents for every person on earth who knew his name. If I were paid two cents for every person who knew my name, I'd get paid about $7,000. That is why Michael Jordan got paid $40,000,000.

Calvin Klein paid $40,000,000 to link one of the world's most loved and best-known people to its product. Underwear. That is what the Law of Association is all about.

When your products and your services are linked to credible, likable, positive-image people, your client will tend to like the products and services.

For years, authors have known that the best way to sell a book is to get people to write favorable testimonials for the dust jacket and front matter of the book. This adds credibility to the book because we respect the people who wrote the quotes.

The power of a testimonial or of someone famous using your products or services can be the key that unlocks the doors of the unconscious mind. If you do not have the ability to have the famous endorse your products or services, ask other people who are using your services to write you a short letter testifying to the fact that your product or service has helped them change their life or their business, or made some significant difference that they didn't have before.

The testimonial speaks volumes about you so you don't have to.

Exercise: How can you utilize the Law of Association in selling your products or services?

> Allow people to see you and your products or services linked to the respected, the famous, and the experienced, and your probability of the yes response is heightened dramatically.

Law of Scarcity

When a person perceives that something he might want is limited in quantity, he believes the value of what he might want to be greater than if it were available in abundance.

What the public finds valuable never ceases to amaze us. Remember the bizarre Christmas season of 1996? That was the year when advertisers promoted Tickle Me Elmo dolls to children and then, to drive the price up, simply refused to produce the dolls in quantity. The price of the dolls grew outrageous. Stores sold out of the dolls after creating huge demand and overpricing them. Within weeks, the *Minneapolis Star Tribune* printed *six and seven columns of classified ads* placed by people offering to sell their Tickle Me Elmo's for anywhere from $300 all the way up to $695!

Imagine this: A mother and child go into the store when the dolls first come out and Mom buys her child a doll for $30. Eventually the media promotes these dolls to the point where stores and shopping centers are flooded with people trying to find Tickle Me Elmo's and are forced to settle for other products in the store for their children's Christmas presents. The marketing campaign was a bonanza for Tickle Me Elmo, radio station giveaways, and retailers, and it was all induced by intentional marketing scarcity.

Which of the following should you use as an indication of scarcity?

- Act now!
- Limited supplies!
- One day only!

All of those are common themes in advertising and marketing. Which works best? "Act now" is third most effective. "One day only" is an effective theme but doesn't even compare to "limited supplies." If you can show that there are only a few of your products or services available, that will increase their perceived value!

The limited-supply frame almost always goes back to your client's childhood. One or two pieces of cake were left, and when your client was four years old he knew that if someone else got the last piece of cake there would be none for him. It was imperative to attempt to get one of the last pieces of cake. Scarcity was installed at an early age and has been reinforced throughout our adult lives. The tension wound into scarcity is very powerful indeed, and you should begin to devise methods to use the principle of scarcity in your daily sales meetings.

> Your client must be made aware that something about you, your service, or your product is scarce. (Scarcity can include quantity of product, the time you have to spend with someone, or a number of specific products at a special low price.)

Real Estate

In the state of Minnesota in the year 2004, many homes were selling literally in days. It is completely ethical to tell your clients "The average house in Minnesota is selling in 31 days. If you want this house, put an offer on paper, now."

Automobile

"There are only three cars like this on the lot. I suspect they will sell out by Monday. That doesn't mean you can't get this car again, but it does mean you could wait weeks or months to get a factory-delivered car with all of these options. It's up to you."

Financial Products

"You can never predict the future, but what happens if this January is like most Januarys and the market goes up 4 percent while you are deciding whether this is the time to open your IRA?"

Exercise: What is it that your client loses if he doesn't buy from you? That is your scarcity point.

Law of Conformity

Most people tend to agree to proposals, products, or services that will be perceived as acceptable by the majority of other people or a majority of the individual's peer groups.

Everyone wants to be accepted. "What will people think?" is something that we all ask ourselves at the unconscious level. We all want to be liked and we all want people to look at what we buy and do with respect and admiration. When your client thinks about how his peers will view his purchase, the sale can be made or broken without going any further. Therefore, it is important to assure your client, at the unconscious level, that his buying your product or service is an outstanding idea.

Conformity is related to consistency in some ways. Conformity is being consistent with your peer group's acceptance. Consistency is being perceived as predictable and ethical within your peer group and even within yourself.

Nonconformists and rebels even tend to conform to their groups that are known to be rebellious against society. Consider that Greenpeace activists are very much nonconformists in the eyes of the public, but among their own group they conform to the nonconformist standard.

Jehovah's Witnesses and Latter-Day Saints are both Christian sects that are considered apart from Christianity by other denominations. They are nonconformists and are proud and honored to be. However, within their own groups, they have clear-cut and definite standards to which members must conform. Your understanding of your client's conforming standards can make or break your sales.

> Allow your client, after purchasing your products and services, to see his future as one where his peers and family not only approve but are excited about his purchase.

"Imagine how your wife will respond when she sees that you have gone out and bought her, and really your whole family, a brand-new car!"

"Imagine how your husband will feel when you show him that you took the initiative to invest in your retirement so his life will be easier—essentially not having to work until he is 77."

Exercise: What can you say to your clients to appeal to their sense of conformity?

Law of Power

People have power over other people to the degree that they are perceived as having greater authority, strength, or expertise in contrast to others.

Power comes with authority and charisma. Power is the ability to change. Power is both real and a perception. Your clients will perceive you as more powerful if you act with confidence but not conceit, with comfort but not disregard. Power is something that exists within you and must be brought out. Once people perceive you as competent, caring, knowledgeable, confident, and certain, then their confidence level in you goes up.

If you attempt to use power *over* other people, instead of *with* other people, then you will lose sales and lose friends. Power with people is perceived by most as strength and is often called charisma. Power over others is normally resented, and people are less likely to conform if they think you are trying to control them.

One recent study that discussed power and authority revealed that 95 percent of all nurses were willing to dispense drugs to patients, after being authorized by physicians, that they knew would indeed likely kill the patient. That's power.

When you are selling a product, it is assumed you are the expert. If you know everything there is to know about your product, you become the go-to guy. Subtly make sure your client knows you are the best or among the best in your company. People like to deal with the guy at the top.

Auto mechanics may not have a highly recognized value for power, but when your car breaks down, they become the most powerful people in the world, don't they? They have the solution to your problem. If they made the solution appear easy, they would have no power. The simple fact that most people are ignorant of how to utilize power is why many of them are perceived as beggars or nuisances.

Exercise: What are three subtle ways you can let your client know you are among the top people with regard to knowledge, client service, and/or sales in the company? How can you show your client that you are not just another salesperson?

Law of Inconsistency

Startling new research explains some things we never understood before about why we buy things that stop us from getting our goals, and why goals themselves can often destroy the achievement of goals.

It was Christmas time in 1975. (See how priming works . . . .)

. . . I was 13 and my Mom was "in" Weight Watchers, as a guest of her friend. She had a postage scale on which she weighed out food that she would eat . . . in ounces. She was about 80 pounds or so overweight, and she wanted to get rid of the excess. She had been going to Weight Watchers since the day after Thanksgiving and would continue to do so until the following summer.

She got home late with Mrs. Jedd from the next street (her friend and Weight Watchers buddy).

"How'd ya' do, Ma?"

"Lost two pounds, Kevy."

(Do not tell anyone she called me Kevy ... I was 13....)

"Good job, Ma."

She and Mrs. Jedd were filled with glee. They had both achieved their goal for the week. I think that meant they didn't gain any weight. It was fairly ambiguous, as I recall.

She got on the phone and ordered Quonset pizza! Sausage and pepperoni. I remember sitting there dumbfounded. It would be ready for pick-up in 45 minutes.

The Chicago area was and is well known for great pizza. You grew up knowing that. Quonset was the best pizza in Waukegan ... and they are still thriving there 30 years later! (No surprise!)

But they were desperately trying to lose weight. My stepdad had just died three months before. She needed to lose weight because she was going to return to the dating scene.

She weighed every single item of every single meal ... every day ... all month. It was the dumbest thing I'd ever seen.

Yet, she'd lost about 5 pounds that month (or so I was told) and now she was going to eat a pound of pizza.

Pizza was a real luxury in those days. It took over two hours' work of Mom's very small income to buy a pizza. We'd get to have Quonset about six times per year. Birthdays, usually.

Now, they ordered an extra large pizza. (She and Mrs. Jedd were both very big women.) I always wondered how people as impoverished as we were in the neighborhood ... could get so big. I didn't know that food that was good for you cost just as much or more than food that was going to make you fat.

They had a goal and it was an important one. And then they celebrated by doing the exact opposite of what would get them their goal.

Three steps forward ... two back.

It made no sense. All week they weighed their food with a postage stamp meter....

Of course, if you were the ad guy for Quonset Pizza, and you knew that this might be your demographic ... you'd probably write an ad that says, "You've had a hard week ... now treat yourself to Quonset."

Maybe you would get more aggressive and run something like, "You sacrificed all week . . . now it's Quonset time." And you'd be hitting the right buttons . . . and sell a lot of pizza.

Research reveals that competing goals, like having a fun night eating pizza and losing weight, not only are normal events for people but causal.

$10,000 Key Point: When people have two or more goals, and are making progress, or perceived progress toward one goal, it makes it *far* more likely that they will take action on another goal (desire) when it contradicts and conflicts with the first goal (desire)!

Another Example

Someone knows they should open a retirement account or invest in their education. They sign the paperwork indicating they will begin to fund their 401(k) account starting the first of the year. The next day they go out and buy a car.

The *perception* that progress is being made toward the goal both consciously and unconsciously *encourages* the individual to *do* things that conflict with the original goal.

$10,000 Key Point: When people feel or think that they are making progress toward a goal (like starting a 401(k) account or starting a weight loss plan) that *perception of progress* triggers the illusion of resources (money, time), making it easier to take action on something else requiring time or money.

When people see future progress from their actions today, they will often take actions that would logically delay the future goal.

We find that expected progress leads to moving away from their goal.

Furthermore, merely planning to make goal progress in the future may facilitate incongruent choice of immediate action. (Fishback and Dhar 2005)

The research was done on numerous experiments in different persuasive and goal-related settings. The results: Always the same.

Problem: How does this square with the Law of Consistency? (See *The Psychology of Persuasion*.)

$10,000 Key Point: Consistency will hold when the actions are framed as defining features of an individual's self-concept. When the actions/desires/alternative choices and goals are about variety-seeking behavior, and not the person's self-concept, their identity, they will take action on the next and conflicting goal.

When presenting yourself, you need to find out whether what you are asking is necessary for the client's variety-seeking behavior or for reinforcing their self-concept. One virtually assures a sale. The other demands that the answer is no.

9 | The Influential Secret of Oscillation

Oscillation is one of the best-kept secrets in human influence. None of the gurus of persuasion or influence will talk about oscillation (and they may not know what it is).

Very few people who understand belief and behavior oscillation want anyone else to grasp the concept. Oscillating beliefs and values are key in successfully understanding and persuading others.

As you learn about managing oscillation in others, I want you to keep the following core concept in mind: Yes is not a true decision. It is agreement or affirmation to a proposal at a particular instant in time . . . *and you had best seize the moment.*

Had you asked for a response five minutes earlier or later, you almost certainly would have gotten a different answer, regardless of what the question was!

Remember when you were 16 or 26 and you were in that moment when you probably were going to be intimate with someone else? Your heart pounded. You knew you could get pregnant, or get her pregnant, or get AIDS or syphilis. You had always thought you believed that you would never have unprotected or possibly premarital sex. Perhaps you:

- Thought it was wrong.
- Knew it was against your religion.
- Would never take the risk of acquiring a life-threatening disease.
- Would never take the risk of pregnancy.
- Believed you should wait to have sex until you were married.
- Were waiting for the right person.

Remember? Your beliefs were strong. Firm. Written in stone. You could have preached a sermon about whichever of these beliefs you held close and lived by. (If this specific example is foreign to you, simply think of the other firm beliefs you had that you violated within a matter of seconds or minutes of first considering doing so.)

And then you were in the moment. And you had this experience that was something you knew you wouldn't do but you did it. Upon reflection, you were surprised at your behavior. Perhaps you were shocked. You now had to try to justify your actions in some way or determine that what you originally believed was wrong. An internal mess. Remember?

Let's examine what happened on that day:

1. You held a powerful, intense, unwavering belief for a long time.
2. You knew that you would never behave in a different fashion than what you believed.
3. With only minutes of consideration, you violated a belief you had had for years and perhaps for your entire life.
4. Afterward you wondered if you really knew who you were, or worse, you experienced tons of guilt because you so easily and instantly wavered on something that was a belief that defined who you were.

You had never oscillated or vacillated about this remarkable subject in the past. You were always absolutely certain about what you believed and how you felt. You knew you could never behave in any other way than what you valued and believed. It was as impossible as a man reaching the moon in the 1960s.

And then you did it.
How is that possible?

I use this extreme example to begin our discussion of oscillation because, in this example, there is essentially no oscillation until the minutes before the ultimate moment. Then, all of a sudden the wavering begins, and it is often experienced as scary because conflicting beliefs now begin to enter the mind. Back and forth, pro and con. Strong feelings/emotions overcome what we might call rational thought, and a lifetime of certainty is transformed after minutes of oscillation to a completely different behavior.

In this case, first there is no oscillation, then there is a burst of oscillation and indecision (often accompanied by confusion), and then a specific behavior occurs. After the behavior, something must happen to make you whole or congruent again. You must reconcile the behavior with the previous beliefs by either establishing new beliefs, condemning yourself, or returning to old beliefs with a renewed vigor realizing you have not been yourself. The oscillations after the behavior are often as dramatic as or more dramatic than those prior to the behavior.

What follows is a completely different example that illustrates this critical point.

(If you don't understand football, you may want to forgive me in advance and dig in for the next four paragraphs.)

> *Strong feelings/emotions overcome what we might call rational thought, and a lifetime of certainty is transformed after minutes of oscillation to a completely different behavior.*

When I first looked at the January 2003 Super Bowl to handicap it, I determined the number should be Oakland −3 at a neutral site. San Diego isn't really quite neutral, because the proximity to the Bay Area versus Florida certainly favors Oakland. I thought the number should be bumped a point or two, perhaps to as much as five. In Vegas the number opened at five and got bet by the pros (smart-money bettors) down to four where it stayed until Sunday.

I previously mentioned the modeling tool I use to handicap football games. One of the key elements that had led me to pick New England the year before was the likely number of turnovers in the game. (The other most important factors are yards per pass for/against.) In 2003, I concluded,

Tampa Bay should be the recipient of about one more interception than Oakland. That means that, if the two teams played millions of times, Tampa would win about 55 to 60 percent of the time, so my money goes on Tampa Bay. (There are other factors that are analyzed in this tough-to-call game, but that isn't the point of this article!)

As soon as I laid a significant number of dollars on Tampa Bay, my mind started to find additional data to support the decision to bet on Tampa Bay. Now as I thought about it, 9 out of 10 of my thoughts supported my decision to bet on Tampa. This large volume of unconscious justification about a decision that is almost a flip of a coin in true probability is uncalled for, based on real world evidence. My emotions started to selectively filter out reasons to bet on Oakland and support my expensive choice of betting on Tampa Bay.

It took me six hours to finally bet the amount of money I did. I vacillated between taking the offensive Oakland scoring machine versus the solid-as-a-rock (Tampa) defense. Back and forth. Then, when my gut said Tampa more often than not, I ran the numbers, and they also pointed to Tampa Bay. Then, as time went on in the week, I became more certain—which of course was only an illusion because it wasn't based on real-world evidence, only on feelings and justifications. (In this case Tampa was kind enough to actually win and allow me another problem, which is believing I am better/smarter than I really am! But, that's okay—I got paid.

Here's what happens: There is typically an *arbitrary decision point that is set* in almost every negotiation/communication/decision. ("I have to know today." "If we don't have a deal by the end of the month, I'll let someone else have it." "If you buy today you get 10 percent off.") A decision needs to be or probably will be made. In some cases, if an obvious decision isn't instantly made (yes, I will pull over for the police officer because I don't want this ticket to be higher than it is now) things could get worse. Almost all decisions that require conscious thought (most decisions require no thought or conscious attention at all) find people oscillating back and forth about what to do, especially *before* the decision point.

Realize that people will make a very different decision at 5:00 P.M. than they will at 5:05 P.M. on something that goes back and forth a lot in the mind! People literally change their mind as each moment passes in many decisions. Unless people have firm beliefs as discussed earlier in the decision about having sex, people are constantly oscillating on decisions. Back and forth. Back and forth. Sometimes with varying degrees of intensity. "No, absolutely not." That was today. Then tomorrow: "Well, maybe." Then the next day: "I don't think so, but it's possible."

You can see the pendulum swing back and forth, or the child on the swing go higher or lower. More important for our discussion is that oscillation is not a day-to-day experience. It is a moment-to-moment experience. Yes and no in varying degrees flip-flop from moment to moment and minute to minute.

The oscillation will continue indefinitely unless a new stimulus enters the equation—and then any decision is subject to further change.

Once persuaded to do anything, there is definitely short-term change in behavior. Instead of doing one thing, a person does another. Instead of believing one thing, a person believes another. Nevertheless, people can and do regularly change even strong beliefs. The more public a person is with their belief/behavior, the more likely they are to maintain that belief. (The minister of the church is more likely to maintain his belief than the parishioner sitting in row 30 because of the weekly public exposition of his beliefs through sermons and prayers.)

Beliefs and behaviors that are not made public are more likely to change due to future attempts at persuasion.

Beliefs and behaviors that are not made public are more likely to change due to future attempts at persuasion.

Someone who begins a diet plan and attends classes or meetings is likely to continue to succeed while attending the classes. As soon as the person stops attending the classes or going to the meetings, the chances are greatly increased that they will stop their weight control program and revert to old beliefs and behaviors.

The more people there are who have opinions and the more important those people's opinions about a person are, the more powerful the desire one has to keep the new belief or behavior consistent with the new belief.

Key Question: Is there anything we can predict will happen after a person has been persuaded?

Yes. Once someone has been persuaded there is a very good chance they will go through oscillations of regret, sometimes so great that they will actually immediately change their mind again and cancel a purchase or not take a job they thought they should, for example.

You can virtually eliminate this specific reaction through the utilization of principles that allow someone to anticipate their regret prior to the decision point so that when they experience the change of belief/behavior, they will be expecting it and will react in a less intense fashion.

Did the firefighters need to be persuaded on 9/11? Did they experience oscillation?

You hire an account to do your books and reduce your taxes.

Your personal trainer's job is to get rid of your gut.

The chef? To cook.

A police officer? To protect public safety.

But what happens when an airplane flies into a building? What happens inside of the mind of the firefighter who is racing upstairs while everyone else is going down?

Specifically there is no way to know. Even the firefighters who lived could only report what they *think* they remembered and thought at the time of the most incredible crisis imaginable, reminiscent of D–Day in some ways. Firefighters train for disasters but they usually have a sense of control about their own safety. Going into the World Trade Center was quite another thing.

We know that many office workers trapped in the buildings who were about to lose their lives called loved ones. The same was true for the passengers on the flight that was heroically downed in Pennsylvania that fateful day. We do know that oscillation probably takes place in these extraordinary circumstances. The desire to be with loved ones. The desire to live. Being able to live your life in the way you choose and ultimately die doing what you love. I imagine there was oscillation and it was fairly rapidly dismissed by the objective, the task at hand.

Veterans of war no doubt experienced similar feelings, thoughts, and oscillations. But what about the more mundane? Buying a car? Saying yes or no to the request for a date? Saying yes or no to the marriage proposal?

There is ample evidence that reveals that the closer one comes to a goal or an objective (the wedding day, for example) the more likely one is to experience regret.

As humans we experience fear and anxiety responses when we lose the freedom options. That's one reason ordering fish or fowl can be such a difficult problem! As soon as a decision is near, anxiety can incapacitate a person, even on little decisions about what to eat in a restaurant.

In fact, reams of research indicate this repulsion to the goal is great as it is approached in many contexts. This often leads to self-sabotage and other destructive behaviors.

This is why people say they would like to invest in their 401(k) plan next year but if they were asked to make a deposit today they would not do so!

Oscillation is not indecisiveness per se. It is a normal and often useful reaction to situations that have unknown variables.

Oscillation is not indecisiveness per se. It is a normal and often useful reaction to situations that have unknown variables.

- Oscillation is wavering between two or more possibilities.
- The wavering can become more intense as the deadline looms.
- The anxiety and fear level increases as the deadline comes closer.
- The desire to move away from any choice that limits future freedom of choice in any way increases as a decision point nears.

A woman who is in love with two men chooses man A. (Men do not choose women, regardless of what religion or theory of evolution you subscribe to that tells you otherwise.) She decides, "I will spend my life with Andrew." But as she comes closer and closer to actually spending the rest of her life with Andrew, she begins to wonder if she has made a big mistake and starts to seriously reconsider Bill! Sure, she dumped Bill a month ago, but really, when she thinks about it, Bill is probably the better choice.

This oscillation doesn't just happen with women. My mom regularly told me that it's a woman's prerogative to change her mind. I always thought that was a lousy excuse. It turns out to be true, though, except that we all change our minds! Most people change their minds as the goal approaches or the other options have been rejected.

Sometimes these oscillations are manifested in behavior. Sometimes they are not. Either way, they are happening in the mind of the individual.

According to Fink, Kaplowitz, and Hubbard (2002), oscillation (wavering) increases when the person or message doing the persuading is perceived as credible. When someone is believable and states an opinion that isn't consistent with what the individual currently believes, credibility becomes a critical issue.

The power of the argument/message is also critical. A well-framed argument will cause people's minds to waver between options. Consider the State of the Union speech by President George W. Bush at the end of January 2003. Bush faced great opposition on his objective of attacking Iraq. In the State of the Union, Bush could not provide the smoking gun that many wanted, so he provided a logical line of thinking that was difficult to refute. I paraphrase: *There were 30,000 missiles that could be used to carry weapons of mass destruction.* Sixteen have been found. Where are the other 29,984?

Indeed. Where were they? Bush clearly and concisely stated the facts of what weapons Iraq had at the end of 1998 and then claimed to reveal what Iraq had not declared. The strategy essentially worked, as 84 percent of the nation had a positive view of the speech. Doubts remained (that is part of what oscillation will always yield!), and perhaps we will never know all the facts. But one thing is certain: The strength of a well-stated argument can cause oscillation. The stronger the argument, the greater and more frequent the oscillation. This means that the more powerful the argument, the more often the person will vacillate between beliefs/choices and the more real both choices become.

What about the 16 percent who weren't convinced and who didn't seem to waver at all? Perhaps they did. Perhaps not. Certainly if their opinion was written in stone, they simply didn't oscillate at all. However, remember the option of having sex or not and how most did so? That was written in stone.

Wavering between two or more options occurs when something is important. Some people hate their jobs, but they want to keep their income, which is high when compared with jobs they would qualify for should they leave their current jobs.

Stay	*Go*
Hate job, well paid.	Less money, more enjoyable work.

This is an important issue, and oscillation could occur dozens of times per hour, day, week, month, and year. Oscillation will generally not happen to any significant degree in issues that are not important to the person. Why would a millionaire care if a cup of coffee is $2 or $1? She probably wouldn't and thus wouldn't waver. Generally speaking, an issue has to be important to engender vacillation. You can tell when you are oscillating when you feel torn or you feel like you are being pulled in two directions.

Generally risk is involved. Staying with the job entails the risk of never enjoying other aspects of life. Going entails the risk of never having the money you have now. People oscillate when something is important and entails tangible risks both in the change and in the status quo.

10 | Mind Reading

How to Know What They Are Thinking

In this chapter I reveal a few of my most closely held secret methods of determining what people are thinking in the moment. I am going to give you some incredible tools. You will learn one of my favorite models for determining current thought, and I am going to give you one of my favorite models for utilizing that specific information in gaining compliance.

Maybe it's just me, but I like to know what other people are thinking. I don't want to guess. I want to know.

When you can *know*, you can determine how best to help that person get what they want in business and in life. Instead of being involved in a long drawn-out process, you can get rapid outcomes that are favorable to everyone involved. Ultimately that's what we all want. Most people experience massive idiopathic fear when it comes to communication in almost any context. In other words, they feel uncomfortable putting their feelings and thoughts on the table for fear that they will be hurt in some way. When people cloak thoughts and feelings, it makes communication incredibly difficult. Honesty becomes compromised and everyone gets poor outcomes. You see this in every aspect of life.

When people don't tell you what they are thinking/feeling, you simply need to discover, calculate, or determine those thoughts in other ways.

You can utilize body language, psychographics, evolutionary psychology, psychobiology, cultural beliefs, religious beliefs, peer pressures, psychological profiles, and expectancies along with prior behavior to determine almost anyone's current thoughts with some significant degree of accuracy.

On larger scales, you can read groups, cultures, specific demographics, and nations using essentially the same tools.

The more you know about someone or some group, the easier it is to gain compliance. It's that simple.

It's true in relationships, it's true in family and friendships, it's true in the selling context, it's true for all aspects of business, it's true for the therapist, and it's true for nations dealing with other nations. Intelligence in the military sense is what separates the wheat from the chaff in every aspect of life.

The ethical use of influence is never more necessary than when you have good intelligence about your client and customer. Knowledge is potential power, and that power can just as easily be used for good as it can be for bad. The line is not always instantly clear, and sometimes the line changes.

Without having excellent intelligence about your clients and consumers, you have little chance of being persuasive beyond random luck. With good intelligence, you can achieve incredible results in gaining compliance. And if you think it's important in business, can you imagine how important it is in personal relationships?

> *The more you know about someone or some group, the easier it is to gain compliance.*

But before we get into utilizing intelligence, I want you to look at some ethical issues that arise in acquiring and utilizing intelligence. Influence hinges on good intelligence, and more than that, the ethical use of persuasion techniques can be compromised if you aren't careful. "Win–win or no deal" is more than a slogan; it is a necessary reality to build long-term relationships that are mutually beneficial for two people or parties.

One of my favorite movies of all time is *Meet John Doe*. This 1941 black-and-white movie starred Gary Cooper. The movie was released as Nazism and fascism were rapidly spreading in Europe, and it was in part a response to those who would find fascism an alternative in the United States. The movie was superb and it did its job.

A young newspaper reporter (Barbara Stanwyck), about to lose her job, concocts a story about a man who is so disgusted with the world that he is going to commit suicide on Christmas Eve. His fictitious note sent to the newspaper office is signed "John Doe." The reporter keeps her job but eventually has to find the would-be martyr—who exists only in her mind. She interviews possible role players and ultimately convinces a homeless man (Gary Cooper) to be John Doe to the public.

Further interviews and the press launch a John Doe movement across the country, based on principles of being a good neighbor, trust, helping others, and making the little guy feel important. Ultimately John has to run for president. The unwilling but trapped John does indeed give the speech of a lifetime to a huge audience. Wondering how he can live with himself as a fraud, John seriously contemplates suicide and is saved only by a throng of John Doe fans. One woman's deception to save her job in wartime turns into a wonderful movement of enormous good. A homeless man's agreement to play the role of John Doe becomes a massive internal struggle between self and public fraud and greater good of the country and the world.

Two paragraphs do not do the movie justice. It doesn't do justice to the ethical issues involved, and it doesn't do the subject of persuasion and influence justice. Rent this two-hour movie to challenge every ethical and moral view you hold. I promise you will be glad you did!

I would venture to guess that if you take advantage of the information I am about to reveal to you, you will nearly double your responses for your sales, adding clients and making successful your influence efforts. (Notice I didn't say, "increase by 10 percent," I said, "nearly double.")

Here is who John Doe is in the twenty-first century. You are selling your ideas, products, and services—and yourself—to John every day. So you may as well meet him (and his dear friend Jane Doe).

- In general people aren't as satisfied as they could be.
- Most people have only a moderate amount of self-esteem.

- Two-thirds of women and one-third of men don't like the way they look.
- Nearly everyone worries and has a deep-seated fear of rejection.
- Almost everyone is afraid to grow old.
- Virtually everyone has a fear of death.
- Almost everyone works to avoid pain, and once in pain will do what it takes to get out of pain.
- People don't have time to be smart shoppers, and they don't comparison shop that much.
- When people get their minds set on something, they want it *now*. (As a rule, people will not delay gratification!)
- Most people still perceive credit cards as not being equal to real money.
- People want to make decisions that will make them look good to others.

That's just a thumbnail sketch of a few of John's and Jane's traits. They are universal because we have all evolved from the same gene pool and in some transactions tend to respond similarly in social exchanges. In other words, people are somewhat predictable.

Realizing this, how do we sell to John Doe and how do we market to him? How do we make use of the information used by the largest advertising firms in the world on our shoestring budgets? How do we talk to John and Jane so they listen and comply quickly? How do we know what they are thinking and feeling?

Once we know what our prospects' needs, wants, and desires are, we can use this information to prepare a message that firmly impresses on the mind how we can help them. We can clearly show our prospects how they will feel better, get out of pain, and look like they make great decisions to the people in their peer group.

Here is a good model for you to present to your prospect:

1. Paint a clear picture for your prospects and bring it up really close. It needs to show your prospects these points about themselves: what you presently have, who you presently are, or how what you presently feel is not satisfactory. You can do, have, or be more, and you can feel better!
2. Product/idea/service X helps many people just like you get that result.

> *Once we know what our prospects' needs, wants, and desires are, we can use this information to prepare a message that firmly impresses on the mind how we can help them.*

3. Try it once. You have nothing to lose and everything to gain.
4. Other people will respect you and like you more for using this product/idea/service.
5. Imagine your future as you deserve it to be. You can reach your dreams and achieve your goals if you use this product/idea/service.
6. This product/idea/service is guaranteed, so you can feel secure in making a decision now.
7. To take advantage of this product/idea/service, call/write now because only Y number of people will be allowed to participate. Here's all you have to do . . .

Now, obviously not all market messages use this model or all components of it. But, based on the market research I have done, this model appeals to John Doe. Research reveals that John and Jane *do* act now when responding to this model!

Now it's up to you. How can you implement this model in your sales or business, and will you start today or wait until tomorrow?

11 | I'll Think About It

What does that mean? It means the client/customer doesn't feel right in at least one way. The client can't quantify it because it is a feeling (or feelings), so you'd better be prepared!

Let's look at feelings and what they mean in the persuasion process.

The pendulum swings back and forth (oscillation). At each moment in time it's in a slightly different place than it was just a fraction of a second before. And so it goes until it stops ... where? Right back in the middle: "I don't know." "Maybe."

The nonconscious mind runs off survival instincts, sometimes with success, sometimes not. The nonconscious mind is very different from the conscious mind. It runs on autopilot. It is basically a stimulus/response mechanism that adapts along the way, but slowly. The conscious mind is that computer, if you will, that thinks, calculates, and can make a decision. But those decisions come at a cost. The nonconscious is often drawn in many different directions, not just one or two, and to cut off any option is a threat to the freedom of the being. (Write that down. This will be referred to by people as, "I have a bad feeling," "I'm not sure," "I don't feel comfortable," and so on.)

Eliminating choices to a human (and many other animals) can be quite an experience. You and I hate to see that freedom say goodbye. And for good reason. Although there are options (escape routes), there is comfort in the status quo. When there is comfort in the status quo (what's going on today), there is seemingly little reason to change. Many animals hunt other animals with this as their guiding fundamental principle: Let them feel secure, safe, then kill. Sun-tzu may have even written about it.

People want to feel good and comfortable so they can live in the illusion that they are happy, when of course the delusion will be shattered in due course. There is no relationship between feeling comfortable today and long-term happiness. I would suggest the opposite.

But is going for the yes response like going for the kill? That seems so wrong! And it would be if you were going to kill someone.

Unfortunately, at the nonconscious level most people perceive every change from the status quo as a threat to their very survival. Someone wants to quit smoking cigarettes, for example. At the conscious level that is a no-brainer: Lung cancer will chew you up and spit you out. But at the nonconscious level the smoking is behaviorally wired into the brain as an adaptation. Just like overeating. You wonder why so many people who live in poverty are grossly obese? They want to feel good and they want the most important choice they have to not be taken away. Think you can change that using conventional thinking? Not likely. It has nothing to do with sense or logic. Someone's feelings will challenge all of your persuasive communication (i.e., just about *all* communication).

Take away the option of smoking and the person goes nuts inside. Anxiety hits stellar levels. Take away the option of choosing more food and the person once again goes nuts inside. They know they shouldn't feel this way but they do. In Hale Dwoskin's book, *The Sedona Method*, he shares Lester Levenson's tools for letting go of feelings of fear, anger, shame, resentment, and grief. Why? Because feelings are the muck of life. They kill. They are the unreliable indicators that destroy lives. When you feel bad and your life is going to heck, you have a double dose of disaster. Most people really believe they should trust their feelings. If you do, you are destined for more than failure in all aspects of your life.

> *Unfortunately, at the nonconscious level, most people perceive every change from the status quo as a threat to their very survival.*

You will never persuade or be persuaded of something you currently don't experience. In other words, you will remain at the status quo for the rest of your life. Feelings aren't a barometer of the quality of life. They aren't a barometer of good and bad, (long-term) happiness, or sadness even. They are a barometer of the nonconscious mind's past experiences and genetic programming.

And when you are attempting to persuade someone, you can bet that the person's conscious mind will analyze your offer and come up with a fairly quick rational decision to do what you ask followed immediately by a flood of anticipated regret. So they say yes, then they feel no.

Now the person doesn't trust you. And they think it's you! You're manipulating them. Really?

Ever see someone buy a $25,000 automobile right after they quit their job? They needed to fill the option void that would likely exist upon further review. Everyone in the car biz knows that once you buy it, it's yours. So the people buy today because they won't have the money tomorrow. This makes no sense because sense doesn't come into play. It's all instinct and behavioral shaping of the nonconscious mind that cause people to feel. As soon as they feel strongly, then everything can quickly go to heck unless something is done and fast.

People's gut instincts took the Twin Towers down. People's feelings caused the trains to be blown up in Madrid. The terrorists were sure their feelings were right. They trusted their gut, and knew they were doing the right thing. History repeats itself every few days or years. In 1999 people were saying "this time it's different" because they felt the greed and euphoria of getting rich fast in the stock market. Um, it's not different. Do not trust those feelings ever. When Saddam gives you the big smile saying you can trust him, just let the mustache remind you of Adolf. Remember the guy who kills his own people for sport? Feelings. They felt totally in the right.

Remember that the next time someone tells you they "don't feel right" or they "have a bad feeling."

Here's the reality principle: *Life really is all about persuasion.*

People must go up one level from feelings to thought and take control of their lives. Part of that is all about being persuaded (changing) and persuading (causing change).

Almost every time you open your mouth you want someone to do something for you:

> You want them to say yes to you and no to the competitor, and to do business just with you.
>
> You want the girl to go out with you, dump her boyfriend, and be eternally devoted to you.
>
> You want the guy to marry you, massage your feet, and bring home the bacon.
>
> You want them to hold the mayo, bring you a fork, and change your $100 bill.
>
> You want them to pick up their clothes, turn the music down, and study.

It's all about persuasion.

I could show you many books that have some pretty funny ideas about what gets people to do things. Sometimes they work, sometimes they rarely work, sometimes they just end up making you look, well, dumb.

My outcome for you is to be able to persuade almost anyone to do almost anything in less than eight minutes. Now, here's the rub.

> I can show you how to get that sale, almost any sale. Once.
>
> I can show you how to get that girl, almost any girl. Once.
>
> I can show you how to get the kids to listen. Once.
>
> I can show you how to get great service. Once.

But after you have that first yes, your personality and who you are become crucial. Getting the first yes can be the toughest. Getting the second is either easier or more difficult, but it's a different ball game completely. Once someone has knowledge about you in a certain area or a certain way, you have to utilize a number of new strategies to get to yes again. And, of course, I'll give you tips along the way about how to do just that. Nevertheless, this book is about getting the tough first yes. It's all about converting her from him to you. About getting someone to switch from them to you. About getting compliance now. And you will be able to do it.

Amazed? I was, too.

You have to deal with the feelings. *You have to get people's feelings positively linked to you.*

Real or illusion, if you have the answer to their problem, the solution to their challenge, you must create positive feelings in that person or you will end up with wider swings of oscillation. You have to assume that people will feel regret or anticipate the feeling of regret, and you need to prepare them for that outcome.

You absolutely must realize that at any moment people are on the pendulum between the conscious mind response, which is probably correct, and their feelings, which are probably all over the map trying to make sense of your proposal or offer.

You must get commitment and reinforce the customer's decision as a good one.

When you have commitment, in most cultures you have psychological pressures from the inside that almost obligate the person to move forward with what they have agreed to. Hopefully, you represent the best product, service, idea, and person in the area you excel in. As you become a master of influence, you truly gain a valuable power that can bring on compliance rapidly in almost all situations.

> **Getting the first yes can be the toughest.**

"No." It's the only thing that is more annoying to hear than "I'll think about it." In both cases there is no intention for further decision making or even thought on the subject at hand. Therefore, the time to act on your part is probably now. Or maybe it was time to act five minutes earlier by precluding "no" in the first place.

Most of the time they (your client, customer, the girl) simply say no. They don't mean anything by no. It isn't even typically an answer that really means "no" or even "probably not." No simply means, "My nonconscious mind doesn't think, it responds, and the response that keeps me in the status quo, which is what I am familiar with, says no."

It is a reaction.

When the doctor tests your knee reflexes, you do not think, "Okay, now, logically I can be reflexive and will swing my knee forward three inches in a third of a second after it is gently struck." Your knee simply moves. It reacts.

Now, this doesn't mean that all no responses are up for grabs. That simply isn't the case. Many times your clients have thoughtfully determined that your service isn't right for them. In these cases *no* means "no," but the person could be either right or wrong. You retain the option of turning no into yes. (They might be wrong in this case and we can present information again in such a way that yes might indeed be the correct response.)

Finally, there are instances when *no* is simply the well-thought-out and correct decision, although it's not common that it's this cut and dry. It never makes sense to ask someone to do what isn't in their best interests, so in these cases you don't.

The nonconscious mind doesn't think or make decisions. By definition it can't and it never will. It has no capacity to come up with alternatives. It reacts in the way it immediately sees the environment and avoids the greatest fear and pain. The nonconscious mind is the dominant force in almost every human being's life—and remember, the nonconscious mind doesn't even think! It's been programmed through genes and through the environment.

In situations where you have made hundreds of decisions (driving a car) the nonconscious mind almost always makes good movements and reacts well to keep you and everyone around you safe. In these cases, a person's intuition tends to be good. (Intuition simply means your immediate reactions and how you feel about them—not what you *think* about them.) In situations in which you have much less experience making essentially all correct decisions, like driving a car, your reactions and feelings about your reactions are completely suspect, and so are theirs.

Think of this: If every time people got up in front of a group they were applauded, they would feel comfortable in that situation and in all likelihood seek it out in the future. Or, if every time they were alone they felt devastated, they would likely seek out the company of others at all costs. The (nonconscious) mind simply adapts to whatever it is given and attempts to avoid fear and pain of things that it has been conditioned to avoid. As for the unknown, it's rarely a better option than the status quo, unless that status quo is enormously painful.

The status quo is painful at the conscious level. Look in the mirror. If you see that extra layer of fat, the conscious mind is very much in pain. But the nonconscious is not. The act of eating feeds the being and, until it experiences pain and fear because of the eating, there is no need for the nonconscious to adjust to anything. The nonconscious mind doesn't see the fat as painful or something to fear. There is no experience in that regard. Therefore, the mind is set on status quo in this situation. To overcome the nonconscious in the status quo takes an enormous amount of conscious determination and internal pressure from commitments to others.

> *To overcome the nonconscious in the status quo takes an enormous amount of conscious determination and internal pressure from commitments to others.*

There are also times when no is a conscious decision that overrides the nonconscious desire of yes.

Everyone has experienced wanting to have just one more piece of pie but saying no because you know you are going to be bloated and uncomfortable later. Here the conscious mind takes over the autopilot.

You've had the situation where someone wanted to have sex with you and although the body was willing, the conscious mind said no. You knew it was too risky or perhaps against your values.

The conscious mind can say no based on rational thought in spite of the nonconscious drives and desires to opt for yes. In these cases, there is also a time and a place to turn the no into yes, and there are times when it is best to leave no at no.

The best way to get past no is to not hear it in the first place. You'll use attractiveness-raising and resistance-reduction techniques, alpha and omega strategies, but even more fundamental is remembering your first objective. In order to accomplish this you must win over the conscious and nonconscious minds in a fairly quick fashion (usually not as easy as you would like to believe). That means that your proposal must make sense, and it must be in line with one of the fundamental desires or drivers of their behavior. This is not the same as emotions, but emotional content is obviously going to accelerate a yes response once the proposal is tracked into a fundamental driver. (Reminder: There are 16 core drivers that you can read about in *Covert Hypnosis: An Advanced Course in Non-conscious Influence.* They include the drives and desires of sex, food, connection, acquisition, learning, competition, altruism, and others.)

If your proposal isn't tracked in one of the 16 drivers that is driving their lives (for example, the desires to eat and to bond could be the driving forces in one life while the desires to have sex and to acquire could be drivers in another person) you're simply going to hear "I'll think about it" or "no."

Obviously this doesn't mean, "Okay, if you go out with me, I'll give you lots of food and be a great person to bond with" or "Now, if you buy a house from me you'll get lots of sex and acquire lots of money." In fact, people are often embarrassed by their core drivers. You don't see people walking around saying, "And I'm proud that altruism and connection drive my behavior."

Those desires that drive our behavior are pretty obvious to ourselves. (For example, I have thousands of books in my library, so do you think that the desires to learn and to acquire might be among my top four or five drivers?)

As is detailed in *Covert Hypnosis: An Advanced Course in Non-conscious Influence*, there is an elegance to tracking your proposal into their core drivers.

Key: You lay down a logical proposal that wires right into a key driver and you get a positive response. You don't have to hear "no" or "I'll think about it" because you are triggering the deep drive to move in the direction of your proposal.

You don't even always have to ask someone to do something in these cases; you simply tell them! I have a good friend who simply says, "This book is going to give you proven insights into human behavior that you've never pondered. Get it now, Kevin." And I do. I trust the source (crucial piece) and it feeds into a driving force in my life that is rarely overridden by anything else.

If tranquility were one of my core drivers, then the same person would say, "This book is going to save you so much research time and reduce your stress levels like you wouldn't believe. Get it."

Granted, it takes a while to be able to identify a person's driving desires. And it takes practice and feedback on your efforts of weaving messages into drivers to begin to understand just how powerful this is. Once you are able to do this, you have the world at your fingertips. You can have as much or as little success as possible. Indeed, this is what power and empowerment are all about.

Think about it.

If you just knew what your most powerful core drivers were, and if you knew how to weave messages to yourself, what would that mean? Then, consider just what happens when you can do the same with others. Then think how big your world would get and just how wide the sphere of your influence would become.

Influence: It's Not How You Ask, But When!

Imagine: July meeting for 2011 benefits plan. . . .

"Okay, everyone, a show of hands. How many of you are going to want to be part of our new benefits program? Corporate is matching up to 50 percent of your contributions to your 401(k). That means if you put $15,000 in your 401(k), the company will put in $7,500."

"Sure thing—I'll make a contribution to my 401(k) plan."

From a simply rational perspective, this is a no-brainer. Every person should say yes, contribute the maximum that the company allows, and chalk up a tidy 50 percent return on investment. (Read that as "I'm smart enough to take all the free money I can get.")

Of course they will!

Now imagine it's six months in the future. In fact, research shows that when you ask people if they intend to do just about anything in a few months or next year, they will affirm that they are going to participate; and then . . . they don't.

They get to December when it's time to fill out the paperwork, which amounts to a signature that affirms that the employee wants free money, and they just can't pull the trigger and watch all that money taken from their paycheck. They opt out—or ask for only a little free money from their company.

But remember, people don't think rationally. They will refuse to take free money, which is why they are working in the first place! Or worse, they realize the value of getting free money and refuse to take all of it! Why? What is wrong with this picture?

Let's look at another example, this one of how the mind works as far as time is concerned.

A friend asks you to do something next week that you only marginally want to do. It would be okay, but it would be just as okay not to do it. You say yes.

As the time approaches you feel more and more like you would rather get something done around the house or go shopping. It now seems like work to do what you previously said yes to.

"My kids are sick and I've got to stay home and take care of them."

And you stay home or go shopping. Or you have this experience:

You're at a Tupperware party and you know the moment is coming. . . .

"Now, if you want to receive a bunch of free gifts like this container that you can stand on and still not break [she demonstrates] you can host a party at your house. But I'm really booked for the next couple of months, so it would have to be in March. Jane, do you want to do one?"

"Sure."

"March 7?"

"Sure, that's fine."

"Great, honey. How about you Jessica? I can do one on the 4th of April."

"Sure, I'll do that."

And so on and so forth.

Now, having a Tupperware party isn't a bad thing. It's probably a very good thing. With a good hostess, the guests will probably have fun and everyone will spend just a little money. But you do have to obligate your friends and family to come, which is a bit uncomfortable for just about anyone. But hey, it's three months out.

As the party approaches you feel torn as you prepare to send out the invitations. You wonder why you said yes in the first place. You still haven't sent the invitations. It's probably going to be fine, but part of you doesn't want to do the party. Life is busy, and this really wasn't necessary. But you said you'd do it—in front of a lot of your friends—and you're going to have a Tupperware party.

When you were asked it didn't seem like that big of a deal, certainly not an obligation that entailed a lot of work. As the date approaches, though, it does seem as though this is going to be an all-day project.

I was watching TV the other night and an annoying commercial came on for Wickes Furniture.

"Two thousand and thirteen," the young suburban housewife says as she sits on her new couch.

"This week only you have no payments till 2013," the young husband parrots.

"Wickes has no payments and no interest till 2013!"

"Wow, no interest?!" the husband feeds the line back, and so the commercial goes:

Is the commercial effective? You bet. The furniture store isn't selling a recliner or sofa; it is selling free furniture . . . until 2012 at least. The year 2013 is 13 months away, and that means that you can have new furniture for free! You look around your house and you think, "You know, we *do* need new furniture."

And you probably do. This is not only an effective promotion, it's also ethical.

When an event is a long way off it's easy to say yes. In fact, the further an event is in the future, the easier it is to say yes.

In each of the preceding examples you discover how easy it is to say yes today.

In the case of the retirement account, the funny thing is that people consistently have regret, as they approach the new year, that they have agreed to participate in something that is completely in their best interest without exception. Unfortunately, people perceive the 401(k) as an expense when, of course, it is a crucial asset. But it does represent money that the person doesn't get to use today. And that feeling of loss of freedom plays a role in the person's feeling that they now are not as certain about the program. (Remember that when feelings come into play, rational thinking often departs.)

When an event is a long way off it's easy to say yes.

In the case of the Tupperware party, you say yes today, partially because you feel obligated to do so, because you are asked in front of a group. It's not unethical, but there is a feeling of pressure involved. Who wants to look bad in front of the group? In this real–life scenario a person's future isn't on the line. It's a Tupperware party and it is helping someone you know earn a living. It's a good thing to do. Nevertheless, as the day approaches, the desire to participate dramatically declines because it takes away your freedom of choice for the party day, in part because you are obligating your friends and family to do something that will be fun but uncomfortable for some.

The furniture store, of course, is the easiest to say yes to today because getting new furniture and spending no money (for at least one year) is more than tempting; it's downright delicious. You *must* do this. The company puts off the payment so far into the future that most people can't even get there in their minds.

Now, you think this is pretty amazing stuff? Obviously it's easy to get people to say yes to something that is going to happen far in the future. Just wait until you learn how to utilize this powerful information in your business and your practice and your life.

And speaking of time, what happens when you ask for an answer at different points in a conversation (early on, in the middle, at the end)? Does it matter *when* you ask for agreement? Does it matter when you ask for a date?

And when you do ask for something, should the event happen quickly (do you take her out tomorrow night or in two weeks?) or do you put it off?

The Most Common Reason They Say No, and How to Overcome It

The reason that word *no* comes out of their mouths is because it is an instant reaction. They did this or something like this before, and they determined quickly it was a bad decision. About 90 percent of all no's come from this background. Pay close attention.

All of a sudden the water turns cold. You turn around in the shower and quickly turn the temp up, up, up. But it doesn't go up. Someone else is using the hot water in the house! You turn it off instantly. That relaxing 20-minute shower has been destroyed. Six months later you still remember it as someone being incredibly rude and that it was a bad shower. You absolutely don't remember the 20 minutes of relaxation.

The next day you take a five-minute shower. It feels good—warm, relaxing. But you remember that someone will probably start using the hot water, so you get out fairly quickly. It was a nice shower—relaxing, if short. And later that week, you remember that it was a good shower.

All relationships have ups and downs. Most of the time they are in the middle and you really aren't in a relationship but working at work, cleaning the house, whatever. Then you go through a period where you argue, fight, bicker. Ugh. It's horrible! Time for a new relationship. You break the news. Arguments elevate. You knew it! And for the rest of your life you tell people that you can't believe you stuck with it for 25 years. A waste of your life.

In order to understand how to influence, you need to understand how people make decisions, how they remember the past, and how they see the future. This is what has been missing for hundreds of salespeople, making persuasion a numbers game instead of essentially selling to everyone.

As you've seen from the examples, people:

1. Remember peak experiences (especially the really bad experiences).
2. Remember how things end.
3. Do not see the future clearly. They do not know how they will feel when certain events transpire, even if they want them to.

All of this is crucial in communication, persuasion, and obviously your business and relationships.

In fact, this might be some of the most important information you have ever learned. Read on. Have you ever been in a conversation with someone and then that person says, "Why did you say ___?"

"I didn't say that!"

"Yes, you did. I heard you!"

"I did not!"

That night in separate conversations (or journal entries) both of you make the other person out to be an idiot or thoughtless or something else that isn't positive!

Clearly one of you is incorrect, but both of you are equally certain that your memory is correct. The fact is that trying to resolve this is impossible. This is the problem of memory. The brain makes stuff up out of thin air to fill in blank spots. Everyone experiences these moments when they said or heard (or saw!) something that actually wasn't articulated or heard (or seen). You can't convince a brain otherwise, because it was there!

Now, if you can't rely on your memory to know what really happened 30 seconds ago, how can you rely on it for accurately representing what happened in the past? Answer: You can't . . . but only you know this. The other person doesn't. Therefore you have to either move past this point or give them a short course in neuroscience. If you choose the latter, you can start with this:

In one recent research study, people were having a necessary colonoscopy. At regular intervals during the process, they were asked to share their level of discomfort. At the end of the process, for one group the scope was allowed to simply not move for a minute right before it was removed. The other group had the scopes removed a minute earlier (when the colonoscopy was actually finished) and with no additional minute of rest.

Results: The group who had the scope in longer but finished easier remembered the colonoscopy very differently from those who had the shorter-time colonoscopy. The patients who had the extra minute of no scope movement while still inserted, remembered the colonoscopy as "not that bad." The group who had no extra moment of rest remembered it as much worse.

> **The brain makes stuff up out of thin air to fill in blank spots.**

Key Point: When matched with how people actually reported they felt at each interval in the process (not later that night in a journal entry), their later recollections reflected the end of the process and not the entire experience. *People remember how an experience ends and generalize the ending back to the rest of the experience.*

Strategy: At each step, know that the people you are talking with do not operate with video cameras in their minds. They operate on their memories, regardless of whether the memories are accurate. Therefore, you need to clearly show how not acting (even though they recall the action as being painful in the past) will have dire consequences.

Then you must show how both decisions could play out, along with the probabilities of both.

For people who lost money in the stock market, you can understand their interest in staying in safe money-market securities! Unfortunately, the reality is that they are probably not going to make much money if they do that. You simply can't tell them to ignore the past. You must point out that it *could* happen again, though it's more likely that more typical returns and results are in the offing.

The research in persuasion is clear. *You must point out both possible futures for you to be successful.* Otherwise, the person will be destined to go with what they feel, instead of what makes sense. The phobia of losing is tough to get past without at least acknowledging and examining those possible outcomes.

Then finish with a very clear picture of a very likely future. If you paint a too-rosy future, you will both lose. Your clients will feel manipulated. If you paint a likely future realistically, there is an excellent chance that people will respond appropriately.

> **If you paint a likely future realistically, there is an excellent chance that people will respond appropriately.**

Ultimately the stock market crashed, the *Titanic* sank, and the Twin Towers went down. But those are not reasons to avoid the stock market, boating, or tall buildings. In fact, having failed in the first two quarters of the game is all the more reason to try harder in the second half.

That is the message that needs to be made clear to your client, and they will get it if you use that metaphor. Never let a bad result in the past phobically turn your client into a nonclient!

Influential Power of Choice Reduction

The more choices you have, the less appealing each of the choices appears. In fact, it is hard to find any exceptions to this in sales literature, academic research, and even politics.

If you were a presidential reelection big shot, you might be thinking, "Man, they are *all* slamming us this week. This is terrible. We are going to suffer in the polls. We have to fight back."

That would be an error. The correct response is to say and do absolutely nothing. Now, that sure seems counterintuitive. But here is the situation at the nonconscious level: The more choices with which you are presented, the less you like *all* of them.

In fact, when someone is presented with one choice, she is more likely to accept that one choice as opposed to declining. When someone is presented with two choices, the likelihood of the person simply not choosing either of them dramatically increases. When presented with three or more choices, the likelihood of selecting any choice is very small indeed.

When medical doctors were presented with a new drug to treat osteoarthritis, 75 percent of them were likely to prescribe the new medication versus 25 percent referring patients to a specialist. When a second medication was placed among the options, 50 percent of the doctors referred patients to a specialist. They simply chose to not choose. Choices cause anxiety, uncertainty, and, believe it or not, depression. And that really seems counterintuitive, doesn't it?

In Barry Schwartz's *Paradox of Choice*, he points out the very interesting research done combining choice and framing. Observe:

Parents divorce. Custody of the child will be awarded to one parent. You are the judge. Would you choose parent A or parent B?

Parent A	*Parent B*
Average income.	Above-average income.
Average health.	Minor health problems.
Average working hours.	Lots of work-related travel.
Reasonable rapport with child.	Very close relationship with child.
Relatively stable social life.	Extremely active social life.

Which parent did you choose?

Interesting, huh? Not easy, but two-thirds of those surveyed chose to award custody to parent B.

But when a new group of people were surveyed and the question was asked like this: "Which parent would you *deny* custody to?" 55 percent chose to deny custody to parent B. Why? Because there are reasons to deny a parent based on the negative aspects of parent B. Choices plus framing can change the world.

Key: Each additional choice or option takes away from the positive light of all other options.

I just bought a new camcorder. I was pondering between getting a professional camera or a small digital one that would do an excellent job like my old Sony. What to do . . .

Canon's Super Professional Camera	*Sony PC 330 Handheld Compact Unit*
Impossible to pack in carry-on luggage.	Easy to pack in carry-on.
$3,000 with accessories.	$2,000 with accessories.
3 CCD.	1 CCD.
1.5 megapixels for still photos.	3 megapixels for still photos.
Easy to use with tripod.	Difficult to use with tripod.
Perfect video quality.	Excellent video quality.
Best low light.	Mediocre low light.

Now, there is no right choice for me or you. There are simply choices—and, frankly, a lot of them. I travel a lot—too much. That's why I prefer a camera I can carry on. I hate checking luggage.

I also want a great picture. This camera will film programs that will eventually be up for sale at kevinhogan.com. In addition, we use a lot of photographs, and I have a four-megapixel camera that is amazing, so I don't have to have this feature if I choose not to.

I pondered and pondered. It took almost five hours just to narrow the field to these two camcorders. What did I finally choose?

I chose the camera I could carry for a couple of reasons. First, I don't have to bring my other digital for still photography. Portability is very important to me. In fact, with all things being close to equal it turned out to be the single most important variable. Had the camera's video qualities been medium or just good, I would have chosen the Canon. Instead, with excellent video (not perfect!) I opted for the smaller unit. Never will this new camera be in Malaysia when I am in Australia.

Had someone simply shown me one or the other and I had not done an exhaustive Web search and comparison project, I likely would have purchased either of these or anything similar in quality in less than five minutes. Need a camera. Need it now. Let's go.

Choices, while theoretically good to have, leave you wishing you had *another* option (great low light) and constantly wondering, "Would it have made a difference to have the other camera?"

Problems of Choices

What do Miss Hawaiian Tropic, keeping a diary or journal, and *Average Joe* teach us about instantly becoming more influential, earning far more money, and having better relationships? Be prepared to be stunned—and take notes.

During the past two years, I have been reevaluating my once firmly held belief that people should journal their lives and their thoughts, especially in terms of their relationships. Why? In recent research studies it has been revealed that people who write down their feelings and thoughts about their partners are much more likely to fail at predicting the success of the relationship. It turns out that what is easy to put into words is not what helps people predict the success of the relationship. In fact, the opposite is true.

So what? It turns out that people who do not (or are asked not to in research studies) analyze their relationships in writing tend to remain in those relationships and the tendency of those who do analyze their relationships in writing tend to not stay in relationships.

Worse? Upon follow-up, those who wrote about their relationships later regretted leaving their relationships. As you're probably already starting to think how this applies in your life and business (especially when tracking employee information!) the ramifications are enormous.

Key Application Concept: If you are going to have your client or customer evaluate you, your product, or your service, have them do so based on specific, preset criteria.

Keep this in mind. I'm coming back to this crucial discovery and its further applications later. . . . About 10 years ago there was a goofy TV show called *Average Joe* or *Average Joe: Hawaii*. I watched a few of the shows in the first installment. Concept: Reality TV show in which a good-looking girl will get to whittle down 16 average joes (men who are average guys) to one guy. (I don't have any idea what the ultimate prize was.)

At first, this girl is appalled. These guys are not what she signed up for. After the initial shock, she gets familiar with the guys to the point where they are very acceptable to her. More: She actually starts to like some of them and enjoy their company quite a bit. Just as you think there is justice in the world, the former cheerleader is brought a half dozen sleek-bodied guys to compete with the average-joe guys for her attention.

The comparison effect is now recalibrated, and ultimately there is no contest. Sleek-bodied guy easily beats out average joe (sorry, guys). The average-joe guys simply can't visually compete with the sleek-bodied guys.

Three key points:

1. When the setting was all average joes, the girl was very much interested in a number of them. There was no frame of reference outside of the average guys for comparison.
2. When the sleek-bodied guys arrived, all the average guys were sharply contrasted and all suffered by the new comparison.
3. Even among the sleek-bodied guys, many of them suffered by comparison with each other.

Have you ever watched a beauty pageant (Miss Universe, Miss America, Miss Hawaiian Tropic)? Up to 100 absolutely stunning women take the same stage. Then under careful scrutiny, as the women stand side by side, then come into view by themselves, you and I begin to see flaws in each of these women! Enough that viewers will say, "She isn't that good looking" or some similar remark. These are not your average-jane women. These are women who come in at 9.8 on the Richter scale that is hard-wired into all men from birth. But side-by-side you become fooled into thinking that Miss 9.8 is really closer to a 7.0 and barely worthy of being on your TV screen. (This reaction is true of both men and women, and by the way women are the primary audience for these shows.)

We all suffer from comparison when we are stacked up next to many other choices. If there are only a few, you can maintain your projection and perception of status, prestige, beauty. Against the backdrop of many applicants, available future partners, and so forth? You sink fast, and so do all the others!

> *We all suffer from comparison when we are stacked up next to many other choices.*

Imagine that you sell a product. Imagine that it has tons of competitors. Imagine that you have two sheets of paper. All the competitors' products should be compared to each other on the first page. Your product should be the only product on the second page.

Key Application Concept: If you place your idea/product/service in with 20 others, it becomes just another piece of the stew. If you set it off by itself, it shines.

Key Application Concept: You work in a cubicle in the same room/office with 20 other people. You are part of a sea of faces. All begin to look alike after a while. If you are going to differentiate yourself, you literally need to find ways to separate yourself from the crowd if you are going to advance, become valued, and gain importance.

Let's go back to our Miss Hawaiian Tropic pageant for a moment. (Don't I ask a lot?) Miss California steps out and introduces herself. You are a judge. You must start to evaluate her and tell her whether, in your mind, she should make the final eight. You must justify your reasons. Ready for this? Those who must articulate or write down their reasons most regret their choices later.

The way the human brain is wired, you instantly come up with a decision, then begin to come up with (or make up) reasons to justify your decision. Here is an interesting fact: The more people have to create reasons for their decisions the more they become disappointed in their choice later! This is true of all decisions.

Key: When you make a decision, you will regret it more later as you discuss the reasons for making the decision.

Key Application Concept: When you get the decision you want from another person, it is time to shut up and move along. If you ask for all the reasons why they decided the way they did, you might just get a reversal in a few days.

Key Application Concept: Once you have a decision, do not encourage people to think about how good their decision was or even set guideposts in the future for them to evaluate it. Be happy they decided in your favor and gave you their business or trust.

TMC. Too many choices! People are becoming responsible for their choices and it is causing an enormous amount of distress, anguish, regret, anxiety, and depression!

Key Application Point: Take the choices others have to make when working with you. If you want your client/customer to be happy with you, and you want to make the sale and then get repeat business, begin to limit options quickly. Do not sell 100 different colored cards. Sell five. Do not sell 100 different customized computers made to suit their needs (unless you are telling them what they need).

Key Application Point: Find the key one, two, or three values or needs a person has as they relate to you and give them those things! Everything else is noise that will cause the person to be less happy with their decision.

I hear someone say, "Well, then give them a money-back guarantee," "They can always exchange it," "Let them swap it for something else if they aren't happy."

This will strike terror in the hearts of just about everyone, but here is a fact based on recent research.

Scary fact: When people have the opportunity to reverse their decision, return a product, or get a refund on a purchase, they tend to be less satisfied with their decision later! Now, that runs contrary to everything I was ever taught 100 years ago in Selling 101!

The odd fact is that when people are buying something or even getting into an arranged marriage (as happens in other countries and was the norm a few centuries ago in most cultures) the people are happier and the relationships last much longer.

Am I suggesting you take back your money-back guarantee and make it more difficult to return products at Wal-Mart? No. It is time to evaluate how you present this information to your customers.

If your client has made a decision to buy a competitor in the past six months and that experience failed, he probably regrets it. However, the experiences that happened years ago that cause the most regret are those things that weren't done.

This is important: You are attempting to influence someone and they made a mistake recently and they are still smarting from it. And they regret it. If what you are proposing is similar to what they regret doing, you need to be prepared for a no: "I did this with them and I really regret it. Been there, done it, not going to do that again." You will need to prepare to frame your proposition differently.

However, if your client has not done something in the more distant past that they wish they had done, this is powerful leverage for them to take action now.

Key Point: The problem is that if people pass up one opportunity in the past they tend to pass up similar opportunities for the rest of their lives!

But there is more about regret that you have to consider. When an Olympian gets a silver medal, the athlete is happy on the stand and probably excited. As time marches on, however, silver medalists realize they were just ticks away from the gold. This is something that breeds depression, disappointment, and frustration forever. If you try to console the person by saying, "My, you were second, good going!" you will not build rapport. These emotional hot buttons are something you will need to work around.

On the other hand, the same Olympian winning the bronze medal is happy. Bronze medalists have done well. They didn't just miss the big medal—there was yet another person between them and the gold. They may have been close. They may have been ticks away, but these athletes are happy with their result as time goes by. They are proud and it sticks. There is no significant regret.

Therefore, when you are communicating with someone about their accomplishments in rapport-building communication be certain that you know whether they are likely to be feeling positive or negative about the subjects of conversation!

What's the right thing to do when you discover regrets?

Here's a quick peek at how to handle this kind of regret so you can get beyond the regret and bring the client into more receptive feelings where they will be more likely to comply with your request. Let's imagine a new auto sales decision.

"The last new car I bought turned out to be okay but it really wasn't my idea but my wife's to buy it."

"You know, at least it was new. It didn't cost you anything to maintain, and it didn't break down. Shoot, she could have made a better choice, but you didn't lose anything. Today we'll get you exactly what you need."

I play blackjack when I visit Las Vegas. I fancy myself a pretty good player. I play quickly and make decisions based on statistical models. There isn't much left to intuition or hunches.

If there are others at the table and someone makes a decision that turns out to be a mistake (at a blackjack table people think that anything that didn't make them money was a mistake—not true), they typically want to see what the next card left concealed is so they could know if making a different decision would have been the right thing to do.

When they see that having made a different decision would have resulted in the same outcome (losing their money) they accept their fate and are annoyed. When they see the concealed card and realize that had they made a different decision they would have *won* money, they feel not only annoyed but disgusted and frankly show symptoms of depression!

In either case, the outcome is the same, but the degree of regret is dramatically different.

I constantly remind my seat partners (if they made the right decision) that they did indeed make the right decision and that shows they know what they are doing. This helps build rapport and keeps things calm, because no one wants to look stupid or feel humiliated when it comes to putting money at risk and losing.

Do the same thing when dealing with your clients! Never let someone feel stupid about past mistakes. Make sure they know that any intelligent person would have done the same thing if they were presented with a similar situation. If you show even a nonconscious body language cue that the person *did* make a foolish mistake or was humiliated in any way, the answer to your request will be no.

Imagine that your neighbor buys a new lawn mower. He had his old one for a decade! Yours is a junker and you should have known better than to buy it, but what do you know about lawn mowers? Nothing. Zip. You can't even spell the words.

"Hey, Mark, what kind of mower did you buy when you tossed yours the other day?"

"Toro XR57Q."

You know what you are going to buy?

A Toro XR57Q.

> ***Never let someone feel stupid about past mistakes.***

If you do not buy a Toro XR57Q and your new lawn mower breaks down, needs repairs, or even conks out after one summer, you are going to look like an idiot! You will massively regret it and that is precisely where your mind goes. Therefore, this is easy. Toro XR57Q.

There can be no regrets if you buy the XR57Q. Sold.

Impact of Emotions

One aspect of influence we've visited several times in the book is the impact of emotions on the results of persuasive communication attempts.

Going back to your medical doctor: If your doctor is in a good mood and feeling positive (gifted with a box of candy in the research project) he makes diagnoses faster and more accurately!

Positive emotions cause us to feel more comfortable in evaluating options and coming up with a correct decision! Is this true only for doctors?

No.

Schwartz reports that when students are offered six essay topics versus 30 essay topics, those students presented with only six topics actually write better essays than those who had a much broader choice. Reduced choice not only makes it easier to choose; it also makes our choices better and more effective!

> *Positive emotions cause us to feel more comfortable in evaluating options and coming up with a correct decision!*

Persuading the Represented Mind: Representation and Exaggeration?

Like everyone else on the planet, you represent the real world in a way that really is a mental interpretation or representation of reality.

Have you ever had this conversation:

"I can't believe you just said that!"

"I didn't say that. I said _____."

"No, you didn't. I heard you say _____."

"I did no such thing. You are dreaming. I clearly said _____."

And the reality–checking pair will never find the answer—because there really is no answer and the two people will permanently represent the event differently. This causes each person to paint a picture of the other person and who they are instead of taking a videotape and storing it in their mind.

What our senses pick up vary from person to person. Other people see slightly different colors than you do. They hear different sounds than you do. They smell different smells than you do . . . or not at all. If you go to a foreign country, people say words that you cannot say because you cannot hear all the sounds in the word. You literally have to be trained to hear them!

All of this is just the tip of the representation iceberg. It does go much further. The implications for influence? Dramatic.

For example, seeing a child starve is a powerful image. Seeing 500 starve logically should give you a much more powerful image—but it doesn't. The difference in empathy or grief is marginal.

Not only do you literally see, hear, feel, taste, and smell a different world than the person next to you, you also literally misrepresent the importance of almost everything in the world. (And so do I!)

People misrepresent the scope, the importance, and the significance of almost every experience in life. All of this causes persuasion to be much more than a game of logic that has an obvious solution. Listen carefully:

There can be no obvious solution because the other person literally sees a different world than you do.

When these differences come up in everyday conversation, one person will attempt to represent the picture or problem to someone using a technique called exaggeration. Sometimes exaggeration helps someone get the leverage needed to create change. Usually it does not.

People often believe that, if you exaggerate your case, you can dramatically improve your sales presentation or your proposal. It often seems that exaggeration in written copy ("251 seats have already been sold") will really make a big difference in your success.

But is this the case? And how do we know?

There is an interesting phenomenon in human behavior that you can call scope neglect.

In a nutshell, scope neglect could be described like this: I'm a millionaire. You tell me that if I give you $100 I will really be helping you out. I decide whether to give you the $100. However much value I feel you will get in your $100 is just about the same as how I will feel about giving you $1,000. Neither amount causes any money pain, but they are seen as very similar numbers.

Here's another example: A fund-raiser is taking place in an actual research study. Some people are told that their donation will immediately help save the lives of 2,000 birds. Another group is told their donation will help save 20,000 birds. A final group is told their donation will save 200,000 birds.

> *Sometimes exaggeration helps someone get the leverage needed to create change. Usually it does not.*

It would seem that the last group should give far more money to the charity than the first group.

But what happened? Group one averaged donations of $80 per person. Group two averaged $78 per person. Group three averaged $88 per person.

I was surprised. I really was! I thought that there would at least be a significant difference between saving 200,000 birds' lives versus 2,000. But there was no significant difference. Increasing the numbers just didn't matter.

What about something other than birds? Residents in four western states were asked to make donations to save either a single wilderness area or 57 wilderness areas. Theoretically the group asked to donate to save 57 areas should give a lot more money (57 times as much?) than those asked to save one area. This wasn't the case. In fact, the group asked to donate to save a total of 57 wilderness areas gave only 28 percent more money than those asked to help save one wilderness area.

Lesson: People neglect the scope of a problem because they develop a representation of it. They don't take the time to put every piece of information up on the board and analyze them all, detail by detail. They get a picture or representation in their mind, then believe that representation is reality. Of course it isn't. The scope of the situation is neglected and usually dramatically so.

Because of this thinking process, there are many ramifications for those who influence others. Exaggerating benefits or possible results from your program is unnecessary and an enormous risk when contrasted with relating facts. It doesn't pay off, and if someone were to find out you were exaggerating, it could destroy your business. Never exaggerate.

And there is more.

In an experiment related to scope neglect (this example is called extension) people were asked to estimate how many murders took place in Detroit the previous year. Another group was asked how many murders took place in Michigan that year. The first group offered a median response of 200 people murdered in Detroit. The second group offered a median response of 100 people murdered in Michigan.

I don't have to tell you that Detroit is just one city in Michigan. One city. But Detroit has a reputation of being dangerous and violent. Michigan has a reputation of being a cold state in the Midwest.

People thought there were twice as many murders in Detroit as in Michigan—and Detroit is only a part of Michigan!

But think about how people think. People don't think in any logical fashion. They think in terms of biases.

What this means is that the painted picture is far more important than any logic when it comes to whether the person will decide on one thing when compared to another. People base their decisions on the pictures in their minds and not on the real-life experiences in the real world. Therefore, you need to be able to find out what those pictures are so you can communicate clearly with your counterpart.

Talking about what is or is not will not make you more persuasive. Finding out what representations your client has will, and this is where you can make dramatic steps forward in the process of persuasion.

Flagging in the Persuasion Process

Flagging is one of the most powerful cutting-edge techniques of persuasion. I've saved it for last in order to leave you on a wow! note. Combining the latest in memory research, neuroscience, real-life selling, and therapeutic skills, you begin to discover some fascinating phenomena. Flagging is one specific technique that you can use to dramatically increase compliance in almost all aspects of influence.

Up until now, you have learned that people remember their (good or bad) peak experiences and how experiences ended, then generalize those two things to an entire lifetime of experience. This is important when attempting to influence people to repurchase your service or product when they might have had a bad experience. Another useful way to prepare for people who have possibly misremembered past experiences with you or a competitor is to prepare your presentation to integrate with that new belief as it is their new reality, if you will.

You learned that people make current decisions (usually in the form of instant reactions) based on past experiences.

You know that if someone has said no to a profitable opportunity in the past, it is very unlikely they will say yes when asked again. This seems counterintuitive; it should be that people will always accept a proposal that obviously benefits them. But this is not how the brain functions. If the brain came to a no conclusion last time, then that will be the instant reaction to a similar proposal this time.

Much like driving to your office, the brain doesn't like to make decisions more than once. Once it has decided, it will typically stick with that. This is not rational per se; it is simply the way you and I were wired to make life easier in the decision-making process!

You know that how people remember their past is crucial to how you must communicate with them today for optimum influence potential. Here is the latest in persuasion research about how people remember the past and its impact on whether they will say yes to you—and then what specifically to do about it.

If you were to ask people what their opinion was last year (or even last week or yesterday) about a political issue, a personal issue, or pretty much anything, there is a surprisingly good chance they will have remembered completely incorrectly.

Studies have been done that show that people remember a movie as being particularly good when leaving the theater, only to change their mind the next day after reading a review in the newspaper that had a contrary point of view.

What past research hasn't shown was specifically who was remembering more correctly and who was remembering more incorrectly. This is a crucial piece of the persuasion puzzle that has been missing—until the twenty-first century. Now it is yours.

Think back to the year 2000. Al Gore and George Bush were in a tight election race. In one experiment participants were asked to predict the percentage of the popular vote each candidate would have. You probably remember that Gore was about five percentage points ahead going into the final days of the campaign. The polls were roughly matched by the participants of this experiment who said (on average) that Gore would win by 4.7 percent over Bush.

After the election, we knew only one fact, and that was that Gore won the popular vote by about 0.3 percent. (We didn't know who would actually be the president, because of chads in Florida!)

When the participants were asked after the election but before the winner was determined in Florida, they remembered saying that Gore would win by (on average) 0.6 percent! What happened to those 4.1 percentage points?

What happened was that people watched the news and discovered that Gore won by 0.3 percent and the actual fact superseded what prediction they made the prior month—and by a great deal.

Let's pause here and quickly analyze this first step: People look in retrospect at what actually did happen and not at what they thought would happen when evaluating how they thought at the time. That's mighty important in persuasion all by itself, but there is more that is going to blow you away!

Key Point: When influencing others, remember that, if you ask them how or what they decided in the past, you will not likely receive accurate information.

Does anyone remember the past correctly? The answer is no, of course. Memory changes with every view of that memory. Experts or people who are directly involved in a situation remember their predictions of outcomes very differently from those who have little investment or interest in the outcomes.

In the Gore/Bush election, those people who admitted to not having political expertise remembered their predictions of the popular vote in a very interesting way (remembering after the fact that Gore would win by 7.5 percent of the vote versus the 4.7 percent they predicted prior to the election, which runs completely counter to the information they had after the election was over). Yes, they remembered that their original predictions were much less accurate than they actually were!

However, those people who felt they had expertise predicted Gore would win by 5 percent but remembered predicting a real horse race with only a projected 0.7 percent difference. Experts or people who have involvement remember things in a different way. In this study experts thought they were almost perfectly accurate in their predictions. They were far from it!

I think one way to utilize the fact that we all have such dismal memories is to help someone feel comfortable with their expertise. A couple of examples:

"You probably figured the Gore/Bush election would be incredibly close, but who would have ever thought it would have been a decision made in court by one vote!"

This kind of approach reduces the insult factor that can happen when you have the kind of knowledge you do about influence, memory, and decision making.

Another way to utilize people's lack of accurate recall is to place a flag in their memory to begin communication with.

"Remember when Gore and Bush debated and Al Gore seemed so arrogant to the public that his numbers started dropping at the very end? Well, that was one of the reasons I thought Bush had a chance."

The flag is Gore's arrogance. The point of placing a flag in someone's memory is that, once it is there, it becomes part of their permanent memory and gives you a point from which to establish a key piece of the persuasion process. Here's a real-life example:

"Remember when you bought this house? Did you want something that would be big enough for your family to live in comfortably?"

> *The point of placing a flag in someone's memory is that, once it is there, it becomes part of their permanent memory and gives you a point from which to establish a key piece of the persuasion process.*

Now, the real estate agent has no clue if this is true, but by flagging the memory of the decision to buy the house you add this specific recollection into their memory as if it had always been there.

If you were to ask, "What caused you to buy this house?" people will generate numerous possibilities internally before giving you a reason. That reason could be helpful in the persuasion process, but one thing is certain: The reason that they state probably had little to do with their decision in the first place!

Therefore, they will be more likely to doubt the generation of their own recollection, and even though you now have a piece of information that is useful, it also has drawbacks.

What, for example? Specifically the person may have generated a number of internal responses of their reason before saying what it was. This causes question marks to pop up in the mind and makes a further conversation more interesting but less likely to persuade.

If you flag a memory you will get one of two responses. Either the people will accept the flag (most typical) and think in terms of *comfortable*, in this case, or they will rapidly tell you just why they did buy the house.

"No, it wasn't space or comfort at all. I needed a home that was near the school."

At this point you have a client with dramatic recall (still as unlikely to be accurate). This allows you to utilize their flag in the persuasion process that has begun.

Once people have a flag anchored in place, it primes mental processes to think in terms of the flag. Yes, you can bet that the nearness to school factor will be a determining factor at this point.

Key Point: You can flag another person's memory through their own generation of the flag or by planting the flag yourself. The flag should always be something that was considered by the other person at some time. If the flag is self-generated by the other person, they are more likely to internally argue or struggle with the flag because, although they originally came up with the flag, they generated other options that they considered and they might recall these other points and begin to oscillate internally.

Imagine I were to say, "Pick a number. I'm thinking of 61,000."

What is your number?

Now, imagine that I say to someone else," Pick a number. I'm thinking of 14."

The responses from the two individuals are going to be dramatically different. Very few people will pick a number higher than 100 in the latter case. In the former case where I said I was thinking of 61,000, people will pick numbers in the thousands, tens of thousands, and even hundreds of thousands.

In both cases I primed the response by stating an anchor or flag—in the first case a big number and in the second a small number.

The faster I ask for a response, the closer to the anchor the response will be. These numbers mean nothing but have direct impact on suggestions given to the person.

Let's move this interesting phenomenon into the persuasion and marketing arena.

Research participants were shown apartments to rent. They were given rental fees for the apartments that varied from very high to very low. When the individuals were given high numbers, the individuals focused on the positive aspects of the apartment. When they were given low numbers they were much more likely to focus on the negative aspects.

In further research, participants who are asked to accept one proposal or another are more likely to focus on the positive aspects of the proposal. Participants asked to reject one of two options are likely to focus on negative aspects of the two.

And there is more, but it all comes down to one key concept: Anchoring is priming and it is an associative error. Whatever you mention to prime their thinking is going to cause error in the thinking toward the anchor—even when you tell someone that this is what you are doing! What does this mean in the real world?

Real estate agents are supposed to be experts in pricing real estate. But take the same property and put a different list price on it by the owner and you get valuations that are biased toward the valuation the owner put on the house!

In courtrooms, judges who are asked for extremely long sentences tend to have their thinking biased toward the long sentence. The same is true for requests for short sentences.

Judges are also biased by anchors in compensation cases. Whether $100 or large sums, judges are more likely to be biased by the number that is requested.

Even more interesting, older adults who should know what percentage of their money is being saved and spent will be biased toward anchors and not what they know to be correct.

"People estimate that Gandhi lived to be roughly 67 years old if they first decided whether he died before the age of 140, but only 50 years old if they first decided whether he died before or after the age of 9" (Strack and Mussweiler 1997).

Why? Because people evaluate hypotheses by trying to confirm them and not by intentionally looking for ways to refute them. The mind pointed in a direction is unlikely to go back the other way without much further thought and consideration.

Here is what is even more interesting. When people come up with their own anchors, they are still biased toward their anchor instead of logically answering the question!

The mind pointed in a direction is unlikely to go back the other way without much further thought and consideration.

Applications

Clearly, if you are selling a service for $1,000 and want to sell the most of them possible, then you probably should set a high anchor. "What you will gain from this experience is easily worth $9,000. I could ask for half of that fee but I'm not going to. Instead I'm going to ask only $1,000 for this experience."

At first glance you might think that the anchor is set too high. As indicated earlier, though, people will set their acceptable price much higher when there is a high anchor. This is true even when the anchor is absurdly high. (Remember the Gandhi at 140 example?) You know that the anchor is set high yet it influences you anyway. This is the power of the anchor or flagging. It's all about how the brain processes information, and that is one of the key pieces we have been missing.

Does this mean that you should flag a high anchor for every promotion you do?

No.

Setting high anchors will get you sales, but don't be surprised if you lose a disproportionately high percentage of these clients because many will buy and then be offered the service later at a lower price by someone else.

If your service is a one-time-only type of service, you might want to try setting a high anchor, then contrast that price with a significantly lower price, compelling the person to buy.

12 | How Their Brain Buys ... You!

When I travel to Warsaw, I ask my sponsor to get me a room at the Sheraton Hotel there. They treat me like a king. I don't think about it anymore, I just instantly know that I want to stay there (stimulus/response reinforced over time). I have the same experience at the W Hotel in Seattle and The Venetian in Las Vegas. There is zero time spent on decision making. It's all done unconsciously, and because these are based on repeatedly positive experiences, they are typically good decisions. Now, if you were to ask me if I seriously compare hotel travel plans to increase my enjoyment factor or get a better price or a better room somewhere else I'd probably say yes, and I'd probably be wrong!

Nine out of 10 consumers leaving the checkout line at a grocery store remember handling the brand they bought and the competing brand to compare it with the one they bought. Hidden cameras reveal that most individuals' memories were completely wrong. In fact, less than 1 in 10 actually handled competing brands. People regularly remember behaviors and actions that don't happen in real life, and this is critical to the influence process, sales, and marketing.

Pay attention: People anticipate purchasing their brand prior to arriving at the store and then they do indeed purchase it. (Just like I am staying at The Venetian in Las Vegas.) They believe they spend time weighing their decisions in the stores, but this isn't true. Where brands are involved, consumers spend only five seconds on average in that category of the store. Five seconds. There is no thought, no decision making. The conscious mind does not engage. Consumers remember comparing products but they don't. They go to the category and purchase their brand choice almost instantly. They made their decision at home at an unconscious level. They never gave it a conscious thought.

The consumer had a good experience in the past with product X. Perhaps it was advertised, and the advertising clicked in the consumer's mind. Either way, the purchase happened with little or no attention (conscious thought). At kevinhogan.com we have a simple rule. Put out programs that no one can match in quality and application. In other words, almost everything is new—cutting-edge new. Ahead of the market. Way ahead. And we have loyal customers who know they will win with every program. It's part of branding. More about that later.

Key: People make many buying decisions in large part because of trust.

It's well known in marketing that individuals will buy the generic painkiller for themselves but only Children's Tylenol for their kids, even though the two products are identical. People trust the brand when the chips are down.

Question: Are you branded for trust? Do people look to you/your company and immediately trust it over all the competing generics?

Case in Point: Each month I put out two or three new CD programs. I love doing it! Each program contains truly cutting-edge material that individuals can immediately use, and there is never a question about whether it will be good, be delivered quickly, and be just as magical (if not more so) as the promotion was for the program. Trust is branded into the name. If it isn't the best, I won't make the program.

My Goal for You: I want you to start branding trust into you/your company name so you become the instant obvious solution to some group's problems. Trust breeds loyalty. It's very hard to switch from someone or something you completely trust. In fact, it's almost impossible to change true loyalty, because the stress of change would be enormous.

There is a lot more to making an indelible positive impression in every human being you meet. Trust is a great starting point. Loyalty is a perfect goal; but what about influence?

Just because you are worthy of trust and loyalty does not mean that you have the ability to initially influence someone; nor does it mean you will be able to influence people to buy *you*. You must have something, some set of solutions that meet needs and wants of other people. And you must be able to influence people to take a chance on you.

Why Most People Fail at Being Persuasive: Why Focus Groups Don't Work

The focus group is nearly the biggest waste of money a company can make. They don't work. They predict nothing. "But Kevin, the focus group said they would buy my product or use my services." For some reason some companies (and small businesses) still use focus groups. Why? (There is an alternative: if you need to know, contact me.)

All the research shows that focus groups don't work. In fact, almost all products that focus group research suggests to launch eventually fail.

> *You must have something, some set of solutions that meet needs and wants of other people.*

Why? Because very little of people's behavior is driven by their conscious minds. Most people cannot explain why they do what they do or predict what they will buy (or do) in the future. The unconscious mind (also known as implicit thought or implicit memory) is not accessible by verbal means. Words can only give an approximation of what the unconscious does, and to analyze why a person does something or what they might do is only a guess on the conscious mind's part.

If people knew what their behavior would be in the future, then focus groups would produce product after product of winners. But they don't and they never will. They are inherently and seriously flawed. "If we put this product on the market, would you buy it?" The answer is failure.

Why do most people fail to influence others? Because they attempt to communicate with the sole intention of having the other person make a logical decision. If they can "just talk some sense into him," they will get him to see things their way.

Of course, people don't decide on the answer to most problems in a logical fashion. Their reactive portion of their brain, the oldest and emotionally driven part of the brain, decides. Then the conscious mind, mostly composed of the cortex, justifies the behavior/emotional decision to make that decision make sense.

Have you ever noticed that sometimes you do something and then someone asks you why you did it? You make something up and then feel guilty because you aren't sure if you are telling the truth. It's completely normal and to be expected because people typically don't think about what they are going to do. They simply do it and then communicate a reason that best fits the circumstances.

Have you ever seen a news story where someone performed a certain behavior, then later realized how foolish it was? They couldn't believe what they had done. Had President Clinton been discreet, his affair never would have been made public and his family would not have been hurt. His mistake (beyond the moral choice of his affair) was to have his meetings with the intern in the White House. There are no secrets in the White House. No one knows that better than a president. Cameras, audio, surveillance, Secret Service everywhere! And this is the place a president selects for an affair? But because of the Inner Dummy, as one author likes to call it, the nation was scandalized for an entire year.

What Causes This Problem?

People live lives in which patterns of experience are repeated over and over. (We go to the same job, drive the same highways, do the same things, every day.) The unconscious mind learns all of this and executes the body's behavior all day long. Rarely does the conscious mind come into play in decision making. It is the client's unconscious mind that is saying yes and no.

Your goal as a professional is to ingratiate the conscious mind of your client/customer and focus most of your attention on the unconscious mind.

What on earth does this mean? It means that you need to persuade the unconscious mind. The conscious mind is only the justifier of unconscious reactions. The unconscious reacts and the conscious tries to explain why you did what you did! And because of this, you want to have a true understanding of the nature of the mind and discharge what you were taught in the past as antiquated and dated. Then realize that people are influenced or buy mostly on their gut reaction, their instincts. These largely flawed responses and reactions to the environment are the triggers to saying yes and buying.

Question: What does your client use you or your product for? What would your client use your service for?

First Answer: This question can only be answered after you get past this fact: Whether you sell yourself, a product, or a service, people are buying and saying yes, to *you*. They are buying you and because of you, if they trust you. If they don't, nothing has a chance to happen. Trust begins and is engendered when reliability is established. Are you always there? Do you respond quickly? Are you helpful? Do you respond to needs beyond making the sale? Do you produce results? Is every client/customer you have as precious to you as a family member? Is this felt by the client?

> *Your goal as a professional is to ingratiate the conscious mind of your client/customer and focus most of your attention on the unconscious mind.*

Second Answer: Secondarily (sometimes primarily), people are buying an experience. Diet Coke refreshes. The trip to the beach will relax the person. The trip to Las Vegas will stimulate and excite the person. The new car will make the person feel good, comfortable, hot, safe, secure, admired, or any of a host of other feelings that are associated with vehicles. A woman buys lingerie from Victoria's Secret to feel sexy. She buys Dannon yogurt because it is wholesome. People want to have experiences. They want to have the feelings that these experiences foster.

My Goal for You: Determine what experience you want to give your clients and customers. Determine what experiences your product or service gives to your customer. The two things could be completely different. If you sell medical supplies, you'd probably like your experience with your customer to be different than their experience with the medical supplies. You should have yourself experientially defined and you should have your product experientially defined. This is part of branding yourself and working with your products at a brand level.

You Can't Get to Yes If You Can't Get Their Attention

Branding is different for you (an individual) versus enormous monster companies such as McDonald's, Burger King, Subway, or any other large franchise. When the big franchises put a big storefront out there, it's different. They can do an enormous amount of evaluation to determine exactly what the customer wants. They can find out exactly what the consumer needs. The idea is to keep adapting and adjusting as people evolve and grow.

Advertising makes sense for those franchisees that already depend on their big brand. Do you need a web site? Yes, your web site address is just as important as your actual location. A web site is so important in today's market. Study kevinhogan.com and kevinhogan.net to determine how we have built the brand "Kevin Hogan." And how are the two web sites different? One is designed to sell influence and body language and the real Kevin Hogan to the public in general (www.kevinhogan.com). The other is designed to sell our services to corporate America (www.kevinhogan.net).

How do you really convince someone that you are the answer to their problems, especially when you are at point zero? What is point zero? It's when you've just started a product line or service. You are brand-new in an industry.

What is it about you that will encourage someone to listen to you in the first place? If you can't get someone's attention, you have no opportunity to influence that person in any way. And why should someone pick you or buy you or buy from you when they have been with someone else for years? This is a critical question.

There must be a process, and there is:

- You must get their attention.
- You must hold their attention.
- You must have a bold promise.
- You must detach any previous commitment.

- You must overdeliver on the promise.
- They need to be excited to tell lots and lots of people whose attention you will eventually want (create a mind virus).

Lots of people have skills in their field and lots of people can get people's attention. The big challenge is to ultimately have what it takes to be skilled and to get the attention of those you want to connect with. It isn't going to be easy, is it? But you know what? You can do it. You can become the answer. You can be seen as the obvious go-to guy (gal). Can you guess what happens when you hit critical mass and everyone knows you are the go-to guy?

> *If you can't get someone's attention, you have no opportunity to influence that person in any way.*

Whether you are trying to win the girl, sell real estate, or heal the world, there must be a very specific brand image that you must have and that you must be able to live up to.

"Wait a minute! You said win the girl? Sell real estate? Heal the world? I'm not a company or cup of soup; I'm a person!"

And that is why you need to be a powerful brand, easily distinguished from and a far superior option to those you compete with. You eventually want to be seen as the obvious choice. If you want to be influential, you want to be the credible, obvious, excellent choice. Period.

Wouldn't it make life so much easier in every respect if you were known as the _____? (You fill in the blank.)

(It would!)

Are you a salesperson? A manager? A therapist? An entrepreneur? (If you are one you are really all of them when you think about it, and I'm not kidding!)

There is an enormous amount of competition out there and yet the arena is even bigger. Not only do you need to be able to promote yourself, but you also must have the character and skills to be among the best in your field.

What makes a brand is far more than promotion and marketing. It is the repeated behaviors of individuals over a long period of time. It is the ingredients in the product. It's the taste (McDonald's french fries). It's the feel. It's the look. It's the sound. If the product is you, it is your character, attitudes, beliefs, and who you are as a person.

> *What makes a brand is far more than promotion and marketing.*

Still don't get it? Try this: What is it that makes you special and different from the rest? It is your ability to self-promote effectively, efficiently, and at a very small expense.

- How do you brand yourself?
- How do you get people to see "brand you"?
- How do you get people to switch to you as a brand?
- How do you develop a long-term relationship with your new client/customer?

I like to think of salespeople, entrepreneurs, and therapists all as real estate agents. The reason is that the real estate agent can't sell for long by accident. That means that the agent can't earn money without making contacts and using effort. That is true for all salespeople. It is true for all successful entrepreneurs and it is true for all successful therapists. In addition, the real estate agent must keep a crystal-clear middle and long-term perspective at all times. The agent realizes that all effort done today will not pay off for 3 to 12 months. Then it is up to the agent to constantly keep up with every contact and his or her home needs.

The real estate agent is a metaphor for almost all businesses. Breaking into real estate, just like starting a therapy practice or your own business or any sales position, puts you at position zero. You are starting with no contacts when everyone else seems to be—and some cases is—selling the same thing you are. Point zero can also mean that you have been in the profession for 20 years but haven't been active.

Answer this: Why go with the new guy on the block when there is a realtor who has sold 150 houses this year and you are looking at his full-page ad in the yellow pages?

That is a critical question not only for the agent but for every person who has a service/product and is at point zero or close to it on the map.

The first answer is that, by being at point zero, you have time. You aren't seeing many clients/customers, so you have time to completely and fully help anyone and everyone who comes your way. Not only do you have time to help but you have time to build a true relationship with each client/customer. You have time to do everything you possibly can for each person you work with while you are at or near point zero. That is a huge benefit.

Being new in a field (or near point zero) also means that you will work harder for your client than the guy who had 150 clients last year. You'll probably let your buyer see twice as many houses or give your client an extra half hour per visit when you are new. You are selling service when you are new. You are selling *yourself*.

- You care. (You wouldn't have chosen the profession/business if you didn't!)
- You work hard for your clients.
- You find out answers that others won't/don't have time to.
- You have time to differentiate yourself from everyone else in your field, and whatever your field is, there are a lot of them out there!
- You have time to create a game plan for life and business.

Capturing attention is simple, but it isn't easy. That means that process is very doable, but it takes effort. Thousands and thousands of commercial messages compete for your pocketbook. There seems to be more TV stations available now than there are stars in the sky. These stations all have thousands of commercials. Then there are radio stations, magazines, newspapers, and—well, there is a lot of competition for attention.

In a certain sort of backward way, the lack of money to compete with those with huge advertising budgets can be advantageous. Now, don't think I have lost my mind. Ever hear of *Chicken Soup for the Soul*? No one made that book a multimillion-dollar seller except the two authors. Every day authors

Jack Canfield and Mark Victor Hansen did radio shows, book signings, presentations, and classes; they appeared on television. They put the world on hold, and the result of branding themselves well is publishing history. They started with very little money but had a strong concept of what they wanted to do. They spent no money on advertising their first book. They put in time and differentiated themselves from every other feel-good book title out there. It worked.

It doesn't take money to build success. It does take tenacity.

It doesn't take money to build success. It does take tenacity.

In fact, most people who have money fall into traps that eventually suck their money away like a Hoover. Those who actually earn their money by offering a great product/service/self tend to treat their reward with respect and tend to achieve long-term success. Money can actually be an impediment to successfully differentiating yourself. People often believe they can buy differentiation. They can't. It takes character and qualities. It takes true differences. It takes true superiority in some way or ways. (Then money can be a big help!)

The best way to get attention is to model Canfield and Hansen. Whether you are a tax accountant, a therapist, or a salesperson, you need to be out there all the time. That might mean something slightly different from field to field and profession to profession, but you need to be in front of your potential client as much as possible.

That is the beginning of accessing the attention you need.

That is the first step: Then you have to keep their attention and make a big promise.

The Attention Model

Produce or represent a product that meets the needs of a *niche market*. There should be a reason that you are different from everyone else. Differentiate yourself; otherwise you are the same as every other salesperson out there. If you sell real estate, specialize in exceptional homes or lakeshore property.

Make your niche specialized so that you can be the go-to person for your market.

Begin to brand yourself—get your face out there. Teach and speak at book signings, community (adult) education facilities, technical colleges, and so on. The process of building the brand snowballs. The more people you are in front of, the more opportunities you have to network and meet people's needs, and the more people want you to provide a service for them.

Make your niche specialized so that you can be the go-to person for your market.

Public relations means free advertising. Don't pay for advertising. There are so many ways out there to get your name before the public for free—or even get paid to do it. Radio stations are always looking for guests. Continuing education centers are always looking for experts to teach on niche topics. Talk before clubs like the Kiwanis, the Optimists, the Eagles. Don't promote yourself, but offer an informational flyer for follow-up with interested parties. Offer real, important information to help people, along with your contact information so it's easy to find you.

Most people's brands fail. They focus on the marketing and promotion, but they fail on the critical factor. You must distinguish yourself from the rest of the crowd. Remember that you are selling *yourself* as the brand.

You are the best. Be seen that way!

13 | "I Will Do the Work for You"

Magic Words That Unlock Minds

"You are beautiful."

"You are the best thing that ever happened to me."

"Just relax, I'll take care of everything."

"I will do the work for you."

Some things we not only love to hear, but the combinations of those words create incredible feelings inside of us all.

Let's set studies and research aside and for the rest of this book let's look at the power of story, empathy, states of mind, and bringing influence into the rest of your life.

Some of the stories in the remainder of the book will excite you. Some will outrage you. Some will make you cry. You will remember them all. They are all woven with Retrieval Cues so they will be recalled when you need them. It's not required that you agree or disagree with the content of the stories, only that you learn how stories can weave into information to generate feeling and emotion that moves people.

One tool I've adopted from the field of hypnosis is the use of . . . those three little dots.

When I want you to drink something in and then raise your antennae for more you will see these . . . .

And you will find that they are uncomfortable until you become familiar with them. Allow that fact to be okay and you will be able to use this very same tool of influence yourself.

Who wouldn't be able to breathe easily when hearing, "I'll do the work for you"?

(At least if you *knew* "it" would get done correctly, efficiently, and quickly.)

Human nature is not as complicated as many would have you believe.

Key Point: Human nature is about right now, in this moment, the next 10 seconds.

- You don't want to experience fear.
- You don't want to exert effort.
- You want to be content.
- You want revenge against the people you feel harmed you or those you love.
- You want to have sex.
- You want to have food, preferably good food.
- You want freedom, independence; while being connected.
- You want to be comfortable.
- You want your children to be safe, secure, and, preferably, happy.

You don't want to do anything in return for these things . . . or at least as little as possible.

Human nature. . .

We want someone to do the work for us.

Of course.

"I will give you National Health Care. I will make your borders secure. I will give you the best education in the world. I will bail out your company and even you . . . or . . . you can vote for the evil guy who wants you to be self-reliant and responsible."

Our Natural Way Is to Experience Hopeful Outsourcing

We will hope that someone out there with the resources will do the work for you and me.

Now the fact is that there are all kinds of problems that don't let you have what you want . . . and you really do want IT whatever it is, now.

- There could be an enemy at the gate. Perhaps many enemies.
- The children (employees) could be crying.
- There might be no one around to have sex with.
- There might be no food convenient.
- There might be someone or something limiting your freedom and independence.
- Those you are familiar with being connected to may not be available.
- The rock or chair on which you sit might be uncomfortable.
- You may not be certain about the whereabouts of your children.

Can't get sex at the office? Is everyone complaining about something? Here are the magic words that would make YOU feel better . . . and buy now.

Magic Words in Business and Personal Relationships

Business and relationships revolve around fixing the problems just noted and bringing your life as close as possible to the things you want. So does politics. Of course, so does pretty much everything.

In fact, the concept of business vs. personal doesn't exist in the human animal, or even the human mind. *Business* is an arbitrary construct and the creation of culture. The human brain has no such understanding of these concepts. It's *all* personal to the brain and there is *no* business.

The reason business often feels so artificial and phony, is because, well it is artificial. Business doesn't really exist outside of mental models made of brain clay.

The brain sees no difference between people at the office and at the stadium.

Behavior, however, is (supposed to be) different at the two locations, of course.

That is simply because the arbitrary cultural rules, later agreed upon, though different from culture to culture...have been put in place in an attempt to regulate behavior (and generally do a fairly good job) at the office.

However, the degree of contentment one has at the office, at least from my quick look at the list, is not very encouraging.

It's no wonder that people don't like going to the office.... going to *work*. And do note the equation of *work* = office, very much like *sex* = a beautiful woman. These constructs are not real, but boy do they shape the thinking processes of a whole bunch of people....

Get rid of the enemies, put a cork in the mouths of the whiney employees, have food and sex handy, feel free with your movements and moment by moment choices and experiences, be comfortable and perhaps content—and work isn't such a bad place to go.

But it isn't like that.

Pretty much all the rules at work run counter to what and how you feel.

You can't regularly yell or smack the guy in the office next to you, or you get written up.

You can't tell the gal across the way what you're really thinking, or you have to go find a different building to depart to each morning.

You can't engage in all the *now* stuff you want to because the rules say you can't, and you'll need a new building to go to if you break the rules.

That would require more discomfort, more unfamiliarity, learning new things, and, thus, people continue to clean the hamster wheel...and keep it well oiled. It's not going anywhere...unless your CEO gets paid $100,000,000 annually and the company loses money, the retirement accounts are almost cleaned out, and you're forced to move the wheel to a new building...nah, that couldn't happen....

And that idea is maddening because we take a *long daily experience* with a low degree of contentment and it then goes lower.

Ouch.

And this is what people want you to say to them:

"I will do the work for you."

Those are Magic Words.

If you can promise someone those words and fulfill them, you can sell and sell and sell and market successfully and never have to worry much about anything as long as you live.

Ask women if they want the guy to do the dishes some of the time, and they will typically say *yes*—that matters . . . shouldn't matter, but it matters a *lot*.

Why do women want you to wash the dishes?

The Gift of Freedom

I was out gift shopping today and there was a section in the store where there are magnets designed as gifts for women. About 5 percent of them have messages on them about *not always* doing the dishes.

But why?

None of the things humans desire happen when the dishes are being done . . . ah . . . so you have an *interpretation* and *assignation of meaning issue* here . . .

. . . Oh, wait, there is a *feeling* attached to one . . . freedom . . . and *freedom* matters especially if it's inferred that something like washing the dishes takes away from freedom.

The funniest, most irrational things always come back to the nature of you and me.

I can go work a 16-hour day, come home with my eyes on top of each other, my brain overheating, and needing to have the hood pulled up, and whether you are roommate, my wife, or whatever, you want me to do the dishes.

There is no logic to feelings, except of course, that they are predictable. I don't need to do the laundry or wash out the sink . . . but I do need to do the dishes. It is a fascinating measurement tool in the *meaning* department of life, yes?

Now you should know that doing the dishes is actually important to me because I'm one of those slightly OCD people who doesn't like to see the dishes on the counter when food is being served. They belong in the dishwasher. And the rest will join them immediately after dinner.

And because I like orderliness, that happens even after 16 hours of work, if necessary. So I *do* do the dishes . . . mostly because of neuroses . . . .

Of course it isn't like this for people in normal mental health.

Those people are going to have problems in the relationship.

The luckiest thing a person can have in the world is someone who is a control freak and also a bit OCD.

Everything gets done, quickly, efficiently, though there may be some grumbling about imbalance. Nevertheless, CF plus OCD = clean house, stable income, and most of human needs met.

Interesting.

But. . .

There are problems, too. That CF/OCD doesn't get her/his comfort/contentment met, she/he only causes it to happen for everyone else and is absolutely certain that Wells Fargo will not correct the 1099.

. . . Oh, I'm sorry, let me explain . . . .

When I received my personal 1099 Misc from Wells Fargo this year, it had all of my interest payments from a business I own reported under my personal tax ID number, making it appear that I earned about 10 times more income than I actually did.

I asked *who* the guy was going to send the fax to when I was at the bank trying to get this sorted out.

"To Whom It May Concern, and they'll take care of it asap."

I must have had a sign on that said, "I am a total idiot. Tell me anything."

I laughed of course. I said I would see him in four months with the same documents . . . and I did on August 1.

Those were *not* the Magic Words.

The Magic Words would have been, "I'll take care of all of this for you, Dr. Hogan, because just like it says on the computer screen in bright green, you are a high-value customer and we are here to help you. I will fax you the documents as soon as I get them back."

Those would have been Magic Words creating some comfort and a sense of familiarity with the way I treat other people . . . .

Of course that didn't happen, and, yes, three weeks ago, I was back talking to Don. (Don also told me that my deposits were all FDIC insured . . . and they aren't . . . oh, well . . . .)

Think about these words: *comfort* and *familiarity*, and then read on.

Comfort and Familiarity

Just so you don't think I was crazy the first go 'round with Wells Fargo, I called Wells Fargo, on February 1. I spoke with people in three states including the office up the street.

"You'll have your 'corrected 1099' in 10 business days."

"Thanks, I appreciate it."

I hang up.

Back to the calendar: I write down on March 15, "Call Wells Fargo for 1099."

There is no chance that people without incentive to work will do anything.

So, when my 1099 didn't arrive, I gave it a few more days and today I called.

"I sure am sorry Dr. Hogan, you'll have your 'corrected 1099' in 10 business days."

"Thanks, I appreciate it."

I hung up and immediately wrote down on the calendar to call on April 1 and also note to write a letter to attach to the incorrect 1099 what happened and enclose the phone number of the Wells Fargo people so the IRS can call to confirm my story.

I'll be calling Wells Fargo back in 13 days asking for my 1099....

When you are CF/OCD you simply don't get surprised by these things.

Nothing gets done if there is no incentive or need for avoidance of pain attached because people are human and human nature requires comfort and familiarity.

Though theoretically possible, I heard nothing but surprise as I had the bankers look at the various certificate of deposit origination papers confirming that my business has a significantly different tax ID number than does the individual Kevin Hogan.

And of course, when I opened my account that day, I knew that if I put my social security number on the form with my tax ID number there was a 50/50 shot that the guy would get it wrong and input the wrong information.

Again, it was anticipated.

Human nature is very predictable.

Being wrong is one of my great pleasures in life.

I just wished it happened more often...

...So, if I can tell you that I will do something for you and it will be done swiftly and accurately, *and* you *believe* it, these are some of the most powerful words on the planet.

Same thing is true with me.

If I believe that and you say it to me, I'll pay any price.

I desperately want people to make me feel *comfortable* and when they do, I'm just like you, I am like a magnet to them . . . which leads us to the most misunderstood advertising factor. . .

The Most Misunderstood Advertising Factor

So we've experienced the words like "I will do the work for you," "familiar," "comfortable," and a few others to this point.

Now, the next level . . . because advertising and marketing firms understand the importance of personal laziness (really just human nature as we are in our raw form, not a pejorative term, except when I say it) it takes no rocket science to create advertising campaigns that work.

Politicians get elected by giving you and me all kinds of interesting things: retirement, education, health care, jobs, and so on. These, of course, are all the things that appeal to laziness and require relinquishing freedom to a group of marginally educated people who often couldn't succeed in business or life or making it to the restroom.

It is certainly not a recipe for the longevity of a society.

But if you want to get elected, you tell those who choose not to work but have a vote that "we'll tax the small business owner."

And then your picture shows up on *Rolling Stone*, and the image of Luke Skywalker comes to mind with the caption in bold: **A New Hope**.

I confess it was a beautiful piece of work. Gorgeous imagery.

WOW!

Now *that* is marketing.

But wait a minute. . . .

How did Jesse Ventura, a wrestler, get elected to be governor for *four years* here in Minnesota? I mean he didn't say, "I'll do the work for you."

In fact, he said, "If you don't get the bill on my desk by May 31, I'm going fishing and hunting, and I'll be back August 15."

They didn't . . . and he did . . . and they were shocked.

They couldn't believe that he'd really leave without the budget signed.

That's what you get when you get an authentic person in government.

They are a mess.

They don't know the rules.

Authentic people don't have a list of people who need freebies and favors.

They didn't B.S. anyone to get elected.

There was no negotiation or clandestine meetings, and such.

And we *knew* that would be the case.

So how could people elect someone like that?

It doesn't work except as a third-party candidate.

With a split vote, about 35 percent were disgusted with fakes and frauds. It was enough to elect a governor.

So don't worry, the person who promises the most comfort and laziness to the most people will win . . . or, more accurately, the person who causes you to believe you will be *more comfortable* and *lazier* each day is the person who will win the presidential election.

It is . . . human nature.

Can *you* overcome *their human nature?*

Will Logic Overcome? Unlikely

Could logic overcome human nature . . . and rational candidates who understand that you can't have things like social security, national health care, and all kinds of other buy-one-get-one-free coupons (money) spread throughout society for no value in return . . . could logic overcome people's personal laziness and personal comfort to strip their children of 9 *trillion dollars* of bills (as of today) . . . could *that person* get elected?

Rhetorical. . . .

Ross Perot tried that twice and got what the 20 percent of logical voters wanted, and everyone else went to the person who would bring them closer to comfort.

Now, I don't know, but am I to believe that an authentic McCain would ever beat The One who promises total and complete creature comforts?

Only if the environmental guy runs like he did in 2000 and gifted the election to the Republicans.

No . . . take out the environmental guy from the equation and it's a simple marketing campaign. "I will do the work for you. Government will pay your bills for you and take care of you and give you tons of free stuff and it will cost you nothing. All courtesy of business and the wealthy."

That's good advertising.

So who gets elected?

Comfort and *familiarity*.

We will tend to sway toward that with which we are familiar.

So the answer is that you promise the free stuff, and then tell them you'll do the work for them. They can go and be comfortable, and tell them that they *deserve* to be comfortable, and then four years later, they are familiar with you and you will get to spend a lot of years in a cool White House. . . .

Now your job is to figure out *how* you can *authentically* do the work for them and make them hear that message.

The difference between you and the people trying to get into that old house is that you will fulfill on your promises and truly serve your customer.

Now, you've seen how story can fit with information and you've learned an overarching principle of influence. Use words to form images that some-one would drink in.

Now let's take this principle to the field of selling.

After all, there is no job in any company or government without those who makes the sale. It's the most basic way to learn influence. It's the easiest to map to other contexts as well.

Imagine you had *new* ways to get clients and make sales. . . .

(See how those . . . can cause one to imagine?)

It is easier to hear yes and hear it more often. You can see people nodding their head. You can see them look at you with a sense of fascination. In your hip pocket you have "The Science of Influence Code Book." (Be patient.) The pages have been earmarked and are tattered. Every person has a different keyhole in their forehead and it's encrypted . . . until you have read the Codebook.

Today, I'm going to show you four proven tactics (not strategies) to increase your sales and get more clients. They're in the Codebook in your hip pocket. . . .

If you will carefully read about and open these four doors to your client's mind, you can't help but make a great deal more money next month than you did this month.

In fact, it would be almost impossible not to . . . unless you don't determine your income! (In this case, read carefully and you will truly gain some incredible distinctions about what gets people to say yes or no.) I guarantee this is surprising and very cool.

What's neat here is that you can just read the tactics, or you can read the tactics and the examples, or you can read the tactics, examples, and how we know these are effective . . . then of course you might want to utilize them today.

Our first tactic is something we wondered about. . . . We just didn't *know* if it was true.

Tactic 1. *Value Shock* occurs when you give someone something of such great value that they are awed.

Get something of yours (your product, your idea, your service) that has value, into your customers' hands/mind . . . as soon as possible! As soon as someone possesses something, they perceive it to be more valuable than they did immediately prior to owning it. In order to implement this strategy the client *must* sense or perceive ownership of a decision, item, idea, or service.

I recently participated in a worldwide promotion in which a number of marketers, coaches, and so forth gave away a bunch of gifts. I participated as someone who had something to offer and as someone who was a consumer as well. A few of the offers were pretty cool. Valuable.

Then there were those that gave me something that wasn't valuable. Something that other people had given me in the past (like recycled gifts).

I loathe that.

Or the person who really doesn't give a gift but plays bait-and-switch, one of the most destructive influence techniques from the field of political propaganda.

As I'm being given this *really* valuable $500 gift, I'm being pushed to upgrade immediately, before I've even test driven the gift.

Don't fall prey to this. Don't do it as a marketer. Don't fall for it as a consumer. Give value *first*. *Then* feel free to offer other opportunities or things of even greater value.

This philosophy influences and builds long-term relationships.

When I'm part of a promotion I try to give away more value than anyone in the promotion.

This isn't just the Law of Reciprocity in action.

It's far more.

It's having so much of value to give someone that they appreciate and acknowledge what has just happened.

I like to give away full-length books if possible. In fact I gave away a lot of full-length books (in e-form) last year.

A lot of people sell—for hundreds of dollars (!)—material that doesn't approach the value of what I give away. What does that tell you?

Recent studies bring these examples to our attention. They are the examples in the Codebook:

1. Individuals who ultimately bet on the Bears (for example) in a football game are often ambivalent about which team to select between the two until they actually place their bet on the Bears. Once they have placed their bet, they tend to dramatically favor the Bears . . . and show little hesitation in sharing their certainty that the Bears will win.
2. Students given mugs in a research setting are given the opportunity to sell the mug. Other students are given the opportunity to buy the mug. On average, students will not take less than $7.12 for the mug they have taken possession of. On average, students will not pay more than $3.12 for the same mug.

Lesson: Possession is nine-tenths of the law. Once you own something, you value it as higher than those who do not own it, even if it has only been owned for 10 minutes!

STOP: If you own someone's truly valuable e-book, a book that takes a few days to read and is filled with tons of information that you can use—if you POSSESS that—how will you rate its value? How will you think about the author?

Exactly. . . .

Tactic 2. *Imagined Value Quo*. Create a frame (a word picture in your customer's mind) that your product/service/idea is something that they already possess, so that it becomes the status quo in their thinking.

"Once our lawn service is yours, we help you eliminate all that crab grass—the crab grass all your old services said they would get rid of but couldn't even keep under control!"

1. Students in one class are given a decorated mug in return for filling out a questionnaire. In another class, students receive a large bar of Swiss chocolate. When given the opportunity to trade with members of the other class, 9 in 10 stayed with what they had.

Lesson: People value what they have and want more of it!

Tactic 3. *Deframing*. Create a word picture that creates a moderate amount of tension if the client doesn't do business with your company. In other words, what will the clients *lose* if they do *not* do business with you?

1. Research on real life applications? It's been done! Loss aversion is more pronounced for safety than money. (People will do more to protect themselves than their money.) Loss aversion is more pronounced for income than leisure. (Losing a chance to travel isn't as powerful as losing income.)

Lesson: People move away from loss. Determine what people lose if they don't do business with you and artfully develop word pictures that clarify the hurt they might experience if they don't. For example:

"For every person who dies this year in the United States, *seven* will become disabled. And if you become permanently disabled, your family will lose everything because you will be unable to work and they will have the added expense of taking care of you. If you carry insurance against this enormous risk, you avoid losing everything and have the ability to maintain a high standard of living no matter what happens to you."

Make sense? It's powerful. Now, here's the best one. . .

Tactic 4. Code Breaker: Know the difference between *opportunity cost* and *out-of-pocket expenses*. Don't confuse opportunity costs with out-of-pocket expenses. Your customer doesn't and is watching you to see how you promote your business. Learn this code breaker in detail and then tell me what happens to your sales.

1. Research was conducted in two cities by telephone sampling:

   Scenario 1. A shortage has developed for a certain popular make of automobile and customers must now wait two months for delivery. The dealer had been selling the cars at list price. Now the dealer prices the cars at $200 over list. Is this acceptable or unfair?

   Acceptable 29 percent

   Unfair 71 percent

   Scenario 2: A shortage has developed for a certain popular make of automobile and customers must now wait two months for delivery. The dealer has been selling the cars at $200 below list price. Now the dealer sells this model at list price. Is this acceptable or unfair?

   Acceptable 58 percent

   Unfair 42 percent

2. Same sampling as in 1.

   Scenario 3: A company is making a small profit. It is located in a city experiencing a recession with substantial unemployment but no inflation. The company decides to decrease wages and salaries this year by 7 percent. Acceptable or unfair?

   Acceptable 37 percent

   Unfair 63 percent

   Scenario 4: A company is making a small profit. It is located in a city experiencing a recession with substantial unemployment and inflation of 12 percent. The company decides to increase salaries by only 5 percent this year. Acceptable or unfair?

   Acceptable 78 percent

   Unfair 22 percent

In both pairs of scenarios the situation presented is identical to the previous situation. However, the consumer reacts very differently to each option.

People do *not* want to perceive money coming out of their pockets. Be certain to frame every promotion in such a way that the consumer is *clearly* saving and assume no mathematical ability on the part of the person.

People behave irrationally, then fabricate information about why they did so. Knowing that one fact can change how you influence for the rest of your life.

14 | The Power of Thinking without Thinking

Imagine if you will, the true force of influence....

There are two different bottles of wine in front of you. A glass is poured from each bottle. Which will taste best?

I bet you're thinking that you won't know until after you taste them. You would be wrong.

The fact is that, on average, the wine will taste good or bad based upon your perception of the label on the wine.

Now *stop*. That is pretty profound. The *label*, the *words*, and the *appearance* of the label determine how much you will like the wine.

And it doesn't just happen with wine. It happens with everything.

Power of Thinking without Thinking

I'll show you some cool research later in this section about how all of this thinking without thinking works, but last week, research was reported that children report that *all food* that comes from McDonald's or in McDonald's, tastes better than those exact same foods served up at home. That includes carrots and asparagus!

And this effect isn't just limited to wine drinkers and kids. It's broad spectrum, and even affects smart people like you and me!

Did you know that, in blind taste tests, when Coca Cola is pitted against Pepsi Cola, that Pepsi is chosen as the better tasting brand about 60 percent of the time?

Here's what's more interesting: When the labels are visible, Coca Cola consistently is selected as the tastier choice! That's how powerful brand is.

What's the lesson? The lesson is what can *you* do to make *yourself* Coca Cola, McDonald's, or the superior appearing wine?

Let's find out. . . .

Recent Coffee Challenge

Recently McDonald's won a surprising title. Consumer Reports reported that, in blind tests, McDonald's *coffee* tasted better than Starbucks.

I think we both know what would have happened if the test had not been blind. But here's what's more interesting yet. . . .

I don't drink a lot of coffee (mostly tea). I was with my friend, Mark Ryan, on our way to a convention, and he wanted to stop at McD's to get something to drink and he suggested coffee. I remembered the white styrofoam cup and I saw no reason to do such a thing, but I was so curious about how good it would taste. The salesperson gave us our coffee and they came in these *very* cool cups that had text and color on them indicating stuff that I remember as environmentally friendly. (I didn't keep the cup nor did I think I'd be writing about it, but you get the idea.) It was almost as cool looking as a Starbucks cup!

My grandfather always talked to me about the power of perception." He wanted me to write a book with that title with him.

Perception Causes Action

Every day I see how perception causes people to do things that logic or reality never would.

Later, at the very end of this section I want to show you some fascinating research about how other people's choices and perceptions change *your* choices!

Basically the concept is this: Everyone is snobby about something. Some people only wear Nike or drink Coke or whatever. And then something interesting happens. People can wear the same clothes for years, but when some other group of people starts to wear the clothes (or whatever) that *your group* wears, you switch to another brand!

Key Point: You and I do a lot of stuff because it *defines* our *identity*. As soon as the products we use fail to differentiate us from others we do not want to be identified with, we change our choices.

More Thinking without Thinking

Changing the label on a wine changed diners' opinions of their wine, opinions of their meal, and their repatronage of the restaurant, according to a Cornell University study.

Forty-one diners at the Spice Box restaurant in Urbana, Illinois were given a free glass of cabernet sauvignon to accompany a $24 prix-fixe French meal. Half the bottles claimed to be from Noah's Winery in California. The labels on the other half claimed to be from Noah's Winery in North Dakota. In both cases, the wine was an inexpensive Charles Shaw wine.

Those drinking what they thought was California wine, rated the wine and food as tasting better, and ate 11 percent more of their food. They were also more likely to make return reservations.

Expectations: If You Think a Wine Will Taste Good, it Will Taste Better Than it Would if You Think it Will Taste Bad

People didn't believe North Dakota wine would taste good, so it had a double curse—it hurt both the wine and the entire meal. "Wine labels can throw both a halo or a shadow over the entire dining experience," according to Cornell professor Brian Wansink, author of the book *Mindless Eating: Why We Eat More Than We Think.*

To confirm this, a similar study was conducted with 49 MBA students at a wine-and-cheese reception. Again, those given wine labeled from California rated the wine as 85 percent higher and the cheese as 50 percent higher.

"Small cues such as origin of a wine or whether the label or name catches your eye often trick even serious Foodies," said co-author Dr. Collin Payne. "He (Wansink) has even conducted demonstrations of this at Le Cordon Bleu in Paris and Apicious Culinary Institute in Florence."

For restaurants and wineries, it's important to keep a keen eye on the possible halo or shadow of wine labels. Diners, on the other hand, should be careful to not overpay for a pretty bottle. The study, published this summer in *Physiology & Behavior*, is one of the few to have investigated the chain effect of sensory expectations.

Now, here is the research about personal identification that I believe you will find exceptionally fascinating. . . .

Personal Identification—Thinking without Thinking

- Consumers often abandon products when other social groups adopt them.
- Teens want to distinguish themselves from their parents.
- Jocks want to separate themselves from geeks.
- Rich Brits stopped buying Burberry once it became the brand of choice for soccer hooligans.
- Shanghai urbanites avoid the Volkswagen model that is preferred by the suburban nouveau riche.

Yet, the same teens who wouldn't be caught dead wearing the same jeans as their parents have no problem using the same brand of detergent!

A new study by Stanford researchers explores why some products are used by people to differentiate themselves from certain social groups.

"Prior work on individual drives for differentiation tells us a lot about who is more likely to prefer unique products or when people might be more likely to prefer them," writes Jonah Berger and Chip Heath (Stanford University) in the *Journal of Consumer Research*. "But these approaches have less to say about where people diverge, or why people diverge more in certain domains."

In a series of experiments, the researchers studied the differences between *products that convey identity information* and products that do not tend to be identified with a certain group. For example, in the first study, the researchers had undergraduates choose options in 19 difference product areas (e.g., power tools, hairstyles, soap, and favorite CD).

In each area, they were told that 65 percent of other students preferred Option A, 25 percent preferred Option B, and 10 percent preferred Option C. They were then asked which option they would choose.

Option C establishes the greatest desire for divergence from the majority. Whereas 67 percent of undergraduates chose Option C for the category of favorite CD, only 6 percent chose it when asked about dish soap. In a national, web-based survey that expanded on the pilot study (median age 38), the results were similar.

A different group of respondents was asked to rate products either on self-expression (how much it contributes to self-expression) or identity inference making (how much people use it to make inferences about others).

Thirty-one percent of participants in the national survey chose Option C (preferred by 10 percent of the population) for products that were ranked as highly identity relevant. For products that were less identity relevant, only 16 percent of participants chose Option C. The researchers wrote:

Consistent with our focus on the social nature of identity-signaling, even though our internet sample came from a range of demographic backgrounds, **participants exhibited strong agreement about which domains were identity-relevant.**

The results underscore the social nature of divergence; **individuals don't establish difference from majorities in every domain or any random domain – they do so more in domains where others look for signals about their identity** (Berger and Heath 2007).

Okay. Now you understand how to cause thinking without thinking. Perhaps you will go forward and **reinvent yourself and your products.**
But wait!

What happens if the people out there don't find you all that phenomenal? What if they see you as ... normal?

Disrupting Their Dislike ... and Influencing Mixed Emotions

Opinions form **rapidly** about you, your product, and your service.

Do you mind if I show you how to cause people to move toward the like-you end of the spectrum as opposed to the don't-like-you end?

Your desired outcome is that opinions about acceptance of you and what you sell form quickly. (They will want to buy you and your product or service.)

Sometimes that desired outcome is easily met to the degree that purchase is desirable and even demanded. (Rockband, XBox 360, iPhone, Avatar, electricity, gas, water, waste disposal, etc.)

However, you don't see salespeople knocking on doors or filling e-mail boxes to sell those products.

There are also products that we simply don't want and wouldn't want. You can think of lots of things that you've seen people spend money on that you wouldn't take as a gift if it was offered to you.

Today you find out how to sell something that people are *initially* more ambivalent about. In other words, they don't hold much of an opinion about it, or if they do, it is mildly conflicted—they have mixed emotions.

Perhaps the product might be dish soap or a cordless telephone. A mutual fund company. A life insurance company. A bank. A hosting company for a web site. A type of tire for your car. A clinic. A computer brand. A throwaway camera.

Research just released shows that negative impressions of mostly neutral products as mentioned earlier, need to first be considered as something they might like. Only when they have determined that they don't like it, do they form the opinion of dislike.

About neutral products:

- Like comes almost instantly.
- Dislike takes some thought.

What should you do when you suspect they have a dislike for you, your product, or service?

What happens if you sense that dislike is their response?

Address it immediately so that the pendulum can swing back in the other direction.

Key Point: Prior to the dislike judgment and when only *considering* the negative/dislike, interject a few questions about irrelevant issues (Who won the game? How are the kids?). This is almost always enough to shut the door to dislike and open the door back up to a possible yes or making a sale!

More interesting is that when presented with neutral products, services, or even people, the bias is to feel positive toward what is presented. And *then* it takes something to get the person thinking about bad things, drawbacks, and so forth.

And that's important, too. When people are presented with a neutral product and asked, "How much do you dislike this?" they do indeed go down that road. Same product, similar group, and this question: "How much do you *like* this?" and the answer is typically the opposite.

Framing is everything . . . yes?

Of course . . .

Framing *isn't everything* is it?

Of course not . . .

Whooooa . . . that was cool. **Framing is *important*?**

Of course . . .

(See how your mind followed all those tracks agreeably?)

It takes longer to determine that someone does *not* like a neutral product than it does for someone to say, "I like it." "I like it," comes quickly to mind, and this is one reason salespeople miss so many sales. They have the product sold, and then they start to tell the customer all the benefits and features.

You know what? Shhhhh . . .

Paul Herr and Christine Page (2004) did a brilliant job of assembling the findings of much of the research I talk about here:

1. Positive and negative emotions are *not* opposites. Both positive *and* negative emotions can and often are held at the same time toward a person, idea, or object. Emotions aren't really positive or negative . . . they are reactions to internal and external stimuli. That's pretty much it. . . .

Point: Just because someone expresses a negative feeling or thought about your product in *no way* means that they won't want to buy it. Just because it's the wrong color or too expensive or doesn't have a better zoom lens or isn't as good in low light . . . does *not* mean they are going to say no. The like and dislike feelings are in no way mutually exclusive of each other!

You can hate the car mechanic, but you appreciate the good job he's doing on your car. You can feel good and bad about owning your new car. You can love your spouse but dislike a lot of things about that person.

> *Like and dislike are not mutually exclusive.*

2. Positive and negative emotions are largely processed in the left and right hemisphere, respectively. I've discussed this discovery at length and how to use this obviously important information in The Body Language Home Study Course, and how it makes or breaks a lot of decisions . . . for no logical reason.
3. Consumer surveys have been shown to be largely useless when they ask individuals whether they like something or dislike a product, service, or attribute of something. (Herr and Leeds have now shown the neuropsychological evidence that liking and disliking are represented in memory very differently from each other.)
4. Consumers who indicate they like x, y, and z about a product and dislike a, b, c about the same product, should not have those scores averaged because they represent *very different* emotions in the brain and the brain does not average the responses to come up with decisions!

5. Positive emotion/motivation toward an object that is greater than the negative emotions/moving away responses ... toward a novel stimulus (an unusual or fascinating object) will cause the consumer to slowly approach the object usually with very little thought involved. They just go in that direction, if the feelings are not too strong either way.

Think of the curious child who is fascinated by a new toy or bug or anything that creates a significant but modest motivational response. The tendency is to go toward it to check it out (my interpretation of Cacioppo, Gardner and Bernston 1999).

Facing neutral or unfamiliar stimuli would be weakly motivated to approach ... and to engage exploratory behavior (unless the flight/fight response is triggered). (Cacioppo et al. 1999)

6. Individuals hold more favorable expectations for their own futures than others (Regan, Snyder, and Kassin 1995 ... and many others). How are you going to consistently frame *that* picture?
7. Individuals attribute lower health risks to themselves than others (Hoorens and Buunk 1993).
   Same!
8. Individuals form slightly positive impressions toward unknown others (Boucher and Osgood 1969).
9. **Unless *intentional thinking* occurs, a person presented with a persuasive message *will be persuaded*** (Gilbert, Tafarodi, and Malone 1993).

Negative versus Positive: Who Wins?

$10,000 Key Point: Extremely negative information is far more powerful than the same extreme of positive information. (Baumeister et al. 2001; Taylor 1991).

This is an absolutely *crucial* factor in persuasion.

Key Point: Negative events elicit *far more* physiological, emotional, intentional thought, and behavioral activity than positive events (according to dozens of studies).

Conclusion of Herr and Page: "Negative information has a more pronounced impact on subsequent cognitive processing." They go on to note that individuals are predisposed to positivity. You lean positive until negative hits; and then it hits really hard.

The only time negativity should hit hard in your communication is when *you* inject it at the right time, with the right intention and purpose. Where there is negativity, *you* must be in control or you will always lose the sale.

15 | Influence in Sales and Marketing Online and in the Real World

What's one of the most important things to know before giving a persuasive selling presentation?

Understanding what motivates people to buy and then pushing all the right buttons. Simple.

Before I launch into creating and presenting your own offer, whether in person, on the web, or in media, we need to do some research to make sure your offer is accepted.

Core Reasons People Buy or Say Yes to Anything

What if I told you that I am going to outline the things that *motivate* people to make purchases, and I'm going to show YOU *how to have control over each of these core factors*, AND I am going to *give you the training you need to master these motivators* to practically cause people to buy from YOU.

Interested? Ready?

What motivates people to buy? These are the major reasons people buy. There are seven.

The Influence of Emotion

One of the reasons people make purchases is because of emotion. Emotions like:

- *FEAR*:
  Fear of gaining weight.
  Fear of missing an opportunity.
  Fear of unemployment.
  Fear of death.
  Fear of a future price increase.
  Fear of what others think about them.
  Fear of the unknown.
  Fear of growing old.
  Fear of being alone.
  Fear of being cheated.

There are hundreds of different phobias that drive people to make purchases.

People buy life insurance because they fear dying prematurely and leaving their family financially strapped.

We buy exercise equipment because we fear gaining weight or getting out of shape.

We buy alarm systems because we fear we are going to be violated in some way.

Key Point: We make a lot of purchases because of our fears, on things that are supposed to ease our fears.

- PASSION:
  Passion for food.
  Passion for money.
  Passion for our children.
  Passion for our partner.
  Passion for our career.
  Passion for success.
  Passion for fame.

We all have those things in our lives that we are passionate about. Whether it is a relationship or a recreation, a possession or a position, we all have those things that we long for.

We all have those things that we love. And we spend a lot of money in pursuit of those things.

I began reading voraciously as a kid. And everywhere I went, people told me more and more of the different kinds of books I could purchase. I bought thousands of books.

Why? Because my passion for reading triggered an emotional response. I wanted to KNOW as much as a human could, and I was as good as sold long before walking into Barnes and Noble.

To this day I own books on and have read everything possible about biblical archaeology, religious literature, the historic Jesus, decision making, illusion of consciousness, consumer behavior, evolutionary psychology, strategic and critical thinking, motivation, rejection, relationship research, well, and a few other—dozens of—areas of interest.

You and I make a lot of purchases based upon passion or love. Things that make us happy, that bring us joy, that increase our pleasure. People buy food in many cases, not because they are hungry, but because they love eating.

People buy self-help books, not because we need to improve our reading skills, but because we long to improve our lives. People buy roses because they love their spouses. **Passion—it fuels a *lot* of buying decisions.**

I touched on fear and passion because those are the two biggest emotional buttons that cause people to make purchases. There are plenty of others: **sorrow, reverence, hate, sadness, surprise, anger, joy, excitement.** We make purchases for all of these reasons.

Key Point: In reality, you and I buy very few things for rational reasons. Instead, we buy things (especially those spur-of-the-moment impulse items!) because of emotions, because of feelings. Now, since people purchase a *lot* of products based on emotions, what can you do to trigger those emotions?

Secrets of Tapping into Emotions

There are two secrets to touching the way we feel about things that work the majority of the time.

$10,000 Key Point: Present problems and offer solutions. Early on in your offer or your presentation is a great place to do this. Outline a problem that your buyer or your target audience is probably facing, and then point out how your product provides the solution.

Online: One of the biggest obstacles facing most people doing business online is generating traffic to their web sites. Let me show you how to *really* get quality people who are interested in *you* and your work, product, service, and/or experience, to *your* web site . . .

I like contrasting my work with others who write about and create products and courses that are about similar topics to what I'm doing, but there is a significant difference.

Because there's no need to replicate information, I produce where others are deficient. I provide depth or value where they don't. That's a huge competitive advantage.

Face it. Someone goes to a seminar for $5,000 and gets nothing but a sales pitch or a bunch of sales pitches. It doesn't take rocket science to know people are angry, knowing that they wanted value, and didn't get it. And that's where an opportunity is created for me to create happy and loyal lifetime relationships.

I mean, think of the last time you went to a seminar that was really a sales pitch for a bunch of other stuff. What emotions are triggered here? Anger? Absolutely! Most likely the reader is angry because she herself has been taken and disillusioned by the event, and the like.

The key is that they are facing a problem (the reason they went to the first event has not been fulfilled), and there is the possibility of a solution for them to take a chance on Kevin Hogan.

Emotion has already been triggered and will continue to be fed throughout the remainder of our hypothetical presentation. (I can feel the emotions of this scenario right now!)

You want to point out what happened with the other event. Let it sting. Then let the reader/prospect/customer/future client see the existing problems that caused them to want to go to that other event in the first place, then offer solutions where possible.

Don't exaggerate, lie, or hype. Offer realistic, reachable solutions that will come to fruition in the near future.

We all have problems and we all want them eliminated. And, we don't mind paying for those solutions—if they are real solutions.

Key Point: Be the *clear alternative*. If you can't be passionate about being the clear alternative, present luxuries and offer opportunities. The flipside to that coin is to present something that triggers your audience's passion and offers them a chance to obtain it. For example, here's one that would get a lot of people now:

"Wouldn't you like to improve your golf game so dramatically that you'll have your buddies scrambling to keep up with you?

"Let me show you how to take at least 10 strokes off your total by the end of the week. You'll drive the ball farther, hit amazingly accurate chip shots, and putt like a pro. Here's how. . ."

What emotions are triggered here? Excitement! Joy! Passion! Pride!

Key Point: There is a certain attraction between our psyches and an opportunity to fulfill something we are passionate about. The idea for you is to capitalize on an *existing* emotional want.

For example, If you get targeted traffic to your web site or the right people in your store, then it is *easy* to present your work to your web site visitors because of their existing desires.

They already want something, all you have to do is be credible enough to persuade them that they can have it.

One reason we buy is because the offer or opportunity triggers some feeling inside of us that prompts us to go for it.

Your job is to let them pull the trigger.

The Influence of Value

We all love a good deal. We buy things because they are valuable to us. Or people buy just because it is on sale and they *might* use the product, whatever it is. Typically people buy something they consider to be of value.

Now, there are two basic ways that we judge value:

1. *Quantity*
   Two for the price of one.
   Buy one get one free.
   Free medium drink with any hamburger order.

Extra value meal.
Free installation with any satellite purchase.
Thirty days free to new members.

These are all ways of providing *more* quantity for the same price. And that, in our estimation, is a determining factor in how valuable something is.

After all, what's more valuable: A large pizza for $14.95 or a large pizza with a free two-liter coke for $14.95? Obviously the free two-liter coke adds more value to the order. That is a quantity increase, and it prompts you and me to order, simply because there is more bang for the buck.

In direct marketing, value was a collection of *thousands* of money-making reports. Online, it's a collection of dozens of e-books. Unfortunately, neither of these usually has a lot of useful information in them, but there sure are a lot of them! And many people buy because of the sheer volume they represent. It just sounds like an awful lot for the price tag that is attached.

2. *Quality*

The other measuring stick of value is quality. Let's stick with pizza as our illustration. I like Godfather's Pizza. It's far and away my favorite. I rarely taste anything as good.

Any store could sell pizza at one-tenth the price of Godfather's, but there's no interest because the quality of Godfather's is supreme.

I am happy to pay a premium because of quality. I would rather pay more to receive something of higher quality. Quality sells.

We make purchases because we see some kind of value, whether quantitative or qualitative. Give us either and you've most likely got a customer. Give us both and it's a done deal.

Influence of Expectation

Herein lies a tremendous motivator for purchases. We buy based on what we expect to achieve from use of the purchase. In other words, we buy based on what we perceive will be the end result of that purchase. For example...

People buy exercise equipment because they *expect to see the results* of weight loss, muscle tone, and overall better health.

They buy grass seed because they *expect to see the results* of a nicer lawn.

They buy cookbooks because they *expect to see the results* of nice meals and desserts.

They buy movie tickets because they *expect to be* entertained.

We make a great many purchases because we *expect* to see some kind of desirable outcome as a result of that purchase.

Key Point: Don't attempt to sell the prospect your product, but rather the end result of using your product.

You aren't selling products or services, you are selling results. You are selling weight loss, not weight loss pills. You are selling an education, not tuition. You are selling a romantic evening for two, not a candlelit dinner.

People buy because they want results. Want to sell more? Start approaching your offer from the end and not the beginning. Ask yourself a simple question: "What does the prospect want to achieve with my product?" Focus on the results.

Influence of Referrals

Many times we purchase based solely on a recommendation from a trusted friend, family member, or associate.

Referrals are SO important in business but most people never get them.

We'll talk about this one in much more detail later and in-depth at *Influence Boot Camp 2011.*

(I'll even show you how to get these referrals for free!) I just want to introduce you to the idea now. People make purchases in a lot of cases simply because someone makes a recommendation.

How many times have you bought something because someone suggested it? I have bought a ton (literally) of books because one of a few trusted friends and colleagues have suggested that I do.

You've made similar purchases yourself.

Influence of Recognition

People often buy things because of *reputation* and/or *recognition*. And of course, everyone buys things because of *name recognition*.

We buy things because of *familiarity*. Why? Because of the scientific principle of priming. It's that simple and it makes companies millions and billions of dollars every year.

Answer these questions without thinking . . .

What is your favorite soft drink?
What is your favorite brand of jeans?
What kind of pain reliever do you use?

Now, why do you drink the same soft drink over and over? You like the taste, right? Why do you buy the same jeans over and over? You like the fit, right? Why do you buy the same pain reliever over and over? You like the lack of pain, right?

In other words, you buy what you are *familiar* with. You buy because of the *reputation* each of those has with you. You buy because you *recognize* them. We make many purchases for that very reason.

Key Point: We buy because of recognition, reputation, and familiarity.

Influence of Necessity

Let's face it, sometimes you and I buy because we *need* to buy. When the tube of toothpaste is depleted, I amble on down to Wal-Mart and buy a new tube. I *need* toothpaste. When my electric bill comes in each month, I pay it. I *need* electricity. Every 3,000 miles (about once annually) I pay to have the oil changed in my car. Why? Because my car *needs* it! We buy a lot of things because we *need* to. That's the principle of necessity. You already knew that, I am sure.

But, did you know that you can *create* need in your offers? And, no, I don't mean, "You need to buy my product now! You need what I've got! Buy from me, buy from me!" That won't get you a sale, *ever*.

Let's recap what we've covered so far. We make purchases in large part because of the influences of persuasive selling presentations. They are:

The Influence of Emotion
The Influence of Value
The Influence of Expectation
The Influence of Referrals
The Influence of Recognition
The Influence of Necessity

And that brings us to number seven, the Influence of Presentation.

Principle of Presentation

People buy because of *presentation*.

This is the most important of all. Master this one and I assure you, you will make more sales than you could ever imagine. You and I buy things because of the way the offer is presented to us. Bottom line: This is **the single most important determining factor in all purchase decisions.**

Why? Because with the proper presentation of your offer, you can **conquer all six other principles at the same time.** You can: trigger the emotion, provide value, build expectation, use referrals, become familiar, and prove there is a need for your product.

All of the other six rest on this seventh. It is the umbrella that covers them all. If you learn to present your offer the *right* way, then selling is the easy part.

Your offer itself (whatever product or service you are selling, for the price you are selling it) must be presented in such a way that it *compels* people to buy. Presentation is just as important as the substance of your product or service.

In fact, it's probably more important. Why? Because no one will ever see your product or service until you present an offer that they must say yes to. As long as they can say no to your offer, as long as they can reject what you are trying to sell them, then your substance doesn't do you a bit of good.

Presentation—that is the key. You've got to make it easier for them to say Yes than it is for them to say No.

Can Higher Prices Cause More Sales Volume?

Each week I receive a few books in the mail that people want me to review for you in *Coffee with Kevin Hogan.*

They know that if I like a book, a lot of people will buy it. If I don't, I almost certainly won't review it because, as a rule, I don't do negative reviews. So they risk $20 and send me a copy. It has little downside and potentially big upside. That's just good promotional thinking.

But, what happens when they tell their audience, "We just sent a review copy to Kevin Hogan for his perusal . . . ," or, "We're so excited that we sent a review copy to Kevin Hogan so he might consider putting the book in his online store."

Is that going to help sell the book?

Would the consumer be happy to hear that I got the book for free and that they have to pay $20?

And what if I didn't actually review the book?

How would *you* feel? Would you simply anticipate that? Does it matter at all? Does it boost your confidence when they tell you they sent a copy of their new book to me? Does it make you feel you got shorted?

The thing is that we know we are lousy predictors of our emotions and feelings, so I'll show you what the latest research says you *should* and *should not* do when promoting your products and services.

Groucho Marx famously said that he wouldn't want to join any club that would have someone like him as a member. But if you are on the outside of some deal that benefits another group more than you, would this make you more or less interested in the product?

> For example, guess how female Victoria's Secret customers would react if they found out that male customers got better deals on the same items?
>
> How would plus-sized women react to a dress that is sold for less in smaller sizes?

According to research from Duke University's Fuqua School of Business, **the excluded consumers would be turned off and would be less likely to make a purchase.**

But how would competitive swimmers react to a product claiming to improve speed if they knew the product is given away free to Olympic swimmers?

How would vodka consumers react to super premium Belvedere vodka if they knew the company offered free tastings exclusively for bartenders?

In these examples, ***the consumer ends up wanting the product more***, said Alison K. C. Lo, a recent doctoral graduate at the Fuqua School of Business.

She and marketing professors John Lynch and Richard Staelin explain why in the article "How to Attract Customers by Giving Them the Short End of the Stick," published in the February 2007 *Journal of Marketing Research*.

Key Point: "As consumers, we sometimes buy things when we feel clueless in telling good-quality products from bad but we think more savvy consumers can tell the good stuff simply by inspecting the merchandise," Allison Lo said. "In such cases, naive consumers are attracted to a product with a freebie that is not available to them but is offered to a more savvy group of buyers, like bartenders or Olympic swimmers."

These savvy buyers presumably would turn up their noses at low-quality merchandise, so naive consumers reason that products promoted to experts must be good.

"On the other hand, *if we are excluded from a deal and the group benefiting is not more savvy or we are more certain of the product's quality, we are put off*," she explained. "We buy less—like the woman who sees that Victoria's Secret is offering a better deal to men than to women."

What happened in another experiment?

Student volunteers in Duke's master of business administration program were asked to choose which of two cordless drills they would prefer to receive as a gift. The researchers tested the effects of varied promotions by pairing the drills with either a $15 Nordstrom gift card or the book "Graphic Guide to Frame Construction: Details for Builders and Designers."

The study participants overwhelmingly preferred the gift card, but ***they thought the book would be more appealing to people with expertise in construction and carpentry.***

Participants then were asked to guess the prices of the drills, and *they gave a higher price to the drill that was paired with the book compared with the one paired with the gift card.*

"This is important because even though the book was not as valuable as the gift card to our participants, they realized the book would be valuable to someone who might know a good drill when he or she sees one," Lynch said. "They reasoned that only a manufacturer of a high-quality drill could lure such an expert to buy."

The research team found similar results in experiments focusing on other products, including camcorders and headphones.

The researchers say the findings challenge some long-held notions regarding consumer reaction to targeted promotions. *"Our findings apply to a specific set of circumstances where the customer is not able to judge the quality of a product, but believes that other consumers are expert in judging that product,"* Staelin said.

"But a lot of marketers sell in exactly those kinds of categories, so our findings can be used to sell products from wine to jewelry to home electronics to financial services."

And now you know how to make it happen too!

You heard it here first.

It's difficult to not see huge amounts of money and resources all around you, and all you have to do is ask for it—and sometimes they'll ask you if you want it . . . and hope like mad you'll take it!

From a *Coffee with Kevin Hogan* reader last year (discussion follows the letter so you can see the piles of gold laying around *you*):

Dear Kevin,

I want to share with you a recent experience with a client of mine:

I offered the client the following two options (verbally and in writing) to complete a project:

Option A: Project costs 2100 pounds ($4,000) and he gets 800 back through a government grant for which it qualifies. The final cost to the customer is 1300 pounds. If the customer wants, he can pay 2000 up front and he will qualify for a 5 percent discount reducing his final cost to 1200 ($2,300). (100 pounds is the grant application fee.)

★★Customer would pay about $2,300 and fills out a short five-minute form.

Option B: The same project as above costs 1600 pounds, but there is no money back from the government. As in Option A, if all the money is paid up front, he gets a 5 percent discount reducing his final cost to 1520 ($2,800) pounds.

To my surprise the customer chose Option B with the discount even though he only had to fill a form to get the government grant (form would take two minutes to fill) and all the bureaucracy would have been taken care of by me (hence the 500 pounds difference in price).

★★Customer preferred to pay $2,800 and not fill out the five-minute form!

After reading your book I have an insight into the possible reasons the customer chose Option B, even though Option A is the most "logical," and everyone I've asked later said the customer would have chosen the A option.

There is one more detail to add. When I asked the customer as to why he has chosen Option B he said that the difference between the two was not big enough to justify choosing Option A.

This does not make any sense to me at all since he is giving away free money, which is a big proportion of the total sale!

Best Regards,
Polyvios Gregoriades

My letter sent to Polyvios:

Polyvios: There is so much behind the story you tell that affects you that we can't appreciate enough that you have written!

Observe:

There are a couple of things at work here. One level in persuasion; and another on the very strange and disappointing fashion in which governments and major corporations do business.

Fact is they are praying to give you a lot of money. . . .

Just Ask, Honey.

First, the person obviously doesn't care about 500 pounds of his company's money.

Why?

It's not his money.

But it is his five minutes in paperwork.

And his superiors don't know anything about the grant!

Spending corporate or government dollars is actually necessary in order for a department to receive the same funding (for the following year) from the absolutely brain-dead budget people that create departmental funding each year.

Here's how it works: Whatever they got last year, they will get this year. *But* they *only* get the money *if* it is spent the prior year!

If money is saved or a department is operated efficiently, it will receive the budget that it got this year, and when it comes to office furniture, picnics, parties, . . . you get the idea . . . it won't be there.

What companies? What governments?

About 85 percent of all corporations with more than 100 employees and 99.7 percent of all city, county, state, and federal governmental bodies in the United States.

Those of you who run your own small businesses must have your jaws on the table!

This is one reason big companies and governments are dying. It is absolutely necessary to literally throw money away, especially at the end of the fiscal year, in order to get budget for next year.

The little known outside-of-government budgeting tool works like this:

Divisions and departments in big companies and government must spend their budget. They fought tooth and nail to get money for x, y, and z in their budget. Sometimes they could get $100,000 for furniture but only a $2,000 increase in salary. Welcome to government and big business.

At the planning meetings for the next fiscal year, budgets aren't questioned, they are simply met, unless the division/department is asking for *more*.

An example from my world: A lot of times a department will have money to hire a speaker but nothing for educational materials or vice versa . . . or maybe they have $15,000 left in training and they need to spend it all!!

Now, part of being creative is figuring out HOW to FRAME what YOU DO into the various line items in the budgets.

I know this all sounds ridiculous but it's how the world works.

Who would want to fill out a five-minute form when, if they did, filling out that form would cause them to lose some of their budgeting for next year?

Not many in corporate America. No one in government.

That's why money gets spent wisely or just blown on everything from parties to consultants, dinners, entertainers, furniture, flowers.

But there is more...less insidious yet something you need to know...

Convenience vs. Cost—The Meta Filter.

The person probably has a "Convenience" meta-program filter instead of a "Cost" meta-program filter. This severe of a meta-program aberration is seen only in about 1 percent of people. Five-hundred dollars or 500 pounds for five minutes of work is not likely to get left on the table when it comes to their own *personal* money.

From a salesperson's perspective, it reminds me what Dottie Walters said to me one day: "Just ask, honey."

You never know when they have to blow their money to have their coffers filled up ... and you aren't taking advantage. They are desperate to spend it!

Think this: They *must* give their business to *someone*. Why not let it be you?!

Now, from the strict perspective of influence, realize that the above is *only one* common cultural scenario that causes a "Cost/Convenience" metaprogram.

Some people simply will do *anything* for convenience, regardless of cost.

Think about it the next time you wonder if you should ask for the order or their business.

There is *so* much money out there. So many people waiting to say yes! All one has to do is ask!

Thanks for writing!!!

Kevin Hogan

16 | The Problem and Opportunity of Memory in Influence

"Buyers are liars."

Having spent half of my life in the world of sales and marketing, I can share with you that a lot of people believe that to be true.

Reality? Maybe . . . but maybe not.

And the same thing that opens the door to their mind . . . opens the gate to you being able to shape *your* mind for wealth, happiness, and more of what you want in life.

Analyze this with me:

Forty-five first-year psychology students were told three stories about their grade-school experiences and asked about their memories of them. Two of the accounts were of real grade-three-to-six events recounted to the researchers by the participant's parents. The third event was fictitious, but also attributed to the parents. It related how, in first grade, the subject and a friend got into trouble for putting Slime (a colorful gelatinous goolike toy made by Mattel that came in a garbage can) in their teacher's desk.

The participants were encouraged to recall the events through a mix of guided imagery and mental context reinstatement—the mental equivalent of putting themselves back in their grade-school shoes. Half of the participants were also given their real first-grade class photo, supplied by their parents.

So a bunch of psych students are told that this event happened when they were kids. Half of the psych students were shown photos of their first-grade class picture. Make sense?

Question One: Estimate the percentage of students who literally believed the Slime story to be true in the groups in which they were not given their class photo.

(a) 3%   (b) 9%   (c) 14%   (d) 20%   (e) 25%   (f) 45%   (g) 67%

Question Two: Estimate the percentage of students who literally believed the Slime story to be true in the groups in which their actual first-grade class photo was shown to the students.

(a) 16%   (b) 28%   (c) 45%   (d) 58%   (e) 67%

So, the mere suggestion of the Slime incident attributed to the parents caused 25 percent of the people to believe it actually happened! That is rather amazing, but consistent with what we know about suggestibility.

One in four people believed an event to be true, even though no such event took place in the person's life!

BUT . . .

Key Point: In the group where the individuals were told the same exact story, but also shown the class picture from that grade, **67 percent** of the students believed the fictional story about themselves to be absolutely true.

Two-thirds of all people believed the fictional story to be true.

Why so much more than the 25 percent in the other groups? Because there was a class photo that apparently helped stimulate some creative storytelling in the brain.

In other words, the false story combined with a true photograph combined for a shocking rewrite of personal history.

"The false memories were richly detailed," said Dr. Lindsay in a press release. His research focuses on memory and he co-authored the paper with a team from the University of Victoria and the Victoria University of Wellington, New Zealand (*see* Lindsay et al. 2004).

Of those who claimed to remember the Slime event, most did so with just as much confidence as for the two real events. When asked which of the events didn't really happen, all but three of the participants said it was the Slime event. Even so, the fact that it was concocted elicited surprised reactions, including the comment, "No way! I remembered it! That is so weird!"

Dr. Lindsay attributes the remarkably high rate of false memory to several factors. These include the plausibility of the Slime scenario (including that a friend was involved); the confidence inspired by the skilled and outgoing interviewee Lisa Hagen, a former student and co-author on the paper; and the role of the photo as both a memory prod and seemingly corroborating piece of evidence.

"The findings support the general theoretical perspective that memories aren't things that are stored somewhere in your head," says Dr. Lindsay. **"Memories are experiences that we can have that arise through an interaction between things that really have happened to us in the past and our current expectations and beliefs."**

The ramifications are startling. The mere presence of a *tangential* (not even corroborating) piece of information (the class photo from two to five years before the Slime event was supposed to have taken place) causes the majority of the individuals to believe a complete fabrication about their own past.

This not only confirms previous research that has been done in the past, but it does it all one better. That extra little visual piece of evidence links the person to the past (false) experience, making it all very real indeed.

The same thing is true in your life about hundreds of things. And the same is true of your clients! The mere suggestion of something that happened to you or your client, verified by a supporting piece of tangential evidence, can cause the immediate creation of an utterly false memory and what shapes beliefs! Yes.

This would be similar to someone in your family showing you a photo of you taken for a Christmas card, and then someone tells a story about you. The mere suggestion combined with a literally irrelevant picture can change the landscape of your mind—just like that.

What Does This Mean for Influence?

This is one of the crucial finds of the last decade, and few will see its relevance in persuasion.

What's the first ramification and how to deal with it?

Avoid Gossip

I advise people I work with in any capacity to never say anything bad about the person they live with—to anyone. (In fact this is a family rule as well.)

Why? The person you tell this information to has a very limited landscape of your reality. Now you create it for them and the relationship between you and the future gossiper will never be the same. Rare events become a way of life. Occasional annoyances become the norm of your life in the mind of the other person.

So what? Each time they communicate with you, they then literally change your memory about your life. Your history. Your relationships. Your experience. Your experience is no longer what it was, but a sum of the conversations you've had with others about your life. That could be a good thing if you follow "the rule"; it could be devastating if you break it.

So, the first thing you must realize is that **your client believes many things about themselves and other people that simply aren't true.** Again these could be constructive beliefs or destructive beliefs.

The power of suggestion combined with tangential evidence is enough to cause someone to believe something ridiculous or even bizarre, something you wouldn't have thought possible.

The brain is completely malleable as far as memory is concerned. I've written about this for a few years now. But now, it is evident that it is even more changeable (and much easier to instantly change) than I, frankly, ever speculated.

The customer tells you anything. Any story. Realize that true or false, **they believe it** and if it is false, *they typically believe it with greater certainty than if it were real.*

Realize that any evidence they show you to support their story will make it much more vivid in their mind, even if the picture/document has nothing to do with the memory.

You've had the experience many times: Someone confirmed something you said about something you remembered and you said, "Oh, yes! I remember now . . ." and perhaps it did happen and perhaps not. The external cue can make something seem to be true, but realize that it might not.

Cue Their Memory

Therefore, you must cue a person's memory on your own. If you are speaking with someone who is a new client, you must create pictures of the past in a way that will not further solidify false beliefs the client might have about you or your company.

Remember when you saw the Super Bowl about eight years ago? There's Justin Timberlake, Janet Jackson (yes, wardrobe malfunction day), Kid Rock, Snoop Dogg all on stage, the camera comes in tight on Janet and Justin, and POOF! there goes the "wardrobe malfunction."

Oh, sorry about that, I had to share a quick thought experiment with you. Snoop Dogg wasn't at the Super Bowl, Kid Rock wasn't on stage when the wardrobe malfunction happened, and the camera didn't zoom in, it actually panned. Amazing huh?

How should you prepare yourself?

How to Prepare Yourself

Now, back to dealing with your client's fallacious memories about your company or you. Be prepared to have photos or video, supporting documents or letters that verify that what you are going to share is indeed true, incredibly useful, and accurate. Those supporting documents (even as simple as a photo of the building you work at—which I'm sure you have noticed as some kind of credibility builder in many people's ads) will add to your story—if you get it out first—or to theirs if they see the photo and then attach it to their fallacious beliefs.

The new model of presenting information demands a very well thought out strategy doesn't it? Each environmental cue will change their memory as you move through your communication. New information will be shuffled with the old and an entirely new picture will indeed emerge.

You need to make sure that picture is favorable . . . and it doesn't take much, does it?!

Now think:

- How are you going to avoid the instantaneous negative review your potential client wants to share with you?
- Can you communicate something with an image or supporting document briefly that will unhook that memory?

Key Point: Never let anyone connect negative information with you.

As soon as they say it and connect it with your face, your office, your product, you are sunk. Best to take 20 seconds and fix this possibility before it is not repairable.

Have you ever seen someone get in an argument with someone else and they use a diary or journal to prove that whatever happened really happened? If you've been with me for long, you know that that journal or diary is just as likely to be incorrect in facts as is the person's memory 10 years later. Why?

People tend to write about **emotional events** and when this is the case, the hippocampus (not an animal, a part of the brain) doesn't store all information. In fact, the information that it does keep is volatile, easily brought to consciousness, and just as likely to be correct as it is incorrect. The same is true with a memory 10 years in the future!

The person's *feeling* will always be the first sorting factor in what a memory will become.

How to Overcome Emotion

This is why I tell people to walk through what their feelings are saying and move completely through it to accomplish your goal. Otherwise, you become fat, smoke more cigarettes, and do everything else your *feelings* tell you to do. Scary, huh?

So ... One picture with one story, true or not, can create a complete memory with a complete set of feelings attached to it. That set of feelings can trigger an entire set of behaviors and actions.

Now, when was the last time someone shared something this amazing with you and you got it for free. I know!

17 | Women

Influencing Women to Buy

For decades women have been the big grocery- and department-store buyers—the drivers of the economy in general.

Today women are now beginning to spend money online as well as just about every other area of the economy. Women are now better educated than male counterparts in the United States. The gender/wage gap has been closed. Women are involved in over 80 percent of all buying decisions.

Influencing women is now the core factor in marketing and sales success for almost all products and services. My personal strongest interest is in building relationships online.

Today women are starting to pay attention to marketing and advertising online. More and more women are active in the buying process in both the cyber and brick-and-mortar world.

And it's costing you money because...

- You don't know how to market to women.
- You don't know how to sell women.
- You probably couldn't get a woman to say yes...well...read on....

Selling to Women Is Often Counterintuitive

Marketing to women, for most products and services (but not all) is very counterintuitive.

Women are becoming a powerful force on the Internet today—a force that will only be increasing in the coming months and years! The fact is that women are responsible, at least in part, of 80 percent or more of the buying decisions in most homes.

Key Point: Millions of women are in charge of the purchasing for divisions, departments, offices, and entire companies that they work for. Women are spending money for products that only men typically once bought.

The man thinking about buying your online product or service just might have his wife, girlfriend, sister, mother, or other female acquaintance taking a look at your sales page to give him a second opinion about whether he should buy your product.

I have two men coming to *Influence: Boot Camp* in March who had to check with their wives for permission to come . . . and we have women coming who *told* their husbands where they would be.

This is nothing new to women in general and particularly to *Coffee with Kevin Hogan* readers, but it surprises a lot of men.

It's fascinating watching marketers who don't understand women. They pander to them, patronize them, appealing to outmoded and outdated thinking processes . . . and then I watch them go broke.

Key Point: Women want the same respect you give men. They don't want to be patronized or pandered to. They recognize when you are BSing them with political correctness, and they would rather do business with someone who irritates them than someone who doesn't respect them.

Most women are way past feminism. They aren't trying to be equal anymore. Visit any university campus. More women will get their bachelor's degree this year than men. Women are keeping their jobs in the recession. Men are losing their jobs at a rate *twice* that of women.

They don't have time to think about ideology because they are too busy putting in nine-hour days at the office and being Supermom at home.

Think about these two key ideas:

1. How much business am I losing by not putting focus on the female market?
2. How much business am I losing (that I am not even aware of) because I don't know the hard facts about marketing to women?

Maybe you already market to the female audience and want to increase your knowledge, sales, and response. Maybe you have been thinking that your product or service would be perfect for women, but you are not sure how to move into this market. Or, perhaps, you are just reading these secrets with an open mind —thinking that maybe you can use this information for a future venture.

So . . . Just Think Pink, Right?

That's what causes business after business to implode.

Unless you are selling Mary Kay, Avon, or Victoria's Secret lingerie, you're thinking the *wrong* color.

Some marketers assume that marketing to women is as easy as changing your colors to pink and sprinkling flowers around your web site. Not so. In fact the opposite is the case.

If you're really serious about reaching your female market, you have to care about her and get to know all about her and her life.

You need to know her desires, the pressures and problems she faces, the dreams she has, and what she is like on the inside.... What her *hot* buttons are, what turns her completely *off* to your offer, and what makes it irresistible!

Key Point: It is critical that you understand her needs and be able to offer solutions for those needs.

Many retailers have had to change their approach to the woman's market as well. Some companies are even devoting entire departments to marketing to women. Compared to men, women are complex creatures. Listening to the politically correct morons, you'll hear that men and women are the same and buy the same. This is blatantly wrong.

Women and men are as different as night and day in how they reach conclusions, *how* they buy, *why* they buy, and *when* they buy.

Look at your client list. How many women are on there?

Tell the politically correct crowd to find their corner so you can do business with clients that are far more loyal to you long term than men ever will be.

In the online world, the companies and individuals that are successful marketing to women online are the ones that understand how to communicate interactively with women.

The most important factor in understanding the mind of women is watching what they *do*. Observe how they behave. How they buy. You don't understand that mind, you make no sale. Simple as that.

Once you understand the mind-set, then you can ask obvious questions:

- What does she need/want?
- What is her life like?
- What makes her buy?
- What are her *hot* buttons?
- What makes a product irresistible to her?
- What keeps her coming back to buy more?

Want to Sell Women?

Put these keys at the forefront of your thinking....

1. Women are busy people! They want you to make their lives easier, smoother, better!
2. Women usually work long hours balancing work, a home, and family, carpooling, and all of the responsibilities that they have on a daily basis. Many women are pressed for time with chores around the house and taking care of the kids. They don't have time to spend researching and analyzing everything they buy, so, they are looking to you for help with that.

3. Women are big relationship builders! They value the opinions of those they feel they can trust. Help them trust you, and you have taken a giant step toward success with marketing to women!

4. Because women are so busy, they want good buys, easy shopping, a relationship with you—the seller—and honesty.

The Online World

Why are women on the Internet?

If you are male, drop all preconceived notions and pay attention.

Women use the Internet for a variety of different reasons. Usually for multiple reasons. Some of the main reasons are:

- For work
- To save time and find information fast
- To improve their lives
- To find solutions
- To connect with others
- For easily researching products
- For shopping
- For advice
- For information
- For entertainment

The Secrets Revealed . . . A Sneak Peek Inside a Woman's Mind

I recently talked in-depth, on the condition of anonymity, with one of the top female marketers in the United States. Her book, about marketing to women, comes out in autumn. (I appreciate you!)

Factor 1—A Woman's Life Revolves around Others: Focus not only on her, but others around her.

If you were to take a look inside a woman's mind, you would find that women spend a large amount of time thinking about and caring for others. This includes her family, kids, spouse, co-workers, you name it.

You can tap into the heart of women by showing them how your products and services can help them take even better care of others in their lives.

Here's what you need to do: Once you have fully shown her how your product or service will impact her and make her life easier, take it one step further. Let her know how this purchase will benefit those around her (directly or indirectly)—her family, her kids, loved ones, friends, and so forth.

This key point alone will dramatically increase your success when marketing to women!

Factor 2—Show Her Your Motives:

When thinking about buying from or doing business with you, a woman wants to know your motives:

- Why are you selling me this?
- Why are you telling me this?
- Tell me your why?

Give her enough information about you and why you created or why you are selling this product or service to her to allow her to trust you and your motives.

Key Point: You want to set her mind at ease and let her know that you genuinely want to help her and you are offering her a real solution, not a chance to get a quick sale on her expense.

Factor 3—A Woman's Secret Questions Revealed:

When a woman is looking at your product or service, here are the questions that she is silently thinking in her mind. Give her an answer to each one of these, and she is likely to do business with you:

- How much time is it going to save me?
- What problem(s) will it solve for me?
- What specifically is your product going to do for my life? What are its benefits?
- If I buy this product, how will it affect how I will be perceived by my peers? Example: If you have an e-book about how she can potty train

her child within 48 hours, you need to let her know that she will be perceived as a Supermom, the envy among other moms, amazing, and so on.

- If I buy this product, how is it going to affect those around me (positively or negatively)? Whose life, other than hers, is this product going to make better? Example: A product to help her make more money will surely give her kids a better lifestyle.
- Who else is buying (has bought) this product? (She wants to know if other women/moms trust you.)
- Is what I am buying part of a high demand market/trend or in a rapidly growing market?
- How long will it take me to earn back my money? (This is her question if it is a money-saving or money-making product or service.)
- Can I really trust you? Give me a reason.

Make sure that your sales copy contains enough information to help women answer most of the above questions.

Factor 4—Help Women "Wade In" Slowly, Then They Will "Jump In":

Women tend to start off very skeptical and then gradually increase their comfort level and belief when buying online. Women are very cautious until they feel comfortable, and that's okay. They like to stick their toes in the water first, and then, if it feels okay, they will venture on in. (Sometimes even jump on in!)

Here are a few ideas that will help her wade in slowly and make your offer irresistible to her:

- Offer a free sample or a sneak peak before she buys.
- Offer a try-before-you-buy.
- Offer a trial version (as in software).
- Offer a reduced price to try your product first (this works well with membership sites).
- Give her a tour (a video tour or some screen shots).
- Let her know step-by-step what she can expect.

It is often harder to make the first sale to women, but after they are confident that you offer a quality product or service . . . and especially after they develop an emotional attachment to your product . . . they will be very eager to spend their money with YOU.

Decide what you can do that will allow women try your product or service before they buy!

Factor 5—Details . . . Details . . . Details, Please:

Women are into details! They want to know everything about a product or service before they buy it. They want to know how it works, how much it costs, what type of support they can expect after the sale . . . and more.

Give them PLENTY of information, but make it EASY for them to scan through and find what they want to read. Remember, women are BUSY people, and if you make it hard for them, they will move on to someone who doesn't.

You can do this by giving your details in small chunks with headings so that they can easily see the things on your site that they need or want to read quickly. When she finds those details that she is interested in, she will read your other details as well . . . and she is much more likely to try your product.

Factor 6—Trust and Security:

The way to a woman's heart (or in marketing, a woman's purse) is trust and security. Without trust, you will not have much business in the female arena. It may take you some time to gain this trust, but it will be well worth your effort as women who trust you and feel secure with your products and services will do business with you again and again indefinitely. This equals long-term security!

Women have money to spend, and in general, they will not spend it with people who don't respect them.

Women are more educated now than ever. In the United States, more women get bachelor's degrees than men.

Women are stuck between the hard-core decisions of being moms, career people, and both . . . and it is a decision they don't like. Parts of them feel unfulfilled as moms, but can't stand the idea of leaving their kids with others while they are away (evolution). Parts of them feel compelled to compete in the business world for their own individual status (culture, identity) . . . and parts of them would like to show they can do it all (some crazy part).

Was it Aretha Franklin who did the song R–E–S–P–E–C–T in capital letters? Don't patronize. Respect me and you go a long way toward hearing yes.

Women do not spend as much money online as they do off line as a percentage of total sales, but they are catching up fast.

I'm going to focus on women who are getting involved online in particular, but everything carries over to brick-and-mortar in very obvious ways.

Okay, those are a few things we've touched on in the past week.

Let's get to the seven specific secrets I've got for you this year.

Factor 7—Let Them Know Where You Are:

When doing business with women, they need to know that you are there.

Before the purchase, if they don't buy right away, keep in touch with them so they can gain trust in you. Let them know that they can contact you with any questions they have. This security is important to their buying process.

After the purchase, let them know that they can count on you after the purchase. Make sure that you keep your word!

Remember women truly are relationship-oriented creatures, and the courting and after-the-fact both matter with women.

This security is a vital part of the trust issue that women need to develop an ongoing relationship with you.

Factor 8—Build a Relationship with Women—and Help Women Build Relationships with Others:

Women shop socially—even online.

Men shop with the mind-set, "Get me in—get me out"!

But, women take their time, gather their information, savor the experience, shop around, compare ... and they listen.

Online, they listen to:

- What YOU have to say on your web site and in your e-mails.
- What others are saying on your site through testimonies.
- What you or others are saying through blogs.
- What others are saying on message boards.

Key Point: Women buy with other women in mind . . . and with the opinions of other women in mind.

Because women are so into building those relationships and listening to what others have to say, even in their shopping, it is imperative that you learn how to be interactive with your female audience.

Through interaction, women find even more information about your product or service and begin to build an emotional bond to it. This builds that gotta-have-it feeling.

For example: "Jenna, Amy, and Victoria say that it has worked for them . . . so, therefore, I must try it myself."

Now . . . Mary, Erika, and Cindy, might be moms in their offline play-group, . . . or they might be ladies on a message board . . . or they might be testimonies from other women on your site. You want to give women as much interaction on your site as possible (without making your site cheesy, cluttered, or distasteful). The more information that they can find from you will help raise their comfort level without feeling the need to check you out in other places.

Check out all the testimonials from women at www.kevinhogan .com . . . just on the front page. Scroll all the way down . . . you get the idea.

Online, here are some ways to be interactive with your female visitors:

- Through testimonials.
- Through pictures on your web site (of other females—women can instantly relate).
- Pictures of you on your site.
- Messages from you on your site.
- Let them learn more about you on your site.
- Let women see testimonials, reviews, or pictures of others who have bought, used, or enjoyed your service or product.
- Through blogs.
- Give them a way to give feedback, submit ideas, or ask questions.
- Have a message board.
- Have an e-mail list where you can be even more personal with them.

Factor 9—Make Them Superwomen!

Women are multitasking achievers and are forever seeking new ways to complete all that they have to do with ease and at a record pace. Help them find ways to do it all with simplicity and ease. You'll have a happy woman and they will forever trust you!

Example: Women with small children want to find ways to "Make money while their babies are napping," or "They want to know how to run a successful business while their children are playing at their feet," or "They want to learn how to paint with a baby in their lap."

Factor 10—Connect with Women:

Women want to feel a connection with the company or individual they are purchasing from. Most women will connect better if there is a female representation in some way associated with your site or your product. I know that this is not always possible, but use these techniques when and where you can.

Here are some suggestions to help connect with your female customers:

- Make everything more personal—let them get to know *you*.
- Use your "about me" page to highlight any female employees—staff members or partners
- If you're female or have female staff in your support area, take advantage of this fact in your support e-mail: For example, on your contact page, instead of using an e-mail contact address, such as support@kevinhogan.com, use danielle@kevinhogan.com.
- If you're a male, consider having a female bridge. This could mean having a female JV (Joint Venture) partner or another woman who really understands women to help you with the product . . . or at least have a female look at your web site, your sales copy, your e-mails, and get her opinion. You want to be careful about how you are coming across to your female market.
- Let her know that your system, service, product was designed with her in mind.
- Let her know that you know how she feels:
  * "I was, too . . . ."
  * "I felt the same way . . . ."
  * Or if you are a male, let her know that was the way that your wife, sister, girlfriend, or mother felt, or you have been told by other women that they felt that way . . . and so on.
- Use pictures of females that they can relate to.
- Use female lingo in your message.

Again, this applies to most women (not all), and simply helps women feel a connection.

Factor 11—Get Her Attention . . . FAST:

Women are so incredibly busy, and they are looking through information quickly. If you don't get her attention . . . FAST, she is off to find her information elsewhere.

Here are some ways to get and keep a woman's attention online:

- Put important things that you want her to see in the top half of your site (above the fold).
- Offer her a sneak preview of your product.
- Offer her a free report.
- Offer her a free sample.
- Include pictures on your site of women she can relate to.
- Make it clear what you site is about.
- Show her EARLY in your site that you offer a solution to her problem(s).
- Let her see testimonials or reviews.

Find a way to stay in touch with her through your e-mail list by offering her something that she can't pass up. This will be critical to keeping her attention and building that relationship over the long haul.

Factor 12—Talk to a Woman Like You're Her BEST Friend:

We have already established the fact that women are incredibly relationship oriented. They bond with others through their conversations and interactions with others both offline and online. They make major and minor decisions based on their relationships with others offline and online.

The secret to writing so that a woman can really understand you (whether you are writing an article, a sales page, or anything else) is to write as though you are her best friend. Use a conversational tone in your writing. Talk to her like you have talked with her before. Make your tone relaxed (but not sloppy) and friendly. Again, using some female lingo will help you get your words across in a more female-friendly way.

Don't be afraid to share information about yourself, your life, and your family with her. Don't hesitate to ask about hers. This builds that relationship, trust, and more. This is a huge step to success in marketing to women online!

Factor 13—Use Imagery:

There are two ways that you can use what I call female imagery. One is on *your* part, and the other is on the part of your female visitors.

First, you need to get a clear picture of the woman or types of women that you are connecting with. Just like men, not all women fit into a cookie cutter mold.

- Which women will fall into the demographic *you* need to reach?
- Which women will *find you*, and what are their demographics and psychographics?

Get out some paper and write down what their lives are like . . . what types of problems they face, what they might be feeling when they are looking for a solution to the problem that your product will solve. If needed, ask another female to help you brainstorm about your target females. Find out as much information as possible. Now, imagine yourself in their shoes. Imagine what they are feeling. Thoughts and ideas will begin to come to you that will help you connect with her on a whole new level!

Next, you need to find ways to get your female customers imagining things about their lives—what they want it to be like. How can you tie visual images into the picture of what they want for their lives? How can you paint them a picture of how their lives will be if they buy your product or use your service?

Key Point: Don't sell them a product—sell them a dream—let them imagine how your product or service will make their lives easier, happier, and better. Let them imagine how taking action NOW will benefit the people around them!

How? Use "female speak" to make it seem more real to her. (I have included a list of *hot* words and phrases in *The Science of Influence 49–60: Triggering the Buying Impulse.*)

Key Point: Use themes—both with pictures and with words. Themes send a mental message to a woman and evoke warm and happy feelings inside.

Here are just a few that you could use:

- Family themes.
- A couple in love.
- Any type of theme that represents joy, laughter, or happiness.
- The successful woman in business.
- A mom with her kids.

There are many more . . . these are just a few ideas.

To get a clear picture of themes, visit other women's sites and look through women's magazines. These should get your creative juices flowing and help you clearly convey your message to her.

Using female imagery both for yourself and for your target market can help you add lots of profits to your business!

Factor 14—Respect Women and Treat Them Intelligently:

Women are intelligent and they want to know that *you* think they are! They want to be recognized, respected, and acknowledged as the powerful force that they are. Show women that you understand this fact and you will reap the benefits!

Compliment women on their decision to do business with you. Talk to them intelligently; ***NEVER-EVER*** talk down to them! Talk to women like they are on your level. They are! (Eventually you'll believe it. I signed on for three gigs in the last three weeks totaling about $45,000.00 . . . all events were offered and negotiated by women.)

Talking down to a woman or showing them that you don't value or respect them will have them clicking off your site faster than greased lightning. And . . . once that impression has been made, there is no turning back.

Those who fail to take these 14 factors into account will find her saying no. Understand why she is saying no.

When Women Say "No"

Did she even *THINK* about it for just *ONE* second?

You meet with your client and they say no, even before they have all the facts about how much you could help them.

They might say, "I've got to think about it." But invariably that means, "No, but I don't want to have to say no." And it doesn't make sense.

Their current person, product, or service they are using is clearly inferior. It makes no sense. *Why would they say no?*

Key Point: When people feel pressured to change . . . they won't. There is one exception and it's about the *type* of pressure.

The Anti-Authority Message Reaction

Your customer could have a $50 bill in her hand and you could offer a $100 bill in exchange, and your customer can easily say no!

WHAT?

Read it again. It's the teen reaction that never went away: the anti-authority message reaction.

Remember from our previous work, that people have a gut level "no" (reactance) to anything that is not familiar . . . and they have a reasoned thought resistance that says no until they've had a chance to step back and evaluate anything that they don't regularly experience.

And then you have additional reactions to authority. There can be a lot to overcome between no and yes.

Key Point: A growing body of research about reactance shows that when people are told to do the opposite of what they believe, they have a tendency to overreact in the direction of their current behavior.

For example: If someone is a cigarette smoker or abuses alcohol, and that person sees authoritarian messages to not do those things . . . you got it . . . the person smokes/drinks *more*.

And that is not just speculation on my part. The research is abundant. The more intense the warning on the cigarette package, the more quickly people go through the cigarettes and the more they smoke.

I travel out of the country quite regularly. When I was in Sydney, Australia, I went grocery shopping (that was an experience that taught me why Americans are fat . . . I'll save that for another day).

I went to a part of the store where they were selling cigarettes. I was drawn to the area because there was a big sign that said, "Cigarettes cause death." There was a skull and cross bones on the sign . . . and a line of people waiting to buy cigarettes.

There is no logic involved here. Cigarettes simply erase years from your life. But the smoker is not smoking for logical reasons.

By telling the person to quit smoking, **you are pushing their anti-authority button. You are telling them they are stupid, or worse, that you are smarter than they are!**

If the pressure you use is directly from you and it is perceived as a win/lose, the other person says no, *and* they hit the brakes and dig in for a fight, defending their position more vigorously every second of the way. That's just how it is. But there is one kind of pressure that does work with women and not men . . . .

Do this: Think of yourself as a magnetic field with a field pushing out away from you. And the other person has the same magnetic field coming out of them. In other words, north faces north. What happens?

Polarity . . . the magnets literally repel each other. It's a fascinating metaphor because it is amazing to watch it happen on your coffee table with two magnets—just like it is in real life with people.

- So, you can't pressure in the commonly understood definition of pressure.
- You can't push.
- You can't have an authoritarian message and expect the customer to say yes.

It won't happen. But your pressure could easily cause them to sign a long-term contract—with your competitor.

Men typically won't cave to any type of pressure. Women will yield to one kind of pressure. You will be surprised . . . .

Does Everyone Have the Same Response?

What's interesting is that not everyone responds with the polarity reaction. Generally there are two groups of people who predictably will react north to north.

1. People who participate in the behavior you are trying to get them to change.
2. People who are normally contrarian in general or to you or your message specifically.

FACT: Reactance is triggered by overt influence attempts that are particularly dogmatic or authoritarian in content or delivery.

Reactance Triggers

Anything else trigger reactance? Yes.

Key Point: A growing body of research shows that low credibility messengers (spokesmen/salespeople/etc.) are regularly met with reactance that ties the person being persuaded more closely to the status quo.

More?
Yep.

Key Point: If some part of a person's freedom is threatened (or perceived to be threatened, which is all that really matters!) in any way, you can know that north will be out in full force.

What About That Teenager?

And what enhances reactance?
The reactant personality of course!
What's that?
The reactant person is one who has a strong desire to make their own choices.

Generally, teens have a much stronger tendency to intense reactance than older people. But of course, reactance is found in all ages.

In one study, the sign, "Danger—Shallow Water: No Diving!" increased kids' diving significantly . . . but only in kids who had dived into the shallow water before. It had no effect on those who had not.

In another study, smokers who saw packs of cigarettes with no health warnings on the packaging caused no change in smoking behavior. Those with strong warning labels caused the individuals to smoke more.

The volume of data here is overwhelming. In the case of using fear in messages specifically, that would need a separate article—or book—but in general it works as described in the following.

Fear and Reactance

Fear is only useful and effective when used mildly. Messages that contain strong or intense levels of fear cause reactance and *cause* the *opposite* behavior.

Key Point: There are exceptions, but, in general, a little fear goes a long way, and a lot of fear kills the message—and causes what you want to change to become more grounded.

Soften Your Message

Obviously we all experience reactance, and often, but depending on personality and circumstances, a lot of people will react much more intensely than others.

If you had to adopt only one idea to increase success in persuasion and influence it would be to *soften your message*.

Softening the Message Will Influence Men

That isn't going to work with women.

Women require knowledge that authority figures they respect have concluded that what you are proposing is what the authority figures have approved of. When women know that authority figures they respect, both men and women, have overwhelmingly concluded that the idea on the table you are presenting is the best, *that* is the *one* and *only* kind of pressure that will predictably turn no into yes.

Most types of pressure simply can't work with 90 percent of people, and that is why salespeople talk about numbers and percentages.

Key Point: Women can and do change their minds in dramatic fashion when they know the respected authorities overwhlemingly agree with a proposal. However, men do not care what the respected authorities over-whelmingly think—and only message softening is effective on the pres-sure/no pressure continuum.

Most people believe the opposite to be true, but that's why most people can't get a yes from someone. They don't know how people think and don't spend the time to learn.

Bibliography

Allesandra, Tony, and Michael J. O'Connor. *The Platinum Rule: Do unto Others As They'd Like Done unto Them.* New York: Warner Books, 1996.

Anastasi, Tom. *Personality Selling: Selling the Way Customers Want to Buy.* New York: Sterling Publications, 1992.

Andreas, Steve, and Charles Faulkner. *NLP: The New Technology of Achievement.* New York: William Morrow, 1994.

Aronson, Elliott. *The Social Animal.* New York: W. H.Freeman & Company, 1995.

Baber, R. E. *Marriage and Family.* New York: McGraw-Hill, 1939.

Baumeister, R. F., E. Bratslavsky, C. Finkenauer, and K. D. Vohs. "Bad Is Stronger Than Good." *Review of General Psychology* 5(4) (2001): 323–70.

Belsky, Gary, and Thomas Gilovich. *Why Smart People Make Big Money Mistakes and How to Correct Them.* New York: Fireside, 1999.

Berger, Jonah, and Chip Heath. "Where Consumers Diverge from Others: Identity-Signaling and Product Domains," *Journal of Consumer Research* 34 (August 2007).

Bernieri, Frank, and Robert Rosenthal. "Interpersonal Coordination, Behavior Matching, and Interpersonal Synchrony," In Robert Feldman and Bernard Rime (Eds.), *Fundamentals of Nonverbal Behavior.* Cambridge: Cambridge University Press, 1991.

Bethel, William. *10 Steps to Connecting with Your Customer: Communication Skills for Selling Your Products, Services, and Ideas.* Chicago: Dartnell Corporation, 1995.

Bloom, Howard. *The Lucifer Principle: A Scientific Expedition Into the Forces of History.* New York: Atlantic Monthly Press, 1995.

Boucher, Jerry, and Charles E. Osgood. "The Pollyanna Hypothesis." *Journal of Verbal Learning and Verbal Behavior* 8(1) (February 1969): 1–8.

Brodie, Richard. *Virus of the Mind: The New Science of the Meme.* Seattle, WA: Integral Press, 1996.

Brooks, Michael. *Instant Rapport: The NLP Program That Creates Intimacy, Persuasiveness, Power!* New York: Warner Books, 1989.

———. *The Power of Business Rapport: Use NLP Technology to Make More Money, Sell Yourself and Your Product, and Move Ahead in Business.* New York: HarperCollins Publishers, 1991.

Burger, Jerry, T. Chartrand, and S. Pinckert. "When Manipulation Backfires: The Effects of Time Delay and Requestor on the Foot in the Door Technique." *Journal of Applied Psychology* 29(1) (1999): 211–21.

Buzan, Tony, and Richard Israel. *Brain Sell.* Brookfield, VT: Gower, 1995.

Byrne, D. "Attitudes and Attraction." In L. Berkowitz (Ed.), *Advances in Experimental Social Psychology.* (Vol. 4, pp. 35–89). New York: Academic Press, 1969.

Cacioppo, J. T., W. L. Gardner, and G. C. Berntson. "The Affect System Has Parallel and Integrative Processing Components: Form Follows Funtion." *Journal of Personality and Social Psycholology* 76(5) (May 1999): 839–55.

Canfield, Jack, and Mark Victor Hansen. *Chicken Soup for the Soul* (10th ed.). Deerfield Beach, FL: Health Communications, 2003.

Carmon, Ziv, and Dan Ariely. "Focusing on the Forgone: Why Value Can Appear So Different to Buyers and Sellers," *Journal of Consumer Research* 27 (December 2000): 360–70.

Cheng, Qiu, and C. W. M. Yeung. "Mood and Comparative Judgement: Does Mood Influence Everything and Finally Nothing?" *Journal of Consumer Research* (February 2008).

Cialdini, Robert B. *Influence: Science and Practice (rev. ed.).* New York: William Morrow, 1993.

Cohen, Allan R., and David L. Bradford. *Influence without Authority.* New York: John Wiley & Sons, 1991.

Dalet, Kevin, with Emmett Wolfe. *Socratic Selling: How to Ask the Questions That Get the Sale.* Chicago: Irwin Professional Publishing, 1996.

Dawson, Roger. *Secrets of Power Persuasion: Everything You'll Ever Need to Get Anything You'll Ever Want.* Englewood Cliffs, NJ: Prentice-Hall, 1992.

Dayton, Doug. *Selling Microsoft: Sales Secrets from Inside the World's Most Successful Company.* Holbrook, MA: Dayton, 1997.

Decker, Bert. *You've Got to Be Believed to Be Heard: Reach the First Brain to Communicate in Business and in Life.* New York: St. Martin's Press, 1992.

Dillard, James, J. E. Hunter, and M. Burgoon. "A Meta-analysis of Two Sequential Request Strategies for Gaining Compliance: Foot in the Door and Door in the Face." *Human Communication Research 10* (1984): 461–88.

Dillard, James, and Michael Pfau. *The Persuasion Handbook: Developments in Theory and Practice.* Thousand Oaks, CA: Sage Publications, 2004.

Dwoskin, Hale. *The Sedona Method.* Sedona, AZ: Sedona Press, 2003.

The Economist. "Persuasion." (Interviewed quote from Brad Sagarin, Northern Illinois University) (May 2, 2002).

Farber, Barry J., and Joyce Wycoff. *Breakthrough Selling: Customer-Building Strategies from the Best in the Business.* Englewood Cliffs, NJ: Prentice-Hall, 1992.

Fink, E. L., S. A. Kaplowitz, and S. M. Hubbard. "Oscillation in Beliefs and Decisions." In J. P. Dillard and M. Pfau (Eds.), *The Persuasion Handbook: Developments in Theory and Practice* (pp. 17–38). Thousand Oaks, CA: Sage Publications, 2002.

Forgas, Joseph P., and Kipling D. Williams. *Social Influence: Direct and Indirect Processes.* Philadelphia: Psychology Press, 2001.

French, Michael. "Physical Appearance and Earnings." *Applied Economics 34*(5) (March 20, 2002): 569–72.

Gass, Robert, and John Seiter. *Persuasion, Social Influence and Compliance Gaining.* New York: Allyn & Bacon, 2004.

Gibson, Bryan. "Can Evaluative Conditioning Change Attitudes toward Mature Brands? New Evidence from the Implicit Association Test." *Journal of Consumer Research 35* (June 2008): 178–88.

Gilbert, D., R. W. Tafarodi, and P. S. Malone. "You Can't Not Believe Everything You Read." *Journal of Personality and Social Psychology, 65*(2) (August 1993): 221–33.

Gilovich, Thomas, Dale Griffin, and Daniel Kahneman. *Heuristics and Biases: The Psychology of Intuitive Judgment.* New York: Cambridge University Press, 2004.

Gitomer, Jeffrey. *The Sales Bible: The Ultimate Sales Resource.* New York: William Morrow, 1994.

Gregory, W. L., R. B. Cialdini, and K. M. Carpenter. "Self-Relevant Scenarios as Mediators of Likelihood Estimates and Compliance: Does Imaging Make It So?" *Journal of Personality and Social Psychology* 43 (1982): 89–99.

Hamer, Dean. *Living with Our Genes: Why They Matter More Than You Think.* New York: Doubleday, 1998.

Herr, Paul M., and Christine M. Page. "Asymmetric Association of Liking and Disliking Judgments: So What's Not to Like?" *Journal of Consumer Research 30* (March 2004): 588–601.

Hoffer, Eric. *The True Believer.* New York: HarperCollins, 1954.

Hogan, Kevin. *The Psychology of Persuasion: How to Persuade Others to Your Way of Thinking.* Gretna, LA: Pelican Publishing Company, 1996.

———. *New Hypnotherapy Handbook.* Eagan, MN: Network 3000 Publishing, 1998.

———. *Talk Your Way to the Top.* Gretna, LA: Pelican Publishing, 1998.

———. *Irresistible Attraction: Secrets of Personal Magnetism.* Eagan, MN: Network 3000 Publishing, 2000.

———. *Covert Hypnosis: An Operator's Manual.* Eagan, MN: Network 3000 Publishing, 2003.

———. *The Science of Influence* (CD Program). Eagan, MN: Network 3000 Publishing, 2004.

Hogan, Kevin, with Wil Horton. *Selling Yourself to Others.* Gretna, LA: Pelican Publishing, 2003.

Hogan, Kevin with Mary Lee LaBay. *Through the Open Door: Secrets of Self-Hypnosis.* Gretna, LA: Pelican Publishing Company, 2000.

———. *Irresistible Attraction: Secrets of Personal Magnetism.* Eagan, MN: Network 3000 Publishing, 2001.

Holt, Charles. *Markets, Games and Strategic Behavior: Recipes for Interactive Learning.* University of Virginia, 2003.

Hoorens, V. and A. P. Buunk. "Social Comparison of Health Risks: Locus of Control, the Person-Positivity Bias and Unrealistic Optimism." *Journal of Applied Social Psychology 23* (1993): 291–302.

Iyengar, S. S., and M. Lepper. "When Choice is Demotivating: Can One Desire Too Much of a Good Thing?" *Journal of Personality and Social Psychology 79*(6) (2000): 995–1006.

Johnson, Kerry L. *Subliminal Selling Skills.* New York: AMACOM, 1988.

———. *Sales Magic: Revolutionary New Techniques That Will Double Your Sales Volume in 21 Days.* New York: William Morrow, 1994.

Kahneman, D., J. L. Kntesch, and R. Thaler. "Anomalies: The Endowment Effect, Loss Aversion, Status Quo Bias." *Journal of Economic Perspectives* 5 (Winter, 1991): 193–206.

Kahneman, D., P. Slovic, and A. Tversky (Eds.). *Judgment under Uncertainty: Heuristics and Biases.* New York: Cambridge University Press, 1982.

Kahneman, Daniel, and Amos Tversky. *Choices, Values and Frames.* New York: Russell Sage Foundation, 2000.

Kennedy, Daniel S. *The Ultimate Sales Letter* (2nd ed.). Avon, MA: Adams Media Corporation, 2000.

Kent, Robert Warren. *The Art of Persuasion.* Surfside, FL: Lee Institute, 1963.

Knapp, Mark, and Judy Hall. *Nonverbal Communication in Human Interaction* (3rd ed.). Fort Worth, TX: Harcourt Brace College Publications, 1992.

Knight, Sue. *NLP at Work: The Difference That Makes a Difference in Business.* Sonoma, CA: Nicholas Brealey Publishing, 1995.

Knowles, Eric, and Jay Linn. *Resistance and Persuasion.* Mahwah, NJ: Erlbaum, 2004.

Kostere, Kim. *Get the Results You Want: A Systematic Approach to NLP.* Portland, OR: Metamorphous Press, 1989.

Krosnick, Jon. *Rethinking the Vote: The Politics and Prospects of American Election Reform.* New York: Oxford University Press.

Lavington, Camille, with Stephanie Losee. *You've Only Got Three Seconds: How to Make the Right Impression in Your Business and Social Life.* New York: Doubleday, 1997.

Lewis, David. *The Secret Language of Success: Using Body Language to Get What You Want.* New York: Carroll & Graf, 1990.

Linden, Anne, with Kathrin Perutz. *Mindworks: Unlock the Promise Within— NLP Tools for Building a Better Life.* Kansas City, MO: Andrews McMeel Publishing, 1997.

Lindsay, D. S., L. Hagen, J. D. Read, K. A. Wade, and M. Garry. "True Photographs and False Memories." *Psychological Science* 15(3) (March 2004): 149–154.

Lo, Alison K. C., J. G. Lynch, and R. Staelin. "How to Attract Customers by Giving Them the Short End of the Stick." *Journal of Marketing Research* 44 (February 2007): 128–41.

Lynn, M., and R. Gregor. "Tipping and Service: The Case of Hotel Bell-men." *International Journal of Hospitality Management* 20 (2001): 299.

Lynn, M., and K. Mynier. "Effect of Server Posture on Restaurant Tipping." *Journal of Applied Social Psychology 23* (1993): 678–85.

Lynn, M., and T. Simons. "Predictors of Male and Female Servers' Average Tip Earnings." *Journal of Applied Social Psychology 30* (2000): 241–52.

McCroskey, J. C., and T. J. Young. "Ethos and Credibility: The Construct and Its Measurement after Three Decades. *Central States Speech Journal 32* (1981): 24–34.

McNeil, B. J., S. G. Pauker, H. C. Sox, and A. Tversky. "On the Elicitation of Preferences for Alternative Therapies." *New England Journal of Medicine 306* (1982): 1259–62.

Mehrabian, Albert. *Silent Messages: Implicit Communication of Emotions and Attitudes.* Belmost, CA: Wadsworth, 1981.

Mills, J., and E. Aronson. "Opinion Change as a Function of the Communicator's Attractiveness and Desire to Influence." *Journal of Personality and Social Psychology I,* (1965): 173–77.

Moine, Donald J., and John H. Herd. *Modern Persuasion Strategies: The Hidden Advantage in Selling.* Englewood Cliffs, NJ: Prentice-Hall, 1984.

Moine, Donald J., and Kenneth Lloyd. *Unlimited Selling Power: How to Master Hypnotic Selling Skills.* Englewood Cliffs, NJ: Prentice-Hall, 1990.

Myers, David G. *Intuition: Its Powers and Perils.* New Haven: Yale University Press, 2003.

O'Keefe, Daniel J. *Persuasion: Theory and Research.* Thousand Oaks, CA: Sage Publications, 1990; rev. ed. 2003.

Ornish, Dean. *Love and Survival.* New York: Perennial Books, 1999.

Overstreet, H. A. *Influencing Human Behavior.* New York: Norton, 1925.

Patton, Forrest H. *Force of Persuasion: Dynamic Techniques for Influencing People.* Englewood Cliffs, NJ: Prentice-Hall, 1986.

Peoples, David. *Selling to the Top.* New York: John Wiley & Sons, 1993.

Perloff, Richard. *The Dynamics of Persuasion.* Hillside, NJ: Erlbaum, 1993.

Piirto, Rebecca. *Beyond Mind Games:The Marketing Power of Psychographics.* Ithaca, NY: American Demographic Books, 1991.

Plous, Scot. *The Psychology of Judgement and Decision Making.* New York: McGraw-Hill, 1993.

Qubein, Nido. *Professional Selling Techniques: Strategies and Tactics to Boost Your Selling Skills and Build Your Career.* Rockville Centre, NY: Farnsworth Publishing Company, 1983.

Redelmeier, D., J. Katz, and D. Kahneman. "Memories of Colonoscopy: A Randomized Trial." *Pain 104*(1–2) (2003): 187–94.

Regan, P. C., M. Snyder, and S. M. Kassin. "Unreaslistic Optimism: Self Enhancement or Personal Positivity?" *Personality and Social Psychology Bulletin 21* (October 1995): 1073–1082.

Richardson, Jerry. *The Magic of Rapport.* Capitola, CA: Meta Publications, 1988.

Robbins, Anthony. *Unlimited Power.* New York: Fawcett, 1987.

Robertson, James E. *Selling the Mind's Eye: What They Didn't Teach You in Sales Training.* Portland, OR: Metamorphous Press, 1990.

Romano, S. T., and J. E. Bordieri. "Physical Attractiveness Stereotypes and Students' Perceptions of College Professors." *Psychological Reports 64* (3, Pt 2) (1989): 1099–102.

Rosenthal, R., and L. Jacobson. *Pygmalion in the Classroom: Teacher Expectation and Pupils' Intellectual Development.* New York: Holt, Rinehart & Winston, 1968.

———. "Pygmalion Effects: Existence, Magnitude, and Social Importance." *Educational Researcher 16* (1987): 37–40.

Ryan, R. M., and J. H. Lynch. (1989). "Emotional Autonomy versus Detachment: Revisiting the Vicissitudes of Adolescence and Young Adulthood. *Child Development, 60*: 340–56.

Sadovsky, Marvin C., and Jon Caswell. *Selling the Way Your Customer Buys: Understand Your Prospects' Unspoken Needs and Close Every Sale.* New York: AMACOM, 1996.

Schwartz, Barry. *The Paradox of Choice: Why More Is Less.* New York: Ecco Publishing, 2004.

Sherman, S. J., M. T. Crawford, and A. R. McConnell. "Looking Ahead as a Technique to Reduce Resistance to Persuasive Attempts." In E. S. Knowles and J. A. Linn, (Eds.), *Resistance and Persuasion* (chapter 8). Mahwah, NJ: Erlbaum, 2004.

Strack, F., and T. Mussweiler. "Explaining the Enigmatic Anchoring Effect: Mechanisms of Selective Accessibility." *Journal of Personality and Social Psychology 73* (1997): 437–46.

Strohmetz, D., B. Rind, R. Fisher, and M. Lynn. "Sweetening the Till: The Use of Candy to Increase Restaurant Tipping." *Journal of Applied Social Psychology 32*(2) (2002): 300–09.

Taylor, S. E. (1991). "Asymmetrical Effects of Positive and Negative Events: The Mobilization-Minimization Hypothesis." *Psychological Bulletin 110*(1) (July 1991): 67–85.

Thaler, Richard. *The Winner's Curse: Paradoxes and Anomalies of Economic Life.* Princeton, NJ: Princeton University Press, 1992.

Thompson, George J., and Jerry B. Jenkins. *Verbal Judo: The Gentle Art of Persuasion.* New York: William Morrow, 1993.

Tracy, Brian. *Advanced Selling Strategies: The Proven System of Sales Ideas, Methods, and Techniques Used by Top Salespeople Everywhere.* New York: Fireside, 1995.

Tversky, Amos, and Daniel Kahneman. "Loss Aversion in Riskless Choice: A Reference Dependent Model." *Quarterly Journal of Economics 106*(4) (1991): 1039–61.

Tykocinski, O. E., and T. S. Pittman. "The Consequences of Doing Nothing: Inaction Inertia as Avoidance of Anticipated Regret." *Journal of Personality and Social Psychology 75* (1998): 607–16.

Vitale, Joe. *The Seven Lost Secrets of Success.* Houston: VistaTron, 1994.

Wegner, Daniel. *The Illusion of Conscious Will.* Cambridge, MA: Bradford Books, MIT Press, 2002.

Weiner, David, and Gilbert Hefter. *Battling the Inner Dummy: The Craziness of Apparently Normal People.* New York: Prometheus Books, 1999.

Willingham, Ron. *The Best Seller: The New Psychology of Selling and Persuading People.* Englewood Cliffs, NJ: Prentice-Hall, 1984.

Wilson, Timothy D. *Strangers to Ourselves: Discovering the Adaptive Unconscious.* Cambridge, MA: Belknap Press of Harvard University, 2002.

Witte, K., and M. Allen. "A Meta Analysis of Fear Appeals: Implications for Effective Public Health Campaigns." *Health, Education and Behavior 27* (2000): 291–615.

Zimbardo, Philip G. *The Psychology of Attitude Change and Social Influence.* New York: McGraw-Hill, 1991.

Index

Stewart, Martha, credibility of, 63
Stories, generating feeling and emotion via, 219–242
Street-smart businesspeople, versus academics, 65
Strong feelings, versus rational thought, 159
Success
    credibility and, 57
    decisions and, 124
    future, 103
    long-term, 216
Suggestion
    false memory, 260, 261
    power of, 262
Superwomen, making, 276–277
Supporting documents, 263–264
Survival
    competition and, 74–75
    threats to, 174
Survival instinct, 20, 21

Talk Your Way to the Top (Hogan), 64, 90
Target audience, self-referencing for, 54
Targeted promotions, consumer reaction to, 254
Team reasoning theories, 80–81
Tenacity, 216
Tenth Law of Persuasion, 100
Testimonials, 60
    power of, 147–148
Thinking without thinking, 233–242
Thought, models for determining, 167–171
Three ways to change, 9–12
Through the Open Door: Secrets of Self-Hypnosis] (Hogan & LaBay), 91
Tickle Me Elmo promotion, 148
Time, ways to experience, 137
Time perspective
    changing, 136–139
    shifting, 100–103
Time-sharing presentations, 112
Time track therapy intervention, 101
Tips, increasing, 96–98
Tone, leading with, 42
Too many choices (TMC), 193
True Believer concept, 69
Trust
    branding into company name, 208
    effect on buying, 211
    women and, 274
Trustworthiness, 62, 64
21-Point Delta Model, 38–47

Unattractive women, 27
Uncertainty, choice-related, 188
Unconscious filters, 24
Unconscious mind, persuading, 210–211. *See also* Nonconscious mind
Understatement, power of, 45–46
Universal laws, 131
Unknown, fear of, 5
Unusual claims tactic, 55

Valuations
    ownership and, 114–115
    priming, 204–205
Value. *See also* Values
    influence of, 247–248
    providing, 246
    ways of judging, 247–248
Values, customer, 31
Values Determination Model, 35
Value Shock tactic, 229–230
Variety-seeking behavior, 155
Ventura, Jesse, 226–227
Verbal signals, 14
Virus of the Mind (Brodie), 90
Vocal cues, gaining rapport via, 37
Vocal pacing, 40
Voice
    gaining rapport via, 40
    leading with, 42

Walters, Dottie, 50, 51, 257
Wansink, Brian, 236
Warnings, power of, 104, 105
"We All Need Someone to Love" principle, 76–78
Wealth, attractiveness and, 20
Web sites, 212
Web site traffic
    generating, 246
    targeted, 247
Weight issues, 22
Well-stated arguments, oscillation and, 164
"Win-win or no deal," 168
Woman's mindset, factors affecting, 271–280
Women. *See also* Female entries
    connecting with, 277–278
    desire for details, 274
    getting the attention of, 278
    influencing to buy, 267–285
    keeping in touch with, 275
    keys to selling to, 270
    making offers irresistible to, 273–274
    marketing to, 268–269
    meeting with, 32
    partner preferences of, 28
    relationships with, 275–276
    respecting, 280
    softening the message for, 284–285
    talking to, 278–279
    unattractive, 27
    understanding, 268
Women's secret questions, 272–273
Work rules, 222
World view, differences in, 197–198

"Yes" response, 174, 176, 179
    core reasons for, 243–251
    for future events, 181–184
Young, Jim, 29

Ziglar, Zig, 38

Need a Speaker?

Kevin is a guaranteed victory for your meeting and will leave your group motivated with new knowledge and skills. He has spoken throughout the world from Sydney, Australia to Warsaw, Poland. Call Kevin *personally* at (612) 616-0732 and discuss your next meeting with Kevin. You can also visit Kevin on the web: www.KevinHogan.com.